To my 'Big Bruv' Ian
To remember the
'gathering of the clan'
Paul *August 2010*
RAuxAF

THE FAITHFUL FEW

Worcestershire's Fighter Boys

Andrew Long

Victory Books International

Dedication

For my late mother, Pam Walters.

THE FAITHFUL FEW: *Worcestershire's Fighter Boys*
© Andrew Long, 2007
ISBN: 1-905768-09-5

First published 2007 by: -

Victory Books International
PO Box 573
Worcester WR5 3WU
UK
Tel: 07921 503105
Fax: 01905 767735
www.victorybooks.co.uk

Layout & design by Victory Books International.
Printed & bound in the UK.

How to achieve your own work in print.

Victory Books International is often approached by new and established authors eager to see new works in print. We welcome submissions on any subject, but in the first instance require a letter briefly outlining your project; all applications will be answered with constructive assistance providing an SAE is enclosed. If positively received we would then ask to see the full work, or if still in preparation, ask you to meet with us and discuss publishing prospects. We are committed to launching first time authors, like Andrew Long, on successful writing careers and appreciate full well how difficult starting off can be. So much excellent material is researched and collated but never appears in print; do not let that happen to your labour of love!

Dilip Sarkar MBE FRHistS, Partner & Managing Editor
www.DilipSarkarMBE.co.uk

Contents

Foreword

I was very pleased when Andrew Long asked me to write a foreword to introduce his book 'The Faithful Few'. However, I felt a little disappointed that he had not included my name in the book, as I am after all nearly one of his local boys having been born and bred just a few bends down the river Severn in Gloucester!

Nevertheless I do congratulate him on providing his home county with such a splendid record of Worcestershire's many notable fighter pilots and aircrews. It makes very interesting reading and I think one of the best records of the air battle of the period that I have read. It certainly brings home the intense pressure under which those aircrew were having to operate and his local area produced more than their share of dedicated and brave men; sadly their losses were considerable. Andrew has apologized that the book has been so long in being published but the excellence of the research has made it well worth waiting for.

The first reason why I am pleased to write a foreword is because it gives me the opportunity to recall the very happy relationship that I enjoyed with Nigel Bunting who was a most able and likeable flight commander in my squadron. It brings back the profound sorrow that his death caused me at the time and still lingers in my memory even now I knew many of the characters that Andrew mentions, of course, and a lot of whom, like me, were flying night-fighters throughout the Battle of Britain. The other reason why I welcomed the opportunity to write here is to emphasize, as does Andrew in his book ,the marked differences in the operation of the night-fighter crews and the Spitfire and Hurricane boys, for whom there can only be the greatest praise. By day they operated under constant pressure often having to change airfields between sorties, and flying several sorties a day.

The author several times refers to this difference and I would like to think that it is remembered that during the Battle and forsome times afterwards there were seven night-fighter Blenheim squadrons operating at the same time as the Hurricanes and Spitfires and often from the same airfields (but at night). The day pilots at least could see where they were going and what was going around them and at least had the possible thrill and stimulus of the chance of engaging the Hun They were together operating as a unit with a friend on each

The Faithful Few

wing tip and all enjoying the great advantage of being able to see! But now consider the night fighter crew, waiting in their crew room with night adoption goggles on and fully dressed in their flying kit As with the day boys they wait for the Scramble! Then it is a matter of abandoning their dark goggles scrambling into their aircraft, and doing all their checks in very poor cockpit lighting and a hand torch The aircraft controllers can only handle one aircraft at a time therefore the night fighter takes off alone with only a little hope of being put on to a hostile aircraft. If he is fortunate enough to intercept there is the difficulty of identifying his target on a black night. An essential as demonstrated by Eddy Crew who

Gloucester boy Richard Haine.

unfortunately shot down a Hurricane one night Not for a moment would I belittle the wonderful performance of the Spits and Hurricanes but I would like to think that some thoughts are given to the night fighter crews of whom their were some 80 pilots and aircrew operating in the same space as the day boys often from the same airfields and flying hundreds of sorties always in blackout conditions at night. The many ground crews that serviced the Blenheim also deserve a mention for they were often bombed or shot up as they worked at night.

I do commend this book as I think Andrew has provided a most interesting and absorbing record of the Air Battles over Southern England in the 1940s, and pays just tribute to the surprisingly large number of dedicated aircrew who so bravely took to the air from their Worcestershire homes.

Group Captain Richard Haine OBE DFC RAF (Ret'd), January 2007

Publisher's Introduction

In 1982, I walked into a model shop in Worcester and saw an advertisement pinned to the wall, to the effect that 'A. Long' wanted to start the Worcestershire Aviation Archaeology Society and was looking for members. Key Publishing's now highly successful *FlyPast* magazine had recently been released, which including features on aviation archaeology encouraged by the original editor, the late Mike Twite, and Winston Ramsey's encyclopaedic 'Battle of Britain: Then & Now' had also hit the shelves in 1980; these publications inspired a whole new generation of aviation enthusiasts to become amateur historians. I had personally been spellbound by the Ramsey book, and avidly devoured anything and everything published in *FlyPast* connected with recovering the remains of crashed wartime aircraft and those who sadly perished in them. In those days, however, the majority of aviation archaeology groups were based in southern England, concentrating on Battle of Britain casualties, and what was going on locally in Worcestershire appeared to me so haphazard and amateurish that becoming involved failed to appeal. For some reason, though, I thought that it was worth contacting 'A. Long' to see what he was all about. I was only 21 myself and wrote expressing my great interest both in the subject generally and in becoming actively involved in excavations. Soon after I received a telephone call from 'A. Long', whose knowledge absolutely stunned me – he seemed to know about every single aeronautical incident that had ever happened in the county, the numbers of every aircraft involved, and had some great ideas for future projects. 'A. Long' had, it transpired, been on many digs with the Severnside Aviation Society, based in Gloucestershire, but now wanted to start his own locally based organisation. My appetite was considerably whetted and suitably inspired we agreed to meet; my suggestion of chatting over a beer was a non-starter, however, because 'A. Long', who I had been talking on the phone to for over an hour and who I assumed was an adult, informed me that he was only 14 years old!

A few days later I went and met Andy Long at his home, thus beginning a lifelong friendship. I remember that evening well, as Andy appeared to produce parts of aircraft from every nook and cranny of the house! Not only were the artefacts themselves impressive, but more so was the fact that he seemed to know pretty much everything about the mechanics and history involved. It was clear to me that Andy was no ordinary teenager but a highly intelligent individual with a special gift. His love and enthusiasm for WW2 aviation really was both impressive and inspiring. The proposed society, however, came to nought as mine was the only response Andy received, but we had a few trips out to various local sites until I joined the police and was posted away in March 1983. There our association could easily have ended.

In May 1985, I was sent to work in Malvern, and the following month was on duty at the Three Counties Show when I bumped into Andy by chance. He was still on the aviation archaeology trail and told me about a Spitfire, R6644, that had crashed just outside Malvern, the Polish pilot of which was one of the Few and baled out. He knew where the plane crashed and offered to show me. Well now we were talking! No more boring Tiger Moths from RAF Perdiswell, but a real fighter and a Battle of Britain pilot as well! The rest, as they say, is history: in October 1986, Andy and I co-founded the Malvern Spitfire Team to undertake the recovery of R6644 and research the incident, and this endeavour rapidly expanded to various other local sites. Unwittingly what we had done was start a snowball rolling which rapidly gathered both pace and size! Everything we did we tried to make as professional as possible, out of respect for those whose sacrifices we were trying to remember and honour. We seemed to hit the right note because enthusiasts, veterans and the relatives of casualties all flocked to our banner like moths around a flame.

In 1990, my first book, *Spitfire Squadron*, was published and in 1992 my ex-wife, Anita, and I co-founded Ramrod Publications to produce, promote and distribute my material. Throughout all this time Andy was busy researching various projects himself, and I urged him constantly to write it all up in a book – which we would publish. His research was, I knew, outstanding, his attention to detail incredible, and all of the information he collated original material. Unfortunately, however, Andy became buffeted around a bit by life's slipstream, suffering various major setbacks in life through no direct fault of his own, meaning that his book just never got written – until now.

Over the many years I have known Andy Long he has bombarded me in conversation with snippets of information regarding his various research projects, as each made progress. Due to the depth of detail it was sometimes difficult to keep track of who was who and what was what; it has been absolutely delightful, therefore, to have the opportunity, at last, to read these stories in a coherent and chronological presentation between the covers of this book. I know how hard Andy has worked on this book, the years spent on research, travelling, piecing together the jig-saw and then finally writing up the whole story – no easy task, believe you me, especially when fitted in around Andy's full time job as a Road Safety Officer for Worcestershire County Council and a long distance relationship with his beloved girlfriend, Jacks, who lives many miles away in Reading.

No-one knows Andy better than me after all these years and the strife we have been through together. I am absolutely delighted that after all these years the public will now get the opportunity to enjoy reading the fruits of Andy's labour and share his knowledge, passion and enthusiasm. Sadly Andy's mother, Pam, died suddenly in 2001, as did my own father later that year, but I know that she would be immensely proud of Andy's great achievement – which Victory Books International is proud to support.

Hopefully the story of Andy's long road to authorship will inspire others to step out of the shadows. Already Andy is talking about various other titles – crack on, I can't wait to read them!

Dilip Sarkar MBE FRHistS, Worcester, January 2007

Authors Introduction

Those readers who know me and are aware of this work have most likely said "At last, he's finished it!" It has, for sure, been a long time coming, the journey at times both enjoyable and frustrating, the latter upon reaching certain inevitable dead ends. Whilst I am obviously delighted that this book has finally appeared in print, I am also saddened by the fact that not all of the pilots alive when I started my research survive the present day. Sadly, therefore, those inspirational men died without seeing what has now been written about them; I hope, however, that they would be pleased with this posthumous recognition.

Although the book's theme is WW2 fighter pilots who came from Worcestershire, I make no apology for having included a chapter on Hereford's Flight Lieutenant Ray Henderson. When I started my research the counties of Herefordshire and Worcestershire were one, and so the original concept to was produce a book on fighter pilots accordingly. In April 1998, however, the two counties spilt due to local government restructuring and once more became seperate authorities. A similar case arises with Pilot Officer George Boucher, from Kinver and who spent time in Worcestershire; recent research confirmed, however, that his time working for the Air Ministry was not locally, at Kidderminster, but in London. His story is nonetheless still included. I am of the opinion that the stories of these two airmen still needed telling, along with the others featured in this book. As the reader will see, Worcestershire produced some remarkable men who served in the RAF during WW2. Some were fortunate in enjoying protracted careers, others were sadly cut down in their prime: all remain an inspiration.

The areas of operations in which 'The Faithful Few' served were numerous, including the hectic days over Kent and Britain's south coast during 1940, offensive operations over the Pas-de-Calais in 1941, braving lethal flak on anti armour patrols over Normandy, the debilitating humidity of Burma, the unforgiving North African desert, and finally the freezing night skies over Germany. Between them these men represent an excellent cross section of the fighter pilot's experience 1939-45.

It is perhaps worth mentioning how we decided upon the title of this book. During the English Civil War, Worcester, due to its support of the Royalist cause, became known as 'The Faithful City'. The 'Few', of course, refers to those gallant airmen of Fighter Command who won the epic Battle of Britain. There were, however, many less trained fighter pilots than there were infantryman, for example, and so the same term applies, in my opinion, to all of those brave young men who went to war in the cockpit of a fighter plane. During the war, two officers of No 66 Squadron, Athol Forbes and 'Dizzy' Allen, wrote a book called 'Fighter Boys', telling the individual stories of pilots in their squadron. So, 'The Faithful Few: Worcestershire's Fighter Boys' is, I hope you will agree, a most appropriate title.

I have tried my best to make this book as interesting and 'readable' as possible, whether to readers with an interest in local history or in RAF history. Any mistakes, however, are entirely mine! Naturally I hope very much that you will enjoy this, my first, book.

In conclusion I would share with the reader this appropriate Shakespearean quote: -

'An honest tale speeds best when plainly told.'
(Richard III, Act IV, Scene III)

Andrew Long, Worcester, January 2007

Chapter One

Sqn Ldr David Pemberton DFC, CO of No 1 (F) Sqn during the Battle of Britain. (Andrew Kimbell).

RAF Station Northolt sits just off the A40 on the western approaches to London, a permanent reminder to the RAF's aerial activity during the last war. Now under constant use by VIP and business traffic, and the operations of 32 Squadron, early July 1940 saw the station consumed by activity; but certainly not of the business type. Instead there were several squadrons busy preparing themselves for the ensuing combat against the then all conquering Luftwaffe.

Dispersed over the airfield were two Hurricane squadrons - 1 and 257, whilst 1 also had a detached flight at Hawkinge. Commanding No 1 was Squadron Leader David Pemberton, of Broadway, Worcestershire. He was an experienced pre-war pilot, having joined the RAF in 1930, passing out of Cranwell in 1932 to join 99 Squadron who were a bomber unit equipped with Handley Page Heyfords. There then followed an overseas posting where he spent 2 years in the middle east, before coming back to the UK and joining 601 Squadron for just over a year.

The phoney war in late 1939 saw him attached to 67 Wing HQ before going to 1 Squadron at Berry-au-Bac as their operations officer. Pilot Officer Paul Richey, author of the acclaimed book 'Fighter Pilot' makes several references to Pemberton in this book, and it makes excellent reading into the exploits of the squadron during that time. With the Battle of France in full swing, the squadron were forced to operate from eight locations prior to their withdrawal back to Northolt on June 18th.

Pemberton took command of the squadron from Squadron Leader 'Bull' Halahan, and many of the pilots who had picked up valuable combat experience over France were being sent to instruct. Halahan, Richey, and Pilot Officer Hanks all ended up at 5 Operational Training Unit to pass on their experiences to the pupil fighter pilots, who in a matter of weeks would be embroiled in the Battle of Britain.

Hurricanes of No 1 (F) Sqn during the Battle of France.
(Andrew Kimbell).

The 'B' Flight commander was also from Worcestershire. Flying Officer Harry Hillcoat, from Bromsgrove, was also a pre-war pilot, having served with 605 Squadron, joining them in 1938, before being called to full time service in August 1939. His father was a naval veteran of the Battle of Jutland, and the family were prominent in the motor trade, founding what was to become the Bristol Street Motors chain. After serving with 605, and surviving two forced landings, he was posted to 1 Squadron at Chateadun. On June the 4th 1940, he destroyed a He 111, but not before the top gunner had peppered his Hurricane and damaged his engine, thus making have his third forced landing of the year!

July had started quietly, with patrols being carried out between many practice flights. New pilots were coming in, with Pilot Officer's Elkington and Davey joining. Elkington was another pilot with Worcestershire roots, with the family coming from Grafton, Bromsgrove. More practice flying ensured, until the afternoon of July 19th, when Red Section had an engagement.

The Faithful Few

Squadron Leader Pemberton, with Pilot Officer Browne and Pilot Officer Matthews spotted an He 111 20 miles north of Brighton emerging from cloud. Pilot Officer Browne engaged it first, and succeeded in expending all his ammunition at the bomber. He then tailed the raider, giving constant positional information, and detailing the course of the He 111. In doing so, he became subject to intense and accurate return fire from the bomber, who in turn managed to hit the Hurricane, peppering the glycol tank, and set it ablaze. Browne managed to force land the stricken fighter (P3471) near Brighton and get clear before fire destroyed the aircraft. Pemberton and Matthews searched for the He 111, but it appeared that it had eluded them, and got clean away. This was not the case, as a section from 145 Squadron caught it on the way out, and shot it down into the sea off Shoreham. The He 111 was from 7/KG55, and the entire crew were lost.

Pilots of 605 Sqn, early 1940; Flt Lt Bryan Hillcoat first left.
(Ian Piper).

The following day, the squadron patrolled the south coast without incident and on the 22nd, orders were issued sending the squadron to Hawkinge to pre-empt any German attacks. However, nothing came of it, and they all returned en masse the same evening. They were off again the next day, this time to Tangmere to temporarily replace 43 Squadron, who in turn went to Northolt. A patrol of the Isle of Wight was flown by 'A' flight, and Blue section of 'B' flight, but bad weather hampered operations, with Blue section just getting back before the weather closed in.

The morning of the 25th started briskly with Portland being bombed. The squadron were engaged on convoy protection patrols, but once again they failed to encounter the enemy. During the afternoon, Blue section, Led by Flight Lieutenant Hillcoat, along with Flying Officer Salmon and Pilot Officer Goodman, ran into Bf 109s of JG27. Hillcoat attacked one, but without any visible result before he ran out of ammunition. Flying Officer Salmon hit one Bf 109 which promptly went into a spin. After following it down from 10,000 feet to 2,000 feet, he blacked out and did not see it hit the water. Pilot Officer Goodman was in turn attacked, and as it broke away it went into a stall. By now the combat was pretty close to the water, and with insufficient height to recover, the Bf 109 crashed into the sea. The pilot, *Oberleutenant* Karl Heinz Kirstein of III/JG27 was killed. All three Hurricanes returned to base undamaged.

The next five days consisted of more sorties around the Isle of Wight, covering several convoys, and for the first time the pilots were called upon to undertake night patrols. The last day of July saw Flying Officer Matthews, Pilot Officer Davey and Sergeant Merchant catch a Do 17 eight miles off St Catherine's Point. Flying at 8000 feet, the German crew spotted the approaching Hurricanes, and promptly dived away to sea level, heading for the French coast as fast as it could. The section attacked in line astern, making several passes, but the bomber managed to get away with one damaged engine. The pilots regretted allowing this solitary aircraft to get away from them, however the mood that night was lifted with the news that Flight Lieutenant 'Hilly' Brown had been awarded the DFC. He was one of the most experienced pilots on serving with the squadron, and had destroyed at least 12 enemy aircraft to date. Shot down at the very end of the Battle of France, he had evaded the Germans and managed to get back to Britain.

August opened with Flight Lieutenant Brown DFC, Sergeant Merchant and Pilot Officer Davey being scrambled to intercept an incoming raid. While 10 miles south of Beachy Head, Brown spotted a Do 17 at 800 feet and attacked. The gunners were alert to the incoming Hurricanes, opening fire on them at 400 yards range. Brown managed a short burst before the aircraft disappeared into cloud. Further sorties were flown that day, but no enemy aircraft were encountered, and all the Hurricanes retuned to Northolt, with 43 Squadron going back the other way. Hawkinge was visited the next day, but no sorties were flown. On the 3rd, Hillcoat and Pilot Officer Hancock flew to Dengie Flats for air to ground firing practice, an exercise repeated by many pilots throughout August. Fighter affiliation was another duty carried out when time and operations permitted. On the 4th, six Blenheims arrived at Northolt for such an exercise, with sections from 1 Squadron acting as enemy aircraft performing dummy attacks. In the early evening, the squadron flew to Tangmere and returned at dusk. During the next two days, they flew to Manston on the 5th, and North Weald on the 6th, but no sorties were flown.

No 1 (F) Sqn, late 1940: P/O Elkington on wing, far right; Other known faces in front row are P/O Pat Hancock, S/L Mark 'Hilly' Brown DFC & P/O Charles Cetham. Middle row, left: 2nd Lt Jean Demozay, far right: Sgt Antonin Zavoral. On wing, extreme left: P/O Arthur Clowes DFM.
(Via Wg Cdr J Elkington).

The 11th dawned with three sections scrambled to patrol the coast south of Tangmere. Control vectored the group out over the channel, and when a distance from land, they sighted some Bf 109s. Before any action could be taken, they were bounced by a number of Bf 110s of ZG2, who dived on the formation from up sun. The Hurricanes separated, and Pilot Officer Chetham and Pilot Office Goodman singled out one of their assailants and curved in to attack. Chetham got to the Bf110 first, and with his first burst apparently silenced the rear gunner. The cockpit canopy flew off and the pilot was seen trying to get out. A drogue with 200 yards of cable attached began to trail from the Bf 110, though it is not known as to why this aircraft would have been fitted with such. Chetham set fire to the starboard engine before breaking away. Goodman closed in on the stricken aircraft , and from 50 yards gave a five second burst, after which the Bf 110 hit the sea and broke up. Flight Lieutenant Brown DFC attacked another, and after three close range attacks, left it diving towards the sea with its port engine and fuselage in flames. Pilot Officer Mann observed it explode during its descent. However, the combat proved not to be one sided - Pilot Officer Shaw suffered aileron damage, and Pilot Officer Davey was killed while attempting to force land his badly damaged Hurricane on Sandown golf course, and becoming the squadron's first Battle of Britain fatality. August 11th proved to be Fighter Commands worst day for fighter pilot fatalities - a total of 25 were killed.

During the afternoon of the 15th, the south coast came under concentrated attacks by large escorted formations. Portland was targeted by Stukas of I/StG 1 and II/StG 2, covered by Bf 110s of V/LG2 and up to 60 Bf 109s. 60 Ju88s attacked Worthy Down and Middle Wallop, while further east, Hawking and Lympne were also attacked. At North Weald, Red, Yellow and Green sections were scrambled to counter 16 Bf 110s and nine Bf 109s of Erprobrungsgruppe 210 who were arrowing in to Martlesham Heath. While south of Harwich, at only 1500 feet, the formation was attacked by Bf 109s. The squadron, and in particular Red section was hit hard. Flight Lieutenant Brown DFC had his Hurricane set alight, forcing him to bale out. He landed in the sea, suffering with minor wounds to the face and hands, and was picked up by a nearby trawler. Pilot Officer Browne, who had survived the encounter with the He 111 on July 19th was shot down into the sea, as was Sergeant Shanahan. Both were killed. Flying Officer Matthews sighted the formation bombing Martlesham and attacked three of them, damaging one. Pilot Officer Mann found himself targeted by a Bf 110 which attacked from astern. After shaking it off, he was attacked again, this time by a Bf 109. During the ensuing tail chase, he managed to reverse the situation and get on its tail. After opening fire he blew the top off the cockpit and set it on fire. Pilot Officer Elkington was also attacked by a Bf 109. He later wrote: -

"I was acting as Green 2. When travelling due east from Martlesham at 10,000 feet an Me 109 approached me from head on and to the left, 1000 feet below. The enemy aircraft started to climb and turn to the left, but I turned sharp left and came in behind him and gave him 1 short burst with no known effect. I again fired at the enemy aircraft from astern as it straightened out and went into a steep climb. I gave him a 2 second burst from astern and above. The engine belched fumes and it turned over on its back , staying there for about 3 seconds, and then turned over and dropped like a plummet into the sea. I circled round and saw no one get out."

By the end of the day, Pemberton and Hillcoat had each flown four sorties, without success.

At midday on August 16th, the squadron were ordered to patrol Tangemere. When over Selsey Bill, they again found themselves being bounced by 109s. A fight ensured, but without result. For Pilot Officer Elkington, it was his turn to be on the receiving end of an attack. He had been acting as a 'weaver' above and behind the squadron, when he lost contact with them. However he spotted a Bf 109 over Portsmouth and went after it, but on the approach he failed to see the other Bf 109 that had come in behind him. It opened fire and set the Hurricane alight, leaving him with no option but to bale out. Attempting to abandon the stricken aircraft , he only managed to get half out, held to the side of the fighter by his radio lead. He managed to struggle back in to the cockpit, disconnect the lead, and get clear at the second attempt. Unknown to him, his mother, who lived on Hayling Island, had witnessed a Hurricane get systematically attacked until the pilot baled out, unaware that the life and death situation that unfolded before her actually involved her son! The Hurricane, P3173, buried itself deep in the ground at Manor Farm, Chidham. Elkington was hospitalised with minor injuries, and had become the 18th 'kill' of Major Helmut Wick. He recorded the combat in his log book: -

F/O John Elkington and Hurricane,
Wittering 1940.
(Wg Cdr J Elkington).

" CO leading. In Berry's section. On to P'smoth & ran into 100+ Huns there. Got spilt up doing X over. Ran into 8 109's. Went after one & 3 others were behind. Cannon hit s'tbd. tank and kite burst into flames; ended up by the Nab Light. Baled out and landed at W.Wittering and landed on my ——! Berry blew me onto land with his slipstream. R.W.Sussex hospital by ambulance. Chute pinched. Baled out from 10,000 ft. at 13.40 hours."

During the afternoon, with Pemberton leading the squadron, they sighted a formation of He 111s, approaching in three waves, with 40 aircraft in each. The bombers were from KG55, and were headed for Heathrow. Lurking above them were the fighter escorts, awaiting their opportunity to attack. Pemberton led the squadron in, flying level with the first wave. With them all in line astern, they turned in to make a head on attack on the second wave. Pemberton wrote after: -

"My first burst at the front of an He 111 sent the bomber down in flames. I dived to break away, and came up again to make a second attack , but I saw no results of this second attack. Immediately afterwards, my engine caught fire, and as I got ready to abandon the aircraft the flames subsided and I brought my aircraft back to base. Subsequent examination showed that 2 armour piercing bullets had penetrated to the top cowling and scored the camshaft to depth of 1/16th of an inch. Possibly the fire was caused by oil fumes igniting and burning out."

Meanwhile, while Pemberton had broken away with a burning aircraft, the other pilots were tackling the formation. Pilot Officer Matthews had stuck with Pemberton, but had pulled away when he observed a Bf 110 from a formation of five that was busy attacking a Hurricane. Matthews quickly got on its tail and shot it down. The Bf 110 was one of 6/ZG6, and after partially breaking up, crashed into the grounds of the Aldro School in Darly Road, Eastbourne. The unfortunate pilot, *Oberleutenant* Ernest Hollekamp

Major Helmut Wick, who shot down P/O Elkington on August 16th, 1940, marking his 18th aerial victory.

fell to his death after his parachute failed; his body being recovered from a roof in Gaudick Road.

Pilot Officer Boot claimed a He 111 but received a damaged glycol tank, causing him to force land on the Hogsback near Farnham. Sergeant Clowes tackled another, sending it down in a vertical dive . Upon rejoining the formation he attacked another, but without result. Dropping below the cloud base, he sighted and attacked at Ju 88 giving it one burst. This apparently attracted the attentions of four Spitfires from 602 Squadron, so Clowes broke off leaving the bomber to the others. However, it sees that the bomber in question was the one engaged by Pilot Officer Goodman.

After the initial attack, Pilot Officer Goodman singled out one of the He 111s - this particular one being flown by *Hauptmann* Sabler, the *Staffelkapitan* of 4/KG55. After his first burst, one of the engines stopped , and Sabler force landed at Upper Frithwold Farm near Petworth. Goodman circled the downed bomber at 500 feet and saw the crew emerge from the wreck, which then suddenly exploded. The crew were killed and a chunk of wreckage hit Goodman's Hurricane, affecting the oil pressure, but not endangering him. Flight Sergeant Berry attacked two He 111s and Pilot Officer Salmon, who had been left behind during the initial run in to the formation, climbed up to 22,000 feet to attack from above. Upon commencing his dive, a Bf 110 came into his sights below him, and he promptly attacked, stopping the port engine and causing it to dive away. Pilot Officer Stavert landed at Redhill to refuel, but while on the ground the airfield was attacked by a Do 17. Pilot Officer Hancock had to return to base after tangling with a Bf 110 which in turn shot away his ailerons. Hillcoat flew four sorties that day, but made no claims, unlike Pilot Officer Stavert, who sent a He 111 diving into cloud after the head on attack. After following it through the cloud base he saw the wreckage of the enemy aircraft burning on the ground. That evening the Squadron had claimed four He 111s destroyed, one Ju 88 destroyed, two He 111s as probables and a Bf 110 destroyed - to date their most successful day.

Luckily, the next 24 hours were quieter , allowing practice flying in the morning and afternoon. However, it proved to be the calm before the proverbial storm. The next day was August 18th, a day that would become to be known as 'The Hardest Day'.

During the morning, reconnaissance aircraft ventured over the south coast, focusing on the airfields, and it wasn't until mid day that large formations of German aircraft began to mass over France. Do 17s of KG76 arrowed in at low level, heading for Kenley. At the same time a free hunt of approximately 60 Bf 109s swept the Ashford and Canterbury areas, while behind them came more bombers.

Biggin Hill was hit by He 111's from KG1, while KG76 turned their attentions on West Malling. 1 Squadron had flow twice during the morning of August 18th, but during the afternoon, with Squadron Leader Pemberton leading, and Flight Lieutenant Hillcoat leading Blue section, they flew to North Weald.

By now, the bomber formations which had hit the airfields were racing for the coast. The squadron encountered a formation of Do 17s of KG76 over the South Downs, and performed a beam attack on it. Blue Section, comprising

Hillcoat and Pilot Officers Stavert and Goodman singled out one of the bombers, and promptly shot it down into the sea, killing *Leutenant* Leder and his crew. Pilot Officer Goodman broke away from the section to check out a parachutist, only to spot a Bf 110 with a heavily smoking port engine trying to get away, only 50 feet above the sea.

This was one of the surviving machines from 6/ZG26 that had been subjected to a mauling by 56 Squadron. Goodman turn in to attack the damaged aircraft, and despite it taking evasive action, Goodman hit it and succeeded in setting both of its engines on fire. So intent on destroying the Bf 110, Goodman hadn't seen the Bf 109 which had got into a firing position, and had opened up on him, hitting the Hurricane. Pulling the fighter into a tight turn, he saw the Bf 110 hit the sea, and applied full boost to get away, crossing the coast at Rye.

Mid afternoon, Stukas from St.G 77 hit targets at Thorney Island, Ford, and the radar at Poling, while 1/St.G 3 attacked Gosport, with fighter cover provided by 55 Bf 109's of JG2, who performed a following free hunt, while JG27 were in action over the Isle of Wight.

At 18.15 hours the squadron, airborne, in position near Southend at 21,000 feet. After emerging from a cloud layer, they were attacked by about 12 Bf 109s of JG3, without result. One dived past Squadron Leader Pemberton, and he gave chase. There then followed a high speed pursuit from over the Thames Estuary and out over Kent. Pemberton later wrote: -

"I gave it a 2 second burst from about 250 yards, which made him go down, and the E/A hedge hopped through Kent. I withheld my fire for some time in the hope he would go down, but when it started to regain some height, I gave him a short burst at 500 feet when the E/A crashed in flames between Tenterden and Cranbrook."

The Bf 109 crashed at Blue House Farm, Milebush and exploded. *Obergefreiter* Basell of 8/JG3 was killed instantly.

By the end of the day, Squadron Leader Pemberton, and Flight Lieutenant Hillcoat had flown five sorties.

The following day was much quieter; and during the evening, night patrols were flown. Pilot Officer Birch flew into the balloon barrage over London, hitting a cable and had to bale out. He landed on a rooftop, and as the 1 Squadron ORB put it: -

The Faithful Few

"He landed with very minor injuries on a house top at Finchley and after convincing the inhabitants of his bonafides, he was requested to make another small jump from the eaves to the top of a ladder about 5 feet below into the arms of a fireman who maintained that this manouvre had been practiced frequently. P/O Birch, steeling himself for this second jump, was successfully brought to earth and enjoyed the enthusiastic welcome of the crowd and the hospitality of the Police force."

During the early afternoon of August 28th, Pemberton leading 11 Hurricanes, left base to patrol over Hornchurch, and encountered a formation of Do 17's over Rochford at 15,000 feet, en route to attack Hornchurch. Pemberton filed this report: -

"I was Red one and leading the squadron. When over Rochford at 15,000 feet an enemy formation of about 30 bombers was seen at 12,000 feet. I led the attack from above and ahead and all the pilots engaged the E/A. The enemy formation was not broken up and individual attacks were made the pilots. As a result of the attack, two Do 215's were seen to crash - one at Rochford, and the other at sea near Tongue Lighthouse. Another was seen proceeding out with its engines smoking at sea level, protected by a vic of 5 bombers. These casualties are confirmed by Flight Lieutenant Hillcoat, Pilot Officer Matthews and Flight Sergeant Berry. As no pilot will make any individual claim, I do so on behalf of the squadron."

The Dornier which ditched was from 6/KG3, and had been earlier attacked by 54 Squadron. The crew survived, and were picked up by fishing boats.

On the 30th, the squadron were airborne over north London when they spotted six aircraft being attacked by Hurricanes. They formed up to attack, and began their approach, only to realise the bombers were actually Blenheims, and that they has stumbled upon an affiliation exercise. After breaking away, they then observed a formation of bombers with about 40 fighters giving cover. This was a raid led by He 111s of KG53, heading for the Vauxhall works at Radlett.

Individual attacks were performed on the formation, and despite the attentions of other fighter squadrons, the bombers did get through to their targets. Sergeant Merchant attacked a He 111 of 3/KG53 that had earlier been damaged by Flying Officer Cutts and Sergeant Davies of 222 Squadron, and Pilot Officer Hancock. Two of the crew baled out, but it crashed on Lifstan Way, Southend, killing the three remaining crew members.

Sergeant Clowes engaged another He 111, and one of the escorting Bf 110s, damaging them both. Pilot Officer Mann damaged two Bf 110's, while Pilot Officer Matthews attacked a straggling He 111, only to see a Hurricane of 56 Squadron come in and finish it off. This might have been A1+BN of 5/KG35 which force landed near Halstead with one fatality after being despatched by Flight Lieutenant Gracie.

On the last day of August, the squadron were scrambled early from Northolt. Pemberton wrote: -

"I was Blue 1. The E/A were travelling NW over Chelmsford at about 15,000 feet in formations of tens stepped up to about 20,000 feet, about one hundred of them. They were protected by fighters. I tried to bring the squadron in a head on attack (we were south west of the enemy formation). As I drew alongside I saw another enemy formation above us, composed of fighters and bombers , and the squadron had to engage fighters which came down. After a general mill round of the fighters, I found myself alone, and followed the main formation until I found myself a suitable target, which was a Ju 88 at which I was able to fire all my rounds deliberately at 300 to 250 yards. Although I do not claim this as a victim, one engine appeared to be stopped and the other belching smoke, but he did not seem to be losing height very rapidly. I was unable to watch him as there were other fighters in the vicinity."

Like the ones Sergeant Merchant was tangling with - he had attacked two Bf 110's, damaging one and possibly destroying another, before one of the ZG76 machines peppered his Hurricane and set it alight. He baled out suffering from burns, his aircraft crashing near Halstead.

Despite the attentions of the escorts, Sergeant Clowes DFM, had managed to put in a frontal attack on the formation of bombers, before he too was attacked by Bf 110's. Pulling a loop, he turned the tables on his assailant, and delivered an attack, putting the starboard engine out of action. Following his victim down to ground level, he saw it looking for a place to land. Pilot Officers Boot, Mann, and Dibnah also engaged, and damaged Bf 110s.

September stared with Hillcoat leading the squadron, as he had done several times before, engaging a heavily escorted bomber formation east of Tonbridge. His combat report stated: -

"I was Blue 1 leading No 1 Squadron. At about 17,000 feet I saw anti aircraft fire ahead which helped me locate E/A. I climbed between the sun and the AA

bursts, and then observed 12 bombers , thought to be Do's, escorted by many fighter formations which had dispersed above and around to avoid the AA. The enemy were proceeding south, and presumably dropped their bombs. I saw several fighters coming in behind and decided they could attack us before being in a advantageous position to attack the bombers. I gave the order "Attack the fighters" and turned left. From the ensuing melee, I picked out an Me 109 which managed to keep ahead until just before the coast. My first burst of 1 second hit his radiator and I waited five minutes until he had slowed down a little. My second burst caused smoke to come from his engine. After two more short bursts the pilot jettisoned the hood and waved his arm. I climbed above and behind him to give him a chance to jump out. He landed near a road close to the shore not far from Folkestone. I circled and saw a pilot picked up by the military. The E/A fell about 100 yards from him and blew up."

The Bf 109 was 5087, of 7/JG53, coded 10+I, and was piloted by *Leutenant* H Strasser. Hillcoat's remarkable restraint in combat had saved Strasser's life, when he could have delivered a coup de grace on the stricken fighter.

During the fight, Pilot Officers Boot, Birch and Chetham all tangled with the Bf 109's and subsequently claimed one each. However, it was not all one sided, for Flight Sergeant Frederick Berry DFM was shot down and killed, his Hurricane crashing at Brisely Farm, Ruckinge. He had been with the Squadron since 1938, and had flown courageously during the Battle of France, and was one of, if not the most experienced pilot on the squadron at the time of his death.

Hillcoat led the squadron again on the 2nd, during a combat in the late afternoon, and once more clashed with Bf 109s. Originally detailed to patrol base, and when at 10,000 feet, AA bursts were seen over London, indicating the presence of bombers flying at 18,000 feet. However the formation was heading south east and out over the coast. 1 Squadron went to engage the fighters, and Hillcoat filed this report after: -

"I climbed to 20,000 feet and attacked a formation of Me 109's at 19,000 feet, on the extreme right of their formation, and they promptly formed a defensive circle and were joined by other formations. I attacked one Me 109. After the first burst smoke appeared and glycol poured from the radiator. I gave him five or six bursts of two seconds at about 100 yards, and I could see my ammunition hitting him. My attack was from the rear with slight deflection. I broke off when I was satisfied the E/A could not get home. It went down in a shallow dive about 10 miles inland, north of Dungeness, near Ashford. About

a dozen Me 109s were manouvreing to get on my tail, so I dived to ground level and made my way back to base."

Hillcoat's victim was a machine from 8/JG54 flown by *Unteroffizier* Elbers. He force landed at speed, on Finns Farm, near Kingsnorth, with the aircraft sliding over a field, through a hedge and coming to rest in a ditch.

Pilot Officer Chetham was the only other pilot to engage the Bf 109's with visible results, damaging one before being forced to break away. Turning to another formation, he managed to fire at three of them before having to break away once again.

Sadly, the combat of September 3rd, proved to be the last for Hillcoat. Ordered to patrol Dungeness, they were 'bounced' by Bf 109s who fell on them from above. Two Hurricanes fell from the formation - P3782 of Pilot Officer Shaw, and P3044 of Hillcoat. One pilot baled out, one did not.

Wing Commander (then Pilot Officer) Pat Hancock recalled: -

"My logbook is sparse for that sortie on 3rd September, and shows that we were on patrol north of Dungeness when attacked by Bf 109s. I have no recollection of that action in detail except I thought I saw Shaw land by parachute in the sea and float in his MaeWest. I thought he succumbed to the cold water quickly."

However, this was not the case, as P3782, with Shaw still at the controls, dived inland, and impacted at high speed at Parkhouse Farm, Chart Sutton. It buried itself deep in the earth, and the impact was so severe that the remains of Robert Shaw lie in the wreck to this day.. The site is now known as the Unknown Battle of Britain Pilots Memorial Garden, and is formally marked. So as Shaw crashed inland, it can be assumed that Hillcoat was the pilot who had baled out and landed in the sea. What a tragedy, to survive combat, only to die of exposure in the Channel. He was never seen again.

Hillcoat had made 116 operational flights in the Battle of Britain, and is remembered on panel 4 of the Runnymede Memorial

September 5th was a fruitless day for the squadron, with no contacts being made. On the 6th, nine Hurricanes were ordered off to patrol Kenley, and spotted a group of Ju 88s, protected by Bf 110's. A range of individual combats took place, with Flight Lieutenant Brown damaging one from 6/KG76, only for

Pilot Officer Stavert to finish it off. It crash landed and burnt out at Tanyards Farm, Tonbridge; with the entire crew being taken POW.

Pilot Officer Dibnah had broken away from the squadron as his Hurricane was suffering from airscrew problems, and spotted a group of Bf 110's bombing Brooklands. He followed the formation, and saw a Bf 110 attacking two Hurricanes. He performed a frontal attack on the fighter, and as he passed, one of the crew baled out. The aircraft dived into the ground and blew up. This was S9+BH of 1/*Erprobrungsgruppe* 210, piloted by *Unteroffizier* Gerhard Ruger, with *Unteroffizier* Edmund Ernst as his gunner. Ruger was killed in the crash. Pilot Officer Goodman had attacked another Bf 110, only to be shot down bythe rear gunner, forcing him to bale out.

Just after 1300 hrs, nine Hurricanes were ordered to patrol Maidstone, and were later vectored to intercept an incoming raid over the Dungeness. The fighter escort attacked the Squadron, but without result. Pilot Officer Stavert, however, managed to damage a 109. As a good example of the pressure under which RAF fighter pilots were operating, Squadron Leader Pemberton flew a total of six operational sorties that day, all in Hurricane P2751, which was his regular aircraft during the battle.

Pemberton flew four more times the following day, when the Luftwaffe changed tactics, and began bombing London itself. At 16.25 hours, 11 Hurricanes, led by Pemberton, were scrambled off to patrol base at 15,000 feet. There they saw a massed formation of approximately 300 aircraft, of which 100 were fighters. On the initial attack, Flight Lieutenant Holderness claimed a Do 215 as destroyed, and Sergeant Clowes claimed a Bf 110. The squadron returned to base, and made rapid turn around - refuelling and rearming before scrambling once again. During the second engagement, Flight Lieutenant Finnis and Pilot Officer Homer damaged a Do 215 apiece. And that was the last full scale combat the squadron would have in the Battle of Britain, for on September 9th, they were withdrawn to RAF Wittering in Cambridgeshire.

The opportunity was taken to fit the Hurricanes with VHF radios while out in 12 Group, and a handful of aircraft were dispersed at Collyweston, Wittering's satellite aerodrome. Good news came their way on September 12th, when it was announced that Squadron Leader Pemberton and Pilot Officer Peter Boot (who had been with the squadron since the Battle of France) had both been awarded the DFC. The citation stated: -

"Sqn Ldr D A Pemberton (33036). This officer has displayed outstanding

The Faithful Few

leadership since the return of his squadron from France. He has led the squadron on almost every operation, during which they have destroyed or damaged fifty one enemy aircraft. His qualities of leadership and personal example have contributed largely to these successes."

Whilst at Wittering, the Squadron flew day, and night patrols, but no contact was made with the enemy. Patrol areas ranged from Coventry, Nottingham and Cambridge, while they also covered other RAF Bases at Duxford and Bircham Newton. A regime of re training commenced, with many practice flights being undertaken. They undertook formation flying, aerobatics, and dog fighting, and got to grips with the new VHF radios. At the same time the squadron had an influx of new pilots, with six of them being Czech.

At its new base, the Squadron still encountered the enemy, for on October 8th , Pilot Officers Matthews and Goodman engaged a lone bomber and damaged it, while Pilot Officer Elkington and Sergeant Davies attacked a lone Ju 88 the next day. Pilot Officer Elkington's combat report reads: -

"While on local flying with Blue 2, we were vectored by Control onto a Bogey. I saw a Ju 88 about 1000 feet below when at 7000 feet ravelling in the same direction. I went down to investigate and when about 800 yards away he started firing from top rear gun. He flew in and out of cloud and when he did so I climbed to await him emerging. Eventually I gave him 2 bursts of 3 secs from 600 yards without effect.. While in cloud I passed quite close to E/A. This dodging in and out of cloud kept up while I dived on him to 300 yards , firing a short burst. The E/A turned gently each time to avoid my fire. We eventually came out of cloud over the sea and the E/A came down to about 600 feet and started a dog fight with steep turns. The rear top gunner firing at about 700 yards. After flying straight at me I climbed into the sun and dived on the E/A who turned, and I pulled round to keep with him and fired the rest of my ammunition in a slight deflection from 200 yards closing right in to 20 yards. I pulled out and upwards to 600 feet and blacked out coming out on my back. When I had righted my aircraft I looked around for two or three minutes without seeing trace of E/A. Visibility was very clear and clouds about 10 miles away and I circled up to about 1000 feet could not see anything. I landed at Manby."

That very day the Squadron suffered one final Battle of Britain casualty: Sergeant Sidney Warren went missing during a flight over the Wash. He was never seen again, and it was assumed he had crashed either in the Wash or North Sea.

The Faithful Few

The month finished with three engagements with enemy bombers in five days. Flight Lieutenant Brown, with Pilot Officers Clowes and Kershaw destroyed a Do 17 near St Neots on October 24th, while three days later Pilot Officers Goodman, Elkington and Robinson attacked a Do 17 above Feltwell Aerodrome, damaging it before it escaped in cloud. The combat report said: -

"E/A sighted over Feltwell Aerodrome on return from East Coast patrol at Clacton with Blue 1 and 2. E/A was a Do 17. When sighted E/A was being fired at by Bofors from Feltwell. Blue Section dived low over aerodrome and climbed to attack, but Bofors kept firing and forced us to split up. After a wide left hand turn round one side of the aerodrome, Blue 1 attacked from astern as E/A entered cloud. I was above Blue 1 and kept to the right in case E/A turned in cloud. I came very close to E/A but did not open fire in case Blue 1 was in there. In a gap in the cloud I had 2 bursts at about 350 yards range. After that I lost E/A in the cloud and later saw Blue 1 on his tail again. I then returned to base."

Finally, Pilot Officer Robinson, and Sergeants Page and Jicha destroyed a Do 17 on October 29th .

Sunday November 3rd was a sad day indeed for the squadron. While returning to Wittering from Collyweston in very bad weather, Squadron Leader Pemberton DFC, flying his usual Hurricane P2751, crashed and was killed. It was a bitter blow to the squadron, losing their CO after his excellent leadership in battle, only to be killed in a crash attributed to the exceedingly bad weather conditions. Wing Commander Pat Hancock remembered Squadron Leader Pemberton being killed: -

"It was a sad loss and I had the unpleasant duty of gathering his effects for disposal. In general he was a pleasant man but knew what he wanted and was a good leader. I should say that in those early days there was a big difference between being a Pilot Officer and a squadron commander. On active service a CO was very much the senior officer although he might relax in the mess. So as an ordinary squadron pilot I cannot claim to have had a close friendship with David Pemberton but do say that after all these years I remember him with admiration and still feel his death was a sad loss."

He was returned home to Broadway where he was accorded a full military funeral, while his father, Guy Pemberton, who was the platoon commander of the local Home Guard led the mourners. After the service, he was interred in the family plot in the new cemetery of St Eadburghas. His grave is marked by a white Portland headstone, and inscribed upon it is the phrase 'A hero of the Battle of Britain', and a phrase which is so true. David Alwyne Pemberton DFC was 28 years old.

Pilot Officer Elkington continued to serve with the squadron until April 1941, before joining 55 Operational Training Unit at Usworth, and later their detached flight at Ouston before a short spell with 601 Squadron at Manston in May 1941.

At the end of July, he joined the newly formed 134 Squadron at Leconfield, under the command of Squadron Leader A.G. Miller, with the aim that the squadron were to join 151 Wing operating in Russia. Pilot Officer Elkington joined 'A' Flight, under Flight Lieutenant V.W.Berg. The ground crews embarked on the 'Llanstephan Castle' in Liverpool docks on August 12th, while the pilots were granted three days leave.

They embarked on the aircraft carrier 'Argus' at Port Greenock, flying off the ship on September 7th. Two Hurricanes were damaged by the small ramp at the end of the deck used for Queen Bee launches, but in general it had been a successful take off, considering they only had a 400 foot run to get airborne. The pilots landed at Vayanga, with the Hurricanes of Flight Lieutenant Berg and Sergeant Campbell crashing on landing - these being the two which had struck the ramp on take off.

The Squadron diary recorded: -

"Admiral Kuznetsov, Commanding Forces in Cola Peninsula, and flying staff, entertained officers of No 151 Wing to reception supper at Vayanga. Very enthusiastic welcome extended to guests. Soviet pilots conducted almost successful offensive with vodka, but only one Officer of another unit 'nose-dived'."

The first operation conducted by 134 took place on September 11th 1941, when four Hurricanes patrolled Murmansk, and East to the Finnish border. A second sortie was flown that afternoon, but both missions were hampered by fuel problems thought to be caused by inferior Russian fuel. A number of aircraft and pilots also operated from Afrikander Aerodrome , without success.

Regular patrols were being flown, but with no direct contact with the Germans, though 81 Squadron who were also part of 151 Wing, managed to engage several Bf 109s on the morning of September 17th, and shoot down four. They managed to down another two on September 26th, but to date, 134 had still had no contact, and had also managed to damage another two of their Hurricanes. The airfield was wet and waterlogged in places, and the weather made life difficult for them.

Sqn Ldr Pemberton DFC's grave at St Eadburgh's New Cemetery, Broadway, Worcs.

A tragic accident occurred on September 27th, when Flight Lieutenant Berg, in Hurricane BD825 took off with two groundcrew on the tail of the fighter. It climbed to about 50 feet before stalling and crashing. Flight Lieutenant Berg was seriously injured, and the two airmen on the tail, Aircraftsman 2nd Class Ridley and Thomas were both killed instantly.

The Squadron continued their patrols, and escorted Soviet bombers on sorties, until on October 10th, they finally managed to force combat with the enemy. Six aircraft of 'A' Flight were on patrol when they spotted several Ju 88s diving down onto the aerodrome, and engaged. Pilot Officer Cameron attacked the leading Ju 88, hitting it in the starboard engine, causing it to emit smoke. He also attacked the second Ju 88 in the formation without result, and made a head on attack on another.

Pilot Officer Furneaux made several attacks on one of the bombers, before setting the port engine on fire. A large piece from the starboard engine fell off, and eventually caught fire, before the aircraft crashed. Sergeant Gould also performed a head on attack on a Ju 88, hitting it in between the port engine and fuselage. Pieces fell off this aircraft and it broke away.

Sergeant Kirvan performed at least three attacks, leaving it when another Hurricane from 81 Squadron attacked it and set it on fire. It had been a productive morning, but another engagement occurred late in the afternoon when the aerodrome was bombed. Pilot Officer Elkington and Flight Sergeant

Barnes attacked the Ju 88, with Pilot Officer Elkington hitting the tail, leaving the rudder flapping. It began to dive away, and Flight Sergeant Barnes attacked it several times, killing the rear gunner after his third attack. It was left desperately trying to stay airborne at ground level, and well alight.

No further direct contact was made in the next three week, but the squadron continued to perform escorts and patrols, as well as get the Soviet pilots familiar with the Hurricane, with them undertaking practice flights between October 10th and 13th. The first Soviet success in a 134 Squadron Hurricane came on October 26th, when one of the pilots destroyed a Bf 110.

In early November, orders were issued for the squadron to return to England. All Hurricanes had officially been handed over to the Soviets on October 19th, and had been used to form 'No 1 Hurricane Squadron', and steps were taken to arrange the move out. Flying Officer Elkington, in charge of 'M' party, departed for Rosta for embarkation by minesweeper on November 16th. The squadron came back in several ships : HMS Kenya, Intrepid, Berwick, Bedouin and Offa, with them returning in early December. The Soviet government asked if their return, and that of 81 Squadron from Murmansk, could be kept quiet, and this was agreed by the RAF.

Camship launch: A 'Hurricat' of the MSFU makes a rocket assisted take-off.

134 Squadron officially reformed on December 30th 1941 at Eglington, this time equipped with Spitfires. Flying Officer Elkington stayed with them until April 1942 before joining the Merchant Ship Fighter Unit at Speke. The RAF had developed an idea to be able to give air cover to the convoys on the route to Russia. Too risky to deploy aircraft carriers, they came up with the plan of a single Hurricane launched from a merchant ship off a rail. The problem was that once the Hurricane was launched, it had nowhere to land, and the pilot had to either bale out or ditch near a ship in the hope that he would be picked up.

All MSFU pilots were volunteers, and knew the risks involved. Training commenced, with pilots experiencing dummy launches from a rail set up on the airfield. Pilot Officer Elkington experienced two such practice launches while at Speke, and participated in 'Camship' escorts, but did not perform a 'Hurricat' launch in anger.

He returned to 1 Squadron at Acklington in August 1942, when they were operating Typhoons on sorties over Europe, before joining 539 Squadron the following month. They were a Boston Havoc Turbinelight unit, later re equipping with Hurricanes. Upon disbanding in January 1943, Elkington went to 197 at Drem. They were a newly formed Typhoon squadron, and headed south to Tangmere in March 1943, before leaving them in September of that year.

In December 1943, he was posted overseas, joining 67 Squadron at Alipore, flying Hurricanes. Staying in India to the end of the war, he returned to England in October 1946, and unlike many, many others, continued his career in the RAF. Postings in the following years included 236 Operational Conversion Unit, Kinloss, 240 Squadron, Central Flying School Little Rissington, and a spell at the RAF College Cranwell. He retired in November 1975 as a Wing Commander. The list of different aircraft types flown by him is long and include those of the Axis nations, including the Bf 110 and Zero.

'Tim' now enjoys a well deserved retirement in the idylls of the Gloucestershire countryside, and the author would like to express his thanks and appreciation for all his help with this chapter.

Above: F/O Elkington whilst in Russia with 134 Sqn.

Below: W/C John 'Tim' Elkington & the author, 2006.
(Dilip Sarkar).

Chapter Two

Edgar Norman Ryder was actually born in India, and returned with his family to the England in 1924. In 1931 he joined the Royal Fusiliers and served with them for three years. After leaving the army, he joined Tredinnick School in Worcester, where he became a mathematics master. But what prompted Norman Ryder to join the RAF? He wrote:

"You may not know, but the whole story started at Tredinnick. I had just returned to the Masters Common Room with John - the classics master, after a foray at the Star Hotel. We were quite happy, thank you! John couldn't add up 2 and 2 so, as it was Sunday and thousands of marks had to be presented to the Head the next day, I took on his task, he read the Daily Telegraph. At about 1 am, we discussed the idea of a short service commission in the RAF - local tasks completed.

Having tried the Army and not wanting to be in a destroyer in the Atlantic pretending to be a battleship, I opted for the RAF quite certain that we would be at war within 4 years. This was the spring of 1936. By August I was at Prestwick doing my initial flying training on Tiger Moths - I passed out top and so had my wish for fighters, which held after my stint at 9 FTS Thornaby. I joined 41 Squadron in March 1937 and stayed with the squadron until January 1st 1941. The rest they say is history!"

41 were based at Catterick, and in October 1937 had re equipped with Hawker Fury II biplanes. They continued to operate these until their first Spitfire I's arrived in January 1939. Just after the outbreak of war, the task of training the squadron to fully operational status began. Sadly, just 11 days after the outbreak of war, they suffered their first fatality, when Pilot Officer James Copley was killed in a flying accident. He was just 18 years old.

While based at Catterick, the squadron were tasked with the defence of the north eastern coast, and were to tackle any intruding German aircraft, as well as undertake convoy patrols. Their first kill was on October 17th 1939 when Green section comprising of Flying Officer Blatchford, and Sergeants Shipman and Harris caught and shot down a He 111 20 miles off Whitby. The He 111 was from *Stab* I (F)/122, and two of the crew survived, later making it ashore by dinghy. However tragedy struck the following day, taking the life of Sergeant Arthur Harris.

On October 18th, the squadron were posted to Wick. 12 Spitfires flew from Catterick, with the servicing party to follow on in a Whitley from 102 Squadron. Loaded with ammunition and 5 passengers, it stalled and crashed on take off, exploding on the runway. The crew of the Whitley were killed, along with three members of 41 Squadron, one of them being Sergeant Harris.

The stay at Wick was short, for the squadron returned to Catterick on October 25th. The first major engagement for the by now Flight Lieutenant Ryder came on April 3rd 1940.

With bad weather over the north east, a report came in ordering an investigation of a raid on Whitby. At 12.20 hours, Flight Lieutenant Ryder, in Spitfire N3114 took off from base and headed to Redcar to sweep from there to Whitby. His combat report read: -

" *I was flying on a course 30 degrees 400 feet, sighted A/C at 60 degrees starboard, below cloud base, about three quarters mile distant. I turned towards him and proceeded to identify A/C, my overtaking speed must have been about 100 mph, so I circled anticlockwise and recognised him as a He 111 (by the VIC under his rudder), with his port engine either completely out, or of very little use (very long glass nose in front) starboard cross very faint, invisible at 300 yards. Port cross very clear and very white, with two figures behind it, which I was unable to read.*

His airspeed was only 100 mph, accounting for my excessive speed of overtaking.

He commenced climbing towards the cloud base as soon as he saw me. I then got into a stern position by a left hand turn, (having made a circuit of the machine and turned in) on my turn I noticed very red flashes indeed from the E/A top gun (no tracer seen).

Visibility very dull and murky. Windscreen covered with fog and rain (both sides).

I commenced firing, taking starboard engine as a target for 6 or 7 seconds. I heard two bangs, (may have been a bullet coming in and out - a clack clack) I then broke away to port and came round again for another No 1 attack, and noticed his starboard engine was streaming both light and dark smoke (light smoke over, dark smoke under.) I did not turn in for this second attack, as he was losing height steadily. I positioned myself on his starboard side, and watched him land on the water. I imagined his starboard engine completely out of action though prop was idling. I then circled the E/A, which was floating in horizontal plane, and saw crew climbing out. I circled plane for one minute and saw trawler turn to approach to pick op crew. I estimate E/A floated for five minutes."

It was after this, that events took a turn for the worse. The return fire from the gunner had indeed hit the Spitfire.

"I checked up all the instruments and airframe, to see if I could find marks of what I thought were two direct hits. I then noticed my oil temperature had risen by 20 degrees to 70 degrees. I reported this to control. The cockpit had become very hot and filled with oil fumes.

I then saw a small trawler half a mile distant and circled it, trying to weigh up chances of reaching land which was out of sight. I decided against this, as oil temperature was rising rapidly, opened radiator flap, and continued to circle trawler and carried out conversation with control."

By now he had reported his Spitfire was on fire, and control wanted him to get as close to the coast as possible. Unable to do this, they advised him to bale out by the nearest ship, and that the coastguards were by now on the look out for him. At 12.45 hours he called out that he was landing in the sea. This would be the first recorded ditching of a Spitfire.

"I then decided I would have to land, as the low cloud height made it difficult to position for a parachute descent. I opened the hood and leaving the flaps up, tightened my Sutton harness and closed radiator flap. Then about 40 feet off water I reported to control I was landing.

I stalled on the water at 65 mph with a loud crash. Aircraft immediately dug its nose in and came to vertical position, tail up, and sank immediately. I think the whole touch down and sinking was simultaneous.

My next clear recollection was realising I was below the surface, and that everything appeared green. I undid my harness and commenced to get clear. The A/C was sinking rapidly and when almost clear my parachute caught under the sliding roof. I then got partly back into the cockpit and out again and finally got clear and commenced to swim to the surface. The tail plane passed just in front of my face. Pressure was very great and green light had changed to dull black. By the time I had broken surface my lungs had reached just about the limit. I then undid my parachute and treaded water and had great difficulty in keeping up. There appeared to be rollers at regular intervals, about 5 to 6 feet high.

I passed through the centre of these, except the odd ones. I tried to remove my helmet, but went under each time I tried, then I tried to put more air into my Mae West which I had failed to do in the air, but found this impossible as I was definitely winded.

I then caught a glimpse of a trawler coming approximately in my direction. I continued to tread water, and with slight help of my Mae West kept up for 5 to 10 minutes , during which time I found the weight of my clothes increasing rapidly. I released parachute and immediately realised it was giving me quite considerable buoyancy, so held it with my left hand. It did not commence to submerge for several minutes when it gradually sank to waist level."

Minutes later, Flight Lieutenant Ryder was picked out of the North Sea by the crew of the trawler 'Alaska' who took him below deck and gave him dry clothing. The experience proved most useful to the RAF, as until then, they had no idea what could happen when a pilot might have to ditch a Spitfire. The events provided the core advice to any future pilot in a similar situation. Ted Shipman remembered: -

"I well remember Norman telling us of his experience in this first ditching of a Spitfire. His description was no way given heroically but was detailed and graphic. Thinking of the combat of 3 April '40 when he went out in bad weather - 300' cloud base and visibility of no more than ° a mile speaks for itself."

For this action, Flight Lieutenant Ryder was awarded a well deserved DFC. The entire crew from the He 111 were saved and became POW's.

On May 28th 1940, the squadron left Catterick for Hornchurch to relieve 54 Squadron. 18 Spitfires flew south, piloted by Squadron Leader Hood, Flight Lieutenants Ryder and Webster; Flying Officers Legard, Scott, Gamblen; Pilot Officers Wallens, Lovell, Morrogh-Ryan, Mackenzie, Cory, Stapleton and Shipman; and Sergeants Carr-Lewty, Howitt, Ford and Darling. That same afternoon, they flew an offensive patrol over Dunkirk, but no enemy aircraft were engaged. Further flights were made over the Dunkirk/Calais areas during the following days, with Flight Lieutenant Webster destroying a Bf 109, and sharing a He 111 with Pilot Officer Lovell on May 31st. More claims followed on June 1st, with Flight Lieutenant Webster shooting down two Do 215s, and

Pilot Officers Lovell and Morrough-Ryan a He 111. Squadron Leader Hood also claimed a Do 215. During the same engagement, Pilot Officer Stapleton was shot down and taken POW, while Flying Officer Billy Legard was killed.

There were no more encounters with the enemy during later operations, and 41 returned en masse to Catterick on June 8th. Training and patrols followed, with sections flying to, and operating from Hartlepool. New pilots arrived on June 18th from 6 FTS- Sergeants Usmar and McAdam, and Pilot Officers Langley and Lock, and they all undertook their first Spitfire solos on June 21st. Many patrols were flown between June 9th and July 25th, with Flight Lieutenant Webster claiming a He 111 on June 19th and Flying Officer Lovell and Sergeant Allison, along with three Hurricanes of 249 Squadron, shooting down a Ju 88 of 9/KG4 at Hornsea, Yorkshire on July 8th. The pilot, *Hauptman* Rohloff, was the *Staffelkapitain* of 9/KG4, and was killed. The remaining three crew all baled out uninjured.

On July 26th, the squadron once again moved south to Hornchurch, with 14 pilots making the flight during the early afternoon, and then flying to Manston the next day. There they used Manston as a forward base, returning to Hornchurch when circumstances allowed. During the afternoon of the 28th, they clashed with Bf 109s of JG51. Major Molders of *Stab* JG51 damaged Pilot Officer Lovell's Spitfire, while he in turn was shot up by Flight Lieutenant Webster. Lovell crashed on landing at Hornchurch and was wounded, while Major Molders force landed on the French coast. Webster also damaged another Bf 109 of I/JG51, while Pilot Officer Bennions destroyed the Bf 109 of *Gefrieter* Martin Gebhardt, sending it, and its pilot, into the sea.

A much larger formation was encountered the next day. 11 aircraft were ordered to patrol Manston and then to Dover. Around 80 enemy aircraft comprising of 40 Ju 87s and 40 Bf 109s were heading to Dover, and while attacking the Ju 87s, the squadron were attacked by the fighter escort from JG51. Flying Officer Douglas Gamblen was shot down into the sea in N3038 and killed, and three more crashed on landing at Manston. N3100 flown by Flying Officer Scott and N3264 flown by Pilot Officer Bennions were written off, while Flight Lieutenant Webster's mount, N3113, was damaged. Pilot Officer Mackenzie force landed N3112 in a damaged state at Ringwould. Squadron Leader Hood claimed a Ju 87 and a Bf 109 destroyed, as did Flight Lieutenant Webster, while Pilot Officer Bennions claimed a Bf 109 damaged and Sergeant Carr-Lewty one destroyed.

Despite many more scrambles, and convoy patrols, their next large engagement came on August 8th while defending convoy 'Peewit' in the Channel. Clashing with fighters from JG27, again the erstwhile Flight Lieutenant Webster added to his score - two Bf 109's destroyed (one shared with Pilot Officer Wallens) two more unconfirmed, while Wallens went on to claim a Bf 109 destroyed and a further one as a probable. That same afternoon, the squadron packed up, and returned to Catterick, and returned to their defence of the north east. They had only been back three days when Green section consisting of Flying Officer Boyle, Pilot Officer Wallens, and Sergeant Darling, shot down a Ju 88 of 1 (F)/ 121 at Newton Moor, Whitby. Three crew were taken POW, and one was killed.

All throughout this time, Flight Lieutenant Ryder DFC, had flown operationally, leading 'A' Flight, as well as at times, the Squadron.

August 15th dawned with fine weather, with the Luftwaffe launching 'Eagle Day' whereby they would being to focus on the airfields and radar stations, and destroy the RAF on the ground. *Luftflotte* 5 despatched a force of 134 aircraft to attack bases in the north east. 63 He 111s of KG26, with 21 escorting Bf 110s from ZG76 took off from Sola and Forus, heading for Newcastle and Sunderland. Further south, 50 Ju 88s of KG30 had taken off from Aalborg, heading for Driffield.

The first attack on the He 111 formation was by 72 Squadron at 12.45 hours, and then by 41 Squadron at approximately 12.55 hours. In the action that followed, 41 put in 13 claims, while 72 Squadron put in 11. Flight Lieutenant Ryder DFC filed this report: -

"I took off as Yellow One at 12.40 hours - my R/T failed completely, and I handed section to Yellow Three. I took up position as Yellow Two. Large bomber force and escort fighter force was engaged. I did not fire at bombers but followed Yellow One who climbed to starboard and attacked a section of escort fighters. I got quarter astern and below a Ju 88 and opened fire from approx 250 yards. Return fire soon ceased. Large pieces of cowling flew off port side and passed over my port wing. A violent crimson explosion was observed in the centre of the fuselage. I fired all my ammunition and when breaking away, the target was losing height and looked as if flaps or dive brakes were down. Small amount smoke was observed apart from the time of the explosion."

The raiding force was badly mauled by the fighters from 41, 72, 79, 616, 73 and 605 Squadrons. KG26 lost eight aircraft; KG30 lost seven, with the escorting Bf 110s of ZG76 also losing seven of their number. It had proved to the *Luftwaffe* that not all the fighter squadrons were down in the south east, and it was apparent that they had totally underestimated the response from the

RAF over the east coast.

No more actions were flown until August 21st, when Pilot Officer Shipman destroyed a He 111 off Flamborough Head. This machine was from II/KG53, and was lost with the entire crew.

On September 3rd, the squadron once again went back to Hornchurch, via Debden, with 16 pilots and Spitfires making the trip, and Flying Officer Boyle and Pilot Officer Lock flying down the next day. During the morning of the 5th, 12 aircraft were ordered off to patrol Manston.

At just after 10.00 hours, two sections of 41 Squadron 'bounced' a formation of Bf 109s from JG3. Flight Lieutenant Ryder DFC was leading 'A' Flight and later wrote: -

"When large escorted bomber formation was sighted, my flight was ordered to act as rear escort in Blue and Green sections. Red and Yellow sections in line astern formation dived and picked up Me 109's in open formation. I carried out a diving and finally, astern attack on one Me 109. I opened fire at 200 yards with a considerable overtaking speed. A large light blue smoke explosion and thick steam was seen from the radiator which after approx 15 secs became a steady thin stream. Enemy aircraft went into left hand gliding turn. I was then engaged and had to stop observation of E/A. After watching E/A and investigating stray aircraft, which turned out to be Spitfires (XT) I did not catch up or sight enemy formation again."

Sergeant Carr-Lewty had his Spitfire damaged during this engagement, and had to force land at Stanford-le-Hope.

A second scramble took place that afternoon, with Squadron Leader Hood leading off 12 Spitfires. Flight Lieutenant Ryder was leading 'A' Flight, and acting as rearguard. Squadron Leader Hood led a head on attack on the enemy formation that was making its way up the Thames estuary. Upon doing so, 'B' Flight were 'bounced' by the escorting Bf 109s, thought to be from JG54. In the melee that followed, Flying Officer Lovell had to bale out of R6885 which crashed at south Benfleet; Pilot Officer Wallens force landed his stricken aircraft, and had suffered a serious leg injury; Pilot Officer Lock returned to base with a slight wound, but worst of all Squadron Leader Hood and Flight Lieutenant Webster had been killed. In the engagement, Webster had collided with the Hurricane flown by Flight Lieutenant Lovett of 73 Squadron. He had either bailed out or been thrown clear of his disintegrating Spitfire but his parachute had become detached and he fell to his death. He had an astounding 11 kills to his credit at the time of his death. Squadron Leader Hood was missing - his Spitfire had also broken up in the air. Flight Lieutenant Ryder DFC engaged the Bf 109s: -

"When leading 'A' Flight and acting as rearguard to 'B' Flight, I attacked a one Me 109 who was on the tail of Blue 3. I fired 5 bursts and followed the E/ A to 8,000 feet. It was smoking heavily, and then exploded and caught fire at about 7,000 feet. It was last seen as a ball of flame. There were no further interceptions."

In the absence of a commanding officer, Flight Lieutenant Ryder DFC took to leading the squadron on operations until a replacement was posted in. On the 6th, 12 Spitfires took off to patrol base. Of note in the 41 Squadron Diary is a reference to Pilot Officer Lock: -

"P/O Lock 'passed out' and lost his squadron, sighted a Ju 88 which he attacked and shot down, the enemy crashing in flames 20 miles behind Calais. The rest of the squadron saw nothing."

A second sortie was flown at 12.50 hours by 11 Spitfires, and at 14.45 hours eight Spitfires departed to Rochford, and were scrambled from there at 17.35 hours, to counter a raid on Thameshaven. Once again, the squadron tangled with the escorting Bf 109's above the Thames Estuary and Eastchurch. Flight Lieutenant Ryder DFC again: -

"I was leading the squadron and led Red and Yellow sections down to identify aircraft below. After identifying friendly fighters, the squadron ran into small formations of Me 109's, with considerable numbers higher up. I attacked an Me 109 and carried on attack with short bursts throughout his evasive tactics. The enemy aircraft smoked and finally exploded in flames and fell into the Thames Estuary about 440 yards off Southend Pier. I was then vectored by Control, but no further contact was made."

41 Squadron had clashed with Bf 109's of JG27 and JG53, and Ryder's victim was *Hauptmann* Hans Joachim Schlichting, the *Gruppenkommandeur* of *Stab* III/JG27. He was a highly experienced pilot, with 10 kills to his credit, and was a Legion Condor veteran from the Spanish Civil War. On his last flight, his fighter had begun to develop rudder problems prior to the attack and had lost some of its manoeuvrability. The coup de grace was delivered by Flight Lieutenant Ryder at 50 yards range, before it caught light. *Hauptmann*

The Faithful Few

Schlichting had no option but to bale out and become a POW. While in captivity, he was awarded the *Ritterkruez* for his leadership of the *Gruppe*.

Pilot Officer Bennions claimed two Bf 109's destroyed, Pilot Officer Mackenzie, one and one probable, while Flying Officer Scott and Sergeant Darling claimed a probable Bf 109 each.

A massive change on Luftwaffe tactics came on September 7th. On longer were they targeting airfields and radar stations, but their focus became the cities. On their fifth patrol of the day they sighted and enemy formation comprising 30 plus Do 17s with over 50 escorting Bf 109s. Combat was joined some 10 miles south of Whitstable, with the bombers being attacked first. Ryder: -

"I fired a fairly long burst into a Dornier 17 and saw my fire hitting it, broke away to starboard and a dog fight followed. I fired at an Me 109, but could not wait for visible results. I climbed to 25,000 feet over home base and dived into enemy formation. I fired at an Me 109, obviously hitting it hard, then black and blue smoke belched from the enemy aircraft and it half rolled. I fired another short burst on passing.

Hptmn Schlichting, Grpkdr of Stab III/JG 27, shot down by Ryder on September 6th, 1940. (Gerda Schlichting).

I was then told to make a nuisance of myself by Control. I climbed to over 20,000 feet five times and dived on enemy formations, through fighters to bombers, firing short bursts whenever a target presented. I then pancaked home base."

41 put in total claims for eight enemy aircraft, however they had three of theirs damaged and one destroyed - Sergeant Roy Ford force landed N3266 at West Hanningfield, Pilot Officer Morrough-Ryan force landed X4318 at Great Wakerling, and Pilot Officer Bennions suffered an undercarriage collapse when landing back at Rochford. Sergeant McAdams baled out of P9430 near Rayleigh, the Spitfire crashing at Drakes Farm.

During a late morning patrol near Dover on the 8th, the squadron engaged Bf 109's of JG51 without success, but Flying Officer William Scott was shot down in flames and killed. The Germans claimed two Spitfires, one each by *Leutnant* Heinz Bar of I/JG51 and *Oberleutnant* Richard Leppla of 3/JG51.

By now the pilots were wondering just who would be given the command of 41 Squadron. Most of the pilots, if not all, were certain that Flight Lieutenant Ryder DFC would be promoted to command, after all, he had lead the squadron on many occasions, and it was thought to be the most logical thing - he knew the pilots, he certainly knew how to lead, and the pilots, above all trusted and respected him. This wasn't to be the case as that afternoon the new commanding officer arrived - Squadron Leader Robert Lister came in from 7 Operational Training Unit. A highly experienced pre war pilot, he had been awarded a DFC for his services in India, however this was to be his first time on fighters. But, as the then Sergeant Roy Ford commented: -

"It is an understatement to say the **whole** *squadron was dismayed when he did not succeed Robin Hood in September."*

Frank Usmar agreed: -

"We all hoped he would be promoted to Squadron Leader and take over the Squadron, as he was an excellent leader and always tried hard to position the squadron to get better advantage of the enemy. We were disappointed when it didn't materialise."

Bob Beardsley:

"It was more than apparent that the pilots wanted Norman for their CO and he was most highly regarded by us all, and the ground crews."

On the 9th, they flew a late afternoon sortie against a large enemy formation, engaging between Maidstone and south London at approx 18.00 hours. Pilot Officer Lock and Sergeant Darling claimed two Bf 109s destroyed each, Flight Lieutenant Ryder DFC and Pilot Officer Bennions one Bf 109 apiece, while Pilot Officer Boyle claimed a He 111.

Leading 'A' Flight again during the afternoon of the 11th, Flight Lieutenant Ryder attacked a formation of Ju 88s of KG30 with Bf 110s of ZG76 as escort, 15 miles south east of Hornchurch: -

The Faithful Few

"I Led Red and Blue section in a diving attack on twin engined formation with a view to cutting the formation in two. I fired on passing through at a Ju 88 and had a glimpse of smoke coming from his port engine and at the same time his left wing dropped slightly. This happened very quickly and might have been his evasion. I then attacked another Ju 88 by joining a circle and experienced very great return fire and by good evasion on the E/A's part had to break off the engagement. I fired at a third and was fired on from astern; part of my hood at this moment flew off. Ordered by Control to patrol base and engage 50 plus E/A I returned but did not engage before pancake order."

41 Squadron submitted a further five claims, including a Ju 88 and a Bf 110 destroyed by Pilot Officer Lock.

The squadron continued to operate between Hornchurch and Rochford, with their next encounter with the enemy coming during the early evening of September 14th. Ten Spitfires were patrolling and spotted several Bf 109s at 31, 000 feet. Pilot Officer Lock claimed two Bf 109's destroyed, but Squadron Leader Lister DFC, flying at the rear of the formation, was attacked from above. With his Spitfire mortally hit, he baled out wounded. 41 had now lost their second commanding officer in the space of nine days.

Once again, Flight Lieutenant Ryder was overlooked for the command of the squadron, and in came Squadron Leader Donald Finlay, the well known pre war Olympic hurdler. He had come from 54 Squadron, who he had commanded from August 26th 1940.

September 15th will always be known as 'Battle of Britain Day' with two major attacks on London, and smaller ones on Portland and Southampton. The morning encounter didn't go too well for the squadron for their attempt to get to the bombers was thwarted by the fighter escorts of JG52 and 53. Pilot Officer Gerald Langley was shot down and killed, his Spitfire crashing at Bulphan near Thurrock, while Pilot Officer Bennions destroyed the Bf 109 of *Leutenant* Bertel from Stab I/JG52, and Flying Officer Lovell did the same to the I/JG53 machine of *Feldwebel* Tschoppe. Both pilots baled out successfully.

Ryder led the second sortie during the afternoon, checking the approach of a 70 plus formation comprising Do 17's with Bf 109 escorts. Flight Lieutenant Ryder wrote: -

" I dived through fighter escort expecting to be engaged but was not attacked, so carried out a diving approach on a single Dornier, this aircraft was engaged

before I got to firing range, but I circled once and fired a burst of approx 5-6 secs from astern as E/A entered cloud tops. I feel certain my burst was hitting (tracer) but I could see no results due to cloud. I followed the aircraft with 3 or 4 other friendly fighters until it force landed on Sheppey Isle."

The Dornier was a Do 17Z from 4/KG3 tasked with the bombing of railway targets. Both engines had been disabled, and it had also been attacked by Sergeant Fejfar of 310 Squadron, Pilot Officer Berry of 603 Squadron, and Flying Officer Boyle of 41 Squadron. It force landed and burnt out at Lower Stoke, with the four crew being taken POW, of which three were wounded.

Other pilots of 41 Squadron had success - Pilot Officer Baker shared the destruction of a He 111 from 1/KG26, Pilot Officer Lock destroyed a Bf 109 and shared a Do 17, while Flying Officer Boyle also claimed a Bf 109 destroyed. The squadron suffered no losses from this sortie.

Two days later, the squadron were on the receiving end while countering a large German fighter sweep. The squadron operational diary recorded: -

"Eleven aircraft ordered to patrol Manston, sighted formation of 30-40 E/A. A series of dog fights ensured in which many of our A/C were hit."

Flying Officer Boyle brought X4178 back to Hornchurch in a damaged state, as did Pilot Officer Chalder in N3266. Despite Pilot Officer Mackenzie bringing R6887 back safely, the aircraft was deemed too badly damaged to repair and was listed as a write off. Pilot Officer Baker didn't make it back, having to force land his Spitfire at Stelling Minnis due to battle damage. Pilot Officer Bennions claimed a Bf 109 destroyed, Flight Lieutenant Boyle claimed two destroyed, and Sergeant Norwell two damaged. Only two Bf 109s were lost over England that day, with the machine from 9/JG53 flown by *Unteroffizier* Langer being Pilot Officer Bennions' victim.

On September 18th, the Germans once again went for the oil storage depots along the Thames Estuary. The squadron flew three sorties that day, claiming two Bf 109s probably destroyed by Pilot Officers Lock and Bennions near Maidstone on the first; a further three Bf 109s destroyed plus two damaged in the second, and on the final, late afternoon sortie, three Bf 109s and a Ju 88 damaged. Poor weather restricted operations on the 19th, and after combat on the 20th, Pilot Officer Bennions had to force land at Lympne with combat damage after the squadron engaged a large fighter sweep towards London.

The Faithful Few

A second large force, mostly Bf 109s made another fighter sweep towards London on the 23rd. 41, along with 603 Squadron engaged the raiders, preventing them from reaching the city. A second raid came through in the afternoon but was again stopped from getting to London. Tilbury Docks and Southampton were raided the next day, and the squadron were in action near Dover. In the ensuing fight, Sergeant McAdam had his Spitfire set alight, and he baled out into the sea, being safely picked up later. Meanwhile, Sergeant Darling had to crash land near Dover. The victors were either from 2/JG51 and 3/JG51, but who exactly had shot them down cannot be ascertained as the Germans had claimed a total of seven Spitfires destroyed near Dover, when in fact the only Spitfires lost that day were from 41.

The Squadron lost two more aircraft during the second sortie of September 27th - Sergeant Usmar was hit in the legs, and had to bale out of his Spitfire, it crashing at Mereworth. Sergeant Darling was hit in the shoulder, and he too, had to bale out, with both pilots being admitted to hospital. In turn, Sergeant Norwell shot down the Bf 109 from 8/JG54 piloted by *Oberleutnant* Schon, who was killed attempting a force landing at Boughton near Canterbury. After hitting a fence, the fighter somersaulted over a road and caught light.

The afternoon sortie proved to be a close thing for Flight Lieutenant Ryder DFC. At 15.10 hours, 11 Spitfires were scrambled to join up with 603 Squadron at a low 5,000 feet. They were attacked by fighters, and Ryder's Spitfire was hit twice. He recalled: -

"I was hit, and the aircraft started to smoke. The controls went 'soggy' and I had no option but to get out. I landed near East Malling, I think."

The ferocity of these late September clashes was getting worse, and the casualty rate for the squadron got higher. On the morning of the 28th, they lost Flying Officer Boyle in combat over Charing, his Spitfire impacting at Lynstead. Pilot Officer Chalder baled out of his near Chilham with serious wounds, (from which he died on November 10th) and Pilot Officer Aldous force landed at Pluckley, his aircraft being written off. They had run into the fighters from JG26, with *Oberleutnant* Walter Schnieder and *Unteroffizier* Hugo Dahmer, both of 6/JG26, claiming one each. *Hauptmann* Gerhard Schopfel of *Stab* III/JG26 claimed one as well. It was his 19th kill.

During the lunchtime engagement, Pilot Officer Bennions damaged a pair of Bf 109s, but had his aircraft damaged by 20mm cannon shells, however he managed to get back to Hornchurch.

No combats were flown on the 29th, giving the pilots a brief respite, but they were back in business on the 30th when ordered off to patrol Rochford and Chatham. A formation of Dorniers was spotted west of Dungeness, and the squadron managed to attack the rear of the formation, only to get attacked by the escorts who were above and behind the bombers.

Sergeant Bob Beardsley damaged a Dornier and Bf 109, only for him to receive some special attention from the escorts: -

"During this combat I had a hectic session with 6 x 109s who had chased me back to land on fire at Hawkinge. (Shattered!) I arrived back at Hornchurch by Tube (+ parachute!) and was asked where the hell I'd been?'"

Pilot Officer Lovell had to perform a wheels up landing at Hornchurch as his Spitfire had been struck by cannon shells, and despite several attempts, he could not get the undercarriage down, Both Sergeant Beardsley's and Pilot Officer Lovell's aircraft were repairable. A further sortie was flown late afternoon, without loss.

On October 1st, they suffered a blow when Pilot Officer Bennions was shot down during a high altitude engagement. 'A' Flight went on the attack, and most of the Bf 109s got into cloud. But one managed to hit Bennions' Spitfire and severely wound him. He was hit in the face and head, subsequently losing an eye. He baled out, with his Spitfire crashing at Alborne. At the time of his wounding, he had amassed 12 kills with a further five probable, and another five damaged. In the tail chase that followed, Squadron Leader Finlay and Pilot Officer Adams shot down a Bf 109 of 4/JG26, piloted by *Unteroffizer* Bluder. It went into a vertical dive from 28,000 feet and crashed near Falmer, with such force that no trace of the pilot could be found.

Between September 29th, and October 2nd, six new pilots had been posted in to the squadron. Every effort was made to ensure they at least survived their first operations, and Flight Lieutenant Ryder had a method for such occasions: -

"I made it a rule when in charge of the squadron that the newest or weakest pilot flew as wingman to myself or Tony Lovell who was 'B' Flight commander. We both could do our jobs and take care of the new boy. My rule was that he stayed with me to the point of attack, tried to sort out the scene and then broke off, to return to base - this to be done three times. After three returns I asked the young fellow how he got on, "Fine" he said "I had a 109 filling my screen, then I remembered your orders and returned to base." I was delighted and

The Faithful Few

certain he would do well - he did very well! One's eyes became skinned in time, and then you could see things you had no hope of doing so in the early stages. Some would return with bullet holes in their Spits yet professed to having seen or felt nothing, those who didn't return - the same explanation possibly."

He also held firm in the belief that plenty of training was good for the pilots, and when possible it should be undertaken. Roy Ford remembers a particular pre Hornchurch training flight: -

"It relates to when a fellow V R and I were being checked out for formation flying at low level by Norman, who led the vic of three. Before taking off on the exercise, our leader informed us that his understanding of low level was only achieved when "one could see the colour of the chickens' eyes". During the ensuing fifty perspiring minutes, my close friend 'Birdy' Darling (subsequently changed to Mitzi by Al Deere) and I were far too occupied in riveting our eyes on the leader's very adjacent wingtips to permit the briefest glance at any chicken unwise enough to stand its ground as we passed somewhat rapidly overhead. However, my peripheral vision of treetops disappearing above and behind us and the complete absence of any after flight comment from Norman on our performance, led me to believe that we had, in fact, passed muster by meeting his exacting requirements in every respect. He certainly set himself high standards and expected others to emulate his example."

Sometimes, his exacting standards made it memorable for other pilots. Bob Beardsley said: -

"I joined 41 from 610, and within a week I was joined by Cyril Baker and 'Red' Bamberger so we were the 3 'B's, and both Baker and Beardsley were blonde! This did confuse things in so far as I as No 2 to Norman was rearguard to the fight commander and was berated that I had deserted him in combat and that Baker had done my job! As I explained it was myself who had stuck with him and Baker was looking after someone else and as it had been a very 'hairy' ride I was slightly aggrieved!"

Sorties continued apace, with five being flown on October 5th. Pilot Officer Lock shot down two Bf 109s in two missions and Pilot Officer Lovell returned with a damaged Spitfire. Pilot Officer Mackenzie also claimed a Bf 109 destroyed. Three more sorties followed on the 7th, with Pilot Officer Adams being shot down by return fire from a Do 17 over Folkestone and parachuted clear. Pilot Officer Mackenzie also had his Spitfire damaged by Do 17 gunner.

One fighter engagement was flown on the 9th, but the squadron were heavily attacked by fighters from JG54 and Squadron Leader Finlay had to force land at Hornchurch with the wheels up. 41 accounted for at least two Bf 109s - Feldwebel Schweser from 7/JG54 force landed near Hawkinge, and Leutenant Eberle of 9/JG54 ditched in the sea, but drowned.

The number of sorties, despite this late phase of the Battle of Britain, did not dwindle. On average the squadron were doing four a day. The third scramble of October 11th was a costly one. Fighters were spotted at 31,000 feet, and during the climb, the Spitfires of Flying Officer O'Neill and Sergeant Carter collided. Both baled out, but Flying Officer O'Neill's parachute failed to open. Then, during the ensuing clash, Pilot Officer Lecky was shot down by *Hauptmann* Walter Adolph of Stab II/JG26. Lecky baled out but was killed - he had been with the squadron just nine days.

A further fatality occurred on October 15th when Sergeant Philip Lloyd was shot down into the Channel, possibly by *Hauptmann* Max Dobislav of Stab III/JG27, becoming his seventh victory. Sergeant Lloyd's body was washed ashore 12 days later at Herne Bay.

Two days later, a large formation of Bf 109s (some carrying bombs) headed over Kent and towards London, causing damage mainly to Waterloo Station. Pilot Officer Aldridge attacked a Bf 109, while Pilot Officer Wells caught one heading for France. He turned on its tail and shot it down into the sea. The pilot, *Leutenant* Hans Carl Mayer, the *Gruppenkommandeur* of *Stab* I/JG53 was killed, his body washing ashore 10 days later.

The high flying, bomb carrying Bf 109s were proving to be a problem, and these '*Jabo*' sorties were being flown in large numbers. The combat in the afternoon of October 20th involved between 50 and 60 Bf 109s, once again, heading for London. 41 claimed three destroyed, plus two damaged.

'New' aircraft arrived on the 24th, in the form of 14 Spitfire II's from 611 Squadron, who in turn took on 41's Mk Is, and flew them back to Digby. They soon made use of their Mk IIs - taking them into action on the 25th, once again against a large formation of Bf 109s. Linking up with 603 Squadron over Rochford, they sighted 30 enemy fighters south of Maidstone. They managed to break up the formation, and individual dog fights ensued.

The Faithful Few

Flight Lieutenant Ryder DFC: -

"I led the squadron on to four Me 109 aircraft acting as rearguard with 'B' Flight acting as our rear guard cover.

"Attacked 109 - small amount of smoke followed. Enemy aircraft half rolled and carried out aileron turns. Delivered a long burst and very heavy and dense black smoke and light gycol vapour came from the enemy aircraft. Carried on attack and smoke continued and the enemy aircraft carried out no further evasion and finally entered cloud at 6000 feet in steep dive on an E N E course. Did not sight enemy aircraft below cloud, in spite of search .Ground position area north of Maidstone."

This could well have been the mount of *Oberleutenant* Schypek of 5/JG54, who force landed at Broom Hill, near Lydd with a damaged radiator. Strangely, it was a downed 109 pilot who proved to be quite beneficial to the squadron, as Roy Ford recalled:

"It is difficult to recall anecdotes, but one I do remember concerns one of several 109's that Norman shot down during the Battle. The pilot survived and on being taken prisoner insisted that his Iron Cross First Class, together with a congratulatory letter be presented to the victor. His wish was duly respected by the interrogating officer. This memorabilia proved to be with its weight in gold as its subsequent displays at admiring customers in the local pub in Upminster never failed to result in Norman and his guests enjoying drinks on the house for the rest of the evening!"

The Squadron's last Battle of Britain combats took place on the 30th, with 10 Spitfires joining up with 222 Squadron over Tilbury. 'A' Flight attacked a number of Bf 109s and after successfully scattering the formation; 'B' Flight joined the attack. Picking out individual targets, three were claimed as destroyed. Flight Lieutenant Ryder DFC destroyed one of those: -

"I was Red 1 and led the squadron into attack on 6 Me 109s acting as rear guard at approx 12.15 hours. I fired at enemy A/C and saw smoke and light vapour.

"Followed the E.A down and gave another long burst when the E/A burst into flames and starboard wing broke in half. The pilot not seen to abandon A/C. I saw the 109 entering cloud in a spin burning furiously."

41 Squadron's pilots at Hornchurch, November 17th, 1940.
F/L Norman Ryder DFC second from left.

The pilot didn't get out - *Unteroffizier* Topfer of 7/JG26 was still on board when his aircraft crashed at Brook Farm, Marden. It is likely that he was already dead, as Flight Lieutenant Ryder's last burst of fire into the 109 was delivered at just 40 yards range.

A second sortie during the afternoon by 11 Spitfires finished with the loss of two Spitfires and one pilot. Pilot Officer Draper was injured, and Sergeant Len Garvey was killed when his Spitfire, P7375, crashed at Church Farm, Stanford.

Despite it being known as the 'end' of the Battle of Britain, several more high altitude fights ensued on November 2nd, and 9th. On the 11th, 11 Spitfires went on patrol, and P/O Wells got separated from the rest of the squadron. While over the Channel, he spotted, and attacked Hs 126 damaging it and possibly killing the gunner. During the same afternoon, while on a convoy protection sortie, he spotted a patch of burning oil on the sea. Breaking away to investigate he sighted about 20 Fiat Cr 42s of the *Regia Aeronatica* heading back to their base. He attacked two, damaging one.

Flight Lieutenant Ryder DFC had his last aerial victory on November 27th 1940, another Bf 109. The squadron attacked a formation of fighters between Ashford and Maidstone at 21,000 feet: -

"I followed the CO to attack and took the right rear machine. The E/A turned sharp left and fired a full deflection shot at Red 1 or Red 2. I closed and fired short burst. Light and dark smoke was emitted and the E/A force landed south of Ashford with a dead engine. Pilot got out and looked fed up but was unhurt, 2 civilians ran to E/A."

The fed up looking pilot was possibly *Feldwebel* Erdniss from 3/JG51 who had managed to get his aircraft down at Horton Court, Monks Horton.

Just over five weeks later, Flight Lieutenant Ryder was posted from 41 squadron after a period of three years and nine months, and given his first official command - 56 Squadron. The pilots were saddened to see him go.
Ted Shipman: -

"He was a good athlete, and I believe he enjoyed his cricket. I saw him as a fine officer in all respects and an excellent pilot and section leader - this sounds like a reference - sorry about this, but he seemed to me to be an outstanding officer, pleasant and liked by all his fellows.

"During the two years from early 1937 until the start of WWII, I was responsible for taking all the squadron pilots in a Magister for instrument flying practice. From my logbook I see I took Norman on seven occasions for a total of 4 ° hours, and I can say he offered himself for these trips more enthusiastically than any others I can recall. He certainly was dedicated to the need for bettering his instrumental flying."

Edward 'Hawkeye' Wells also recalled Norman Ryder:

"I was in 'B' Flight so as a humble and very new Pilot Officer I never got to know him as well as I did with my own Flight Commander, Tony Lovell. As well, in those days the two flights had separate dispersal huts more or less on different sides of the grass airfield which Hornchurch then was.

"However, I ,in common with all 41 Squadron pilots, had a very high regard for Norman as a person and as Flight Commander. He was always cheerful (rather important sometimes in those days) steady and one felt absolutely reliable. In fact he was informally referred to as 'Uncle' Norman. I think this

The Faithful Few

in itself reflects the character and personality of the man."

No 41 Squadron had held its own, and had experienced more fighter to fighter combat that most other squadrons. The squadron's participation was summed up by Norman Ryder: -

No 41 Squadron's pilots cut a cake to celebrate their 100th kill; Norman Ryder is cutting the first slice!

"The fighter pilots role is unique, no other cocky aircrew to take off some of the strain - as in a bomber. From the moment he closed the hood he was alone with his thoughts and emotions, if he should turn away from the real test and take on that smoking Heinkel, he alone knew it: another thought to ponder on during the wait on the ground for the next sortie - knowing that if he failed again than all self respect would be gone. Even more serious the squadron would have a weak link.

The weak link was most important for 41 Squadron. We were the first squadron to get VHF, and with the higher standard of communication we were assigned to the higher levels of operation, and therefore pitted against the high flying cover of the 109's. Without positive proof, I believe that when we celebrated our 100th squadron victory, some 80 were Me 109s. We had to weave our way through the lower bomber formations to gain the height to take on our true assignment - the 109 escort, and did so in line astern. This is when the weak link really became serious - if a pilot broke the line, those following would naturally follow and the poor chap ahead of the weak link had no back cover and did not know it. I lost a good friend in this fashion. On several occasions I led 41 up to 36,000 feet - quite high with no body heating, so we all donned 3 or 4 pairs of gloves. Still, frostbite was not uncommon. On one occasion, with a 109 filling my front panel, I was unable to put enough force on the firing button because of frozen fingers."

No 56 Squadron were based at North Weald, and equipped with Hurricane Is, and they had been a squadron heavily involved with the fighting during the Battle of Britain, losing numerous aircraft, and suffering eight pilots killed.

Squadron Leader Ryder DFC flew his first 56 Squadron flight on January 17th, in Hurricane V7105, and did not undertake any operational flying until February 5th, when he took part in Circus 2 - an 11 Group attack on St Omer airfield. There, 56 acted as part of a close escort wing with 302, 601, and 610 Squadrons, providing cover for 12 Blenheims. On the return to England, the squadron were engaged by Bf 109s; with the result that Sergeant Rowland Jones was shot down and killed.

Circus 3 was flown five days later, with the target being the dockyards at Dunkirk. Blenheims from 139 Squadron were escorted by 17, 56, and 249 squadrons, with the loss of one 249 Hurricane. Similar operations were to follow throughout this month, and into March, with the squadron next losing a pilot on April 26th when Pilot Officer Guest was shot down and taken POW during a fighter sweep over France.

Their worst day since the Battle of Britain occurred on June 17th, when the squadron were taking part in Circus 13 - an attack on Kuhlmann Chocques. Acting as part of the close escort wing, they were bounced by Bf 109s with the loss of four aircraft, and three pilots. Pilot Officers Patrick Harris and Peter Robinson, along with Sergeant Richard Carvill, were shot down into the sea, while Flight Lieutenant Frederick 'Taffy' Higginson DFM was taken POW. However, he did evade capture, and made it back the squadron in October. This final operation coincided with Squadron Leader Ryder DFC being 'tour expired', and command of the squadron was taken over by Squadron Leader Peter Hanks DFC, while Ryder went to 53 Operational Training Unit to Instruct.

However, he was soon to be back on operations, this time with a promotion to Wing Commander and sent to lead the Kenley Wing. Generally flying with 485 (NZ) Squadron, he did so until his last sortie October 31st 1941.

That afternoon, 11 Group ran Circus 109B, targeting barges at Bourbourgville. The attacks were to be carried out by Hurricanes from 607 Squadron, with the withdrawal cover to be supplied by the Kenley Wing. During the mission, 607 lost Sergeant Antonin Zavoral to flak, and 615 Squadron, acting as an anti flak flight, has Pilot Officer McCormack wounded.

485 Squadron deployed 12 Spitfires on Circus 109B, but failed to encounter the enemy. Wing Commander Ryder DFC broke away from the formation and was not seen again, but it is certain that at one stage his Spitfire, W3579 was hit by flak, causing him to bale out, and to land near Gravelines where he was captured.

Firstly incarcerated in Stalag Luft I at Barth until April 1942, he was sent to *Stalag Luft* III at Sagan, site of the Great Escape. Six months later, he was sent on again, this time to *Oflag* XXIB at Schubin. It was during his time at Schubin that he managed to escape, hiding in a box with heavy luggage on the back of a truck, before being recaptured two days later on Bromberg Aerodrome while trying to find a suitable aircraft to steal.

Obviously, the Germans weren't pleased, and he was sent back to *Stalag Luft* III at Sagan, spending the next 21 months there. He didn't waste his time, while a POW, as he was involved in no less than nine unsuccessful tunnel attempts, and a further three schemes. His actions were recognised by the award of a Mention in Despatches for his actions as a POW. His final five months of the war were spent at *Stalag* IIIA at Luckenwald prior to liberation.

He continued his RAF career post war, reaching the rank of Group Captain, and retired in 1960 as Station Commander Duxford. He had been awarded a Bar to his DFC in July 1941, and a CBE in 1960 New Year's Honours List. He moved to America, settling in Arizona, where he died in October 1995.

Bob Beardsley remembered the last time he saw Norman Ryder: -

"I last saw Norman before he retired, at the mess at Farnborough Air Show. I was a Flight Commander with 74 Squadron, flying Meteors. He asked me what the best squadron I had flown in. I replied "74". He said "No Bob, the best was 41!" and you know in my old age, he was quite right! The glory days, eh?."

I leave the last part to Norman Ryder, the landmark making pilot, and best officer never to command 41 Squadron, to recall the heady days of the Battle of Britain in his own way: -

The Faithful Few

"Any pilot with worthwhile experience during the battle will match any other on the 'blood sweat and tears' angle, so nough said. Here are some other thoughts-

The first to come to mind was the unreality of it all; the red double decker bus you had to lift your wing over during take off, the white cloths spread in the green fields of Kent for the picnic - the beaches were mined and out of bounds; the meals in the officers mess; the scores for the day on the wireless, rather like the cricket scores; the beer in the pub - if you were lucky enough to be released from ops earlier than usual. Against this background came the came the actual sorties, not just an exercise, but a deadly serious business. The best ground defence organisation in the world was set on getting you up into the enemy formations - and damn good they were at it; up to five operational sorties a day , though I don't know anyone who got in six! Indeed life was a strange and lonely mixture for the fighter pilot."

No 56 Squadron, early 1941. S/L Ryder DFC seated, centre.
(Dilip Sarkar Collection).

Chapter Three

Bertie Wootten & Bugatti pictured in Malvern.

Born on November 5th, 1918, and later educated at St Cuthbert's Prep School, and Kings School, Worcester, before Ernest Waite Wootten became an apprentice electrical engineer at C.A.Parsons in Newcastle in 1934. Four years later he joined the RAF on a short service commission.

He did his ab initio course at Prestwick, his intermediate training at 8 Flying Training School at Hullavington, and then his advanced at 15 Flying Training School at Lossiemouth. By the end of February 1940, he was at No 9 Air Observer School at Penrhos as a staff pilot, before joining No 4 Continental Ferry Pilots Pool at Cardiff, and later Kemble. There, he delivered aircraft from maintenance units to squadrons in France and at home, until he was posted to 234 Squadron at St Eval.

234 Squadron had moved from Middle Wallop to St Eval on September 11th 1940, having fought hard during the Battle of Britain. During their campaign they had lost five pilots, including their commanding officer, Squadron Leader O'Brien, and one of the most successful pilots of that period, Flight Lieutenant Pat Hughes DFC. A further two had been taken POW after clashes way out over the channel.

The Faithful Few

By then, the squadron consisted of a group of highly experienced combat pilots, and gradually new pilots were beginning to be posted in. It was on September 14th 1940, that Pilot Officer Wootten joined 234. His first day on the squadron resulted in him being christened with the nickname which he used right throughout his service career.

When the author asked him about the origins of his nickname, he recalled the moment: -

"How did I get my nickname? Well, it was when I joined 234 Squadron in September 1940. I walked in to one of the crew huts, only to be met with silence, as all the old hands gave me the once over. One of those pilots looked over the top of his newspaper and asked "A new boy! Where are you from?" "Malvern" I replied. My inquisitor said "Malvern? Where the bloody hell is Malvern?"

Quickly, I replied "Near Worcester!" only for the wag with the paper to exclaim "Aha! Bertie Wooster!!" And I've been Bertie ever since!"

The aforementioned wag was Pilot Officer Edward Mortimer-Rose (known in the squadron as 'Morty') and this little 'christening' began a great friendship between the two. The Squadron was under the temporary command of Flight Lieutenant Page, until the appointment of the new commanding officer. In the meantime, the unit continued to fly standing patrols and interceptions on the German bombers which were still intruding across the west country.

His first flights with 234 were in Spitfires P4255, P9508, and N3276. He also flew Spitfire X4036 on numerous occasions. Coded AZ-D, this Spitfire was usually flown by Flying Officer Bob Doe DFC during the sorties from Middle Wallop in August.

On September 22nd, Squadron Leader Minden Blake took charge, and one of the experienced pilots, Sergeant 'Budge' Harker shot down a Ju 88 some 50 miles off Start Point, while Pilot Officer Kane was shot down and taken POW the following day, when he was bounced by Bf 109's not far from the Channel Islands. Three days later, Pilot Officer Mackay crashed near Newquay, and was seriously injured. The next contact with the enemy occurred four days later when Pilot Officers Dewhurst and Zurakowski caught a Bf 110 some 10 miles off Exmouth, and destroyed it. In a second scramble, two Spitfires from 234 were unable to engage a formation of about 10 enemy aircraft as they were too far out off Lands End.

'Bertie' Wootten's first Spitfire, 234 Sqn, St Eval.

It was October 9th when Pilot Officer Wootten first engaged the enemy. Along with Pilot Officer Mortimer-Rose, they damaged a Ju 88 10 miles south of Falmouth during an afternoon scramble, while Sergeant Bell went one better by destroying a Do 17 during the early evening. So elated at the destruction of this raider, Sergeant Bell forgot to lower the undercarriage of his Spitfire on return to St Eval, and gracefully slid to a halt on the grass. This incident generated much hilarity, and anyone on 234 with a camera took advantage of this photo opportunity to capture a picture of a forlorn looking Spitfire!

Sergeant Sharpley damaged a Ju 88 on October 19th; Pilot Officer Mortimer-Rose probably destroyed a Ju 88 on the 26th, while Flying Officer Ritchie damaged another Ju 88, and Sergeant Boddington destroyed another on two separate engagements on October 28th.

Sergeant Michael Boddington opened November by damaging a He 111 off Lands End on the 2nd, then received his commission on the 5th, and to cap it all, he was awarded a DFM on the 12th! During this period, the squadron undertook numerous practice flights, and provided air cover over Plymouth. During a scramble on November 16th, Sergeant Hugh Sharpley crashed into the sea off Porth and was killed.

Further success came on November 24th, when Squadron Leader Blake and Pilot Officer Mortimer-Rose intercepted a Do 215 between St Eval and Falmouth, eventually sending it into the sea off the Lizard with the loss of three of its crew, with one surviving to be taken POW. The next day, Pilot

Officer Wootten intercepted a Ju 88 30 miles south of Lands End and destroyed it.

A 234 Squadron Spitfire lands at St Eval.

The month finished with activity covering a convoy on November 29th, and during the day they had four engagements with Squadron Leader Blake destroying a Do 17, Flying Officer Ritcher damaging another, and Pilot Officers Edwards and Boddington destroying a Ju88, and damaging another. Edwards went on to down a Bf 110 off Plymouth the next day.

F/O Mortimer-Rose, originator of Bertie's nickname!

Duties in December consisted of more scrambles, patrols over the Scillies, and dices with bad weather. Pilot Officer Boddington caught a Do 17 off St Austell on December 5th and shot it down, with Pilot Officer Wootten destroying a Do 17 14 days later off Rames Head. His combat report reads: -

"I was Red 1 engaged with practice flying when I was ordered to Dodman Point at 10,000 feet on reaching patrol point by vectors I was informed bandit was five miles south of my position going west at 1,000 feet. I started an approximate SW course, on reaching cloud base I saw bandit about a mile south of my position. I intercepted the E/A and attacked from starboard rear quarter putting starboard motor out of action. I delivered another attack from rear starboard quarter and one from dead abeam. E/A then held flight at zero feet over the water for a few seconds then for no apparent reason dived straight into the sea. I did not observe any bodies come up, there being just an oil patch and several floating objects."

S/L Minden Blake, P/O Bertie Wootten & F/O Mortimer-Rose, St Eval, late 1940.

The squadron finished 1940 with three more claims for Pilot Officer Mortimer-Rose (with Squadron Leader Blake and Sergeant Pearce) plus the award of the DFC to Squadron Leader Blake on December 20th.

1941 started with more new pilots coming in from Operational Training Units , with some of the more experienced ones being posted out to other squadrons, or to have a stint in training command. January was a poor month, with only Flying Officer Dewhurst damaging a Ju 88 on the 2nd, it escaping into cloud with one engine smoking. Sadly, Pilot Officer Beech and Sergeant Rogers were killed on January 16th - Beech crashing near Rian Lanihorne, near Truro, and Rogers went missing after engaging a Ju 88 over Plymouth. Further tragedy struck on the 20th, when AC2 Tod was killed on flare path duty, and when the airfield was bombed on January 25th, killing one of the pilots, Sergeant Wotton, and two groundcrew, AC1 Browning and AC2 Allan.

The squadron had also received four Tomahawk aircraft for test purposes, but they spent a considerable time unserviceable., before being flown in February.

Exceedingly poor weather wreaked havoc on the flying during early February, with only two engagements during the first two weeks. Pilot Officer Michael Boddington DFM was posted to 118 Squadron at Filton as a flight commander, while the squadron departed to Warmwell on February 24th. Later Flight Lieutenant Gillen was posted out, with the erstwhile Flying Officer Mortimer-Rose taking over one of the flights, and promoted to the rank of Acting Flight Lieutenant. The pilots also flew the Tomahawks that the squadron had received in January, with satisfactory results for the Air Ministry.

Their first sortie of March was to cover a convoy along with HMS Resolution on a course between the Scillies and Plymouth. However, for reasons unknown, Sergeant Bell went missing during this operation, and was not seen again. The squadron intercepted a Bf 110 near Lyme Regis the following day, but despite the attentions of Sergeants Harker, Shepherd and Martin, it managed to get away. A second Bf 110 was engaged on March 11th by Squadron Leader Blake DFC, Flight Lieutenant Mortimer-Rose, and Pilot Officer Wootten, and this one wasn't so lucky. Pilot Officer Wootten submitted this combat report: -

"I was Red 2 patrolling Portland at 24, 000 feet. Red 3 sighted bandit and took the lead, I followed and passed Red 1, as myself and Red 3 were flying Spitfire II's. I was about ° mile behind Red 3 and had closed to about 200 yards behind the bandit on a parallel course with Red 3 when the bandit and Red 3 dived. I followed and got in a short burst from rear quarter after Red 3 had broken away from his first attack. As Red 3 attacked I saw the engines of the bandit catch fire and almost immediately this fire went out. Both engines caught alight again after my attack. I then carried out two more attacks from the rear quarter and then one last one from front quarter when E/A was just above the sea with both engines burning."

This aircraft is likely to have been the Bf 110E-3 of 3 (F)123 which was later posted missing along with the two crew of *Feldwebel* Ziegenbalk and Ruschenburg.

A second Bf 110 was encountered the next day, but without result. The squadron continued to operate out of Warmwell, with the odd section despatched back to operate from St Eval. One of the sections was detailed for ferry duty, collecting several Tomahawks from Eastleigh. The squadrons last claim of the month occurred on March 23rd when Flight Lieutenant Mortimer-Rose, Pilot Officer Masters and Sergeant Shepherd shared in damaging a Ju 88 south east of the Isle of Wight.

April started with a bang. Literally. Three He 111s managed to bomb the aerodrome on the 1st, and damaged some of the huts the pilots used. The hut which Pilot Officer Wootten used, had the side blown away, but luckily he wasn't in it. The only casualty was Sergeant Budge Harker, who was wounded in the arm. The squadron redressed the balance the next day, with Flight Lieutenant Mortimer-Rose probably destroying a Ju 88 off Lyme Regis, and Sergeant Shepherd intercepted a Ju 88 about to attack a convoy. The Ju 88 dumped its bombs, and rapidly headed for home.

On April 12th, the entire squadron performed a fly past over Weymouth for the opening of the War Weapons Week, with the Air Officer Commanding of 10 Group taking the salute. The same day news came through that Budge Harker had been granted a commission to Pilot Officer, and much partying ensued!

April 13th saw the squadron fly to Westhampnett, leaving there just after lunchtime, to meet up with 66 and 501 Squadrons to escort some Blenheims to Cherbourg. The squadron saw no action, and returned to Westhampnett during the late afternoon. A practice wing scramble was undertaken later in the month - to Middle Wallop with 66 and 501 Squadrons, and a practice wing formation with 501 was flown to Newquay and back.

Numerous flights were flown by Pilot Officer Wootten during the first half of May, providing air cover for passing convoys and coastal towns. He had spotted an He 111 on patrol during early May, and recorded it in his log book: -

"Heinkel sighted over Portland and was an absolute sitter. Span off climbing turn A.S.I u/s. Lost the bastard!"

The squadron was scrambled to Portland on May 12th, and engaged some Bf 109s, with Squadron Leader Blake and Sergeant Martin destroying one apiece. On May 13th, the squadron performed a Channel sweep as part of a 10 Group Roadstead off Cherbourg, but during this sortie, the Spitfires of Sergeant Stoodley and Pilot Officer 'Shorty' Goodall collided. Pilot Officer Goodall went straight into the sea, but Sergeant Stoodley managed to bale out, however no trace was found of him.

Pilot Officer Wootten also recorded this in his log book: -

Bertie's hut at Warmwell, hit by German raiders.

"Channel sweep to Cherbourg to strafe a German convoy. Shorty Goodall and Sergeant Stoodley collided on the way out. One baled but neither of the poor chaps picked up, but four dead 'plucky Jerries' rescued. What a day!! Both must have been injured and gone straight down."

Two more Spitfires were lost in the morning of May 19th, when Green Section were attacked by Bf 109s from III/JG2 during a convoy patrol. Pilot Officer Budge Harker managed to force land his stricken fighter, but Sergeant Parker had to bale out into the sea. Happily, he was picked up by an Air Sea Rescue launch none the worse for his ordeal. The afternoon's events were much more in the favour of 234 Squadron. Red and Yellow sections were despatched on a convoy patrol, and were then vectored

Sgt John Bean Shepherd. Later an 'ace', both in terms of enemy aircraft & V1s destroyed. Later he commanded 41 Squadron but was killed in a post war flying accident.

to counter several Bf 109s in the area, these being from I/JG2. Pilot Officer Wootten wrote in his combat report: -

"I was Red 1 and ordered to patrol a convoy two miles S.SW of Portland Bill. I was informed that one bandit was 5 miles south of convoy, going N.W. A few minutes later I saw three yellow nosed 109s circling just south of the convoy and below my section. I warned Yellow 1 that Me 109's were in the vicinity and told my number 2 to follow me. I made a head on attack on what appeared to be the leading 109, but he turned in towards me and I could not get on enough deflection , but I gave a very short burst without any apparent effect. As I broke away, I saw two more 109's in line astern , going in a southerly direction. I gave chase and they both saw me coming and climbed through a thin layer of cloud.

Bertie and his Bull Terrier, 'Poopdeck' - who had more flying hours than any other dog in 10 Group!

The Faithful Few

They then flew more or less straight and level thinking no doubt they had thrown me off. I closed in to approximately 150 yards and gave the rear 109 a 4 or 5 second burst, he immediately blew up and went down out of control into the sea, nobody baled out. The first 109 evidently saw what had happened, started violent evasive action, and after a short while tried a steep turn which gave me opportunity for a short burst which caused black smoke to come back from his engine, he then recommenced his southerly flight, still using violent evasive action, he then straightened up and I gave him a fairly long burst and then saw a flash above me and to starboard a row of 25 to 30 Me 109's coming down on me, at the same time the pilot of the 109 attacked by me baled out. I then dived through cloud for base and was not followed more than 10 miles by the 30 109's. First 109 went in about 15 miles S.SW of Portland and the second about 40 - 45 miles S of Portland."

The other pilots also engaged the 109's, with Flight Lieutenant Mortimer-Rose shooting down two, and Flying Officer Baynham one. Pilot Officer Wootten recorded the engagement in his log book in slightly different terms: -

"Chased two yellow nosed bastards and shot the rear one down in flames. The leader was an old hand and took violent evasive action but managed to get a few bursts in and he baled out 45 miles from Portland. Was chased by 30 yellow noses , went like hell for home. "he who fights and runs away!!" Morty got two and Geoff B got one. Earlier in the day Budge and Parker shot down "Oh, what a surprise!!" Both ok. Sqn bag 87."

A well deserved DFC was awarded to Flight Lieutenant Mortimer-Rose on May 26th. By then he had accounted for no less than six enemy aircraft, with several others damaged. June saw the squadron (and sometimes flights) operate from Exeter, but bad, misty weather hampered flying during the first part of the month. Operations were also flown from Middle Wallop, covering Bournemouth, and Portland. On June 17th, the squadron took part in a Roadstead on shipping off Querqueville. Engaged by Bf 109s, they lost Flight Sergeant Armitage, but Flight Lieutenant Mortimer-Rose and Sergeant Shepherd destroyed a 109 each. Pilot Officer Wootten wrote this about the sortie: -

"High cover for 7 Beauforts and close escort 118 Sqn. Baynham and myself top cover 15,000. Lost main formation (due to lack of information at start) over Alderney. Patrolled Alderney for 15 minutes + returned. F/SG Armitage missing, Fawkes shot up. Morty & Shep 1 109. Torpedoes missed destroyers. What a shambles!"

The Faithful Few

This proved to be their main sortie of the month, and they went back to patrolling the south coast, and covering more passing convoys, as well as providing aircraft for Army co-operation flights. However, they were back in action on July 7th, escorting Blenheims to bomb the dock yards in Cherbourg. Bf 109s tangled with 234 Squadron, with Squadron Leader Blake downing two Bf 109's, and Sergeant Jacka probably destroyed another. Sergeant Pearce was killed during this engagement in Spitfire P8659, and Sergeant Newman was wounded. Squadron Leader Blake was also shot down after having his radiator holed, and ditched in the sea. Pilot Officer Wootten recorded this mission: -

" Very successful raid engaged by 109s, returned to base without engaging anything . S/G Jacka got a probable. F/Lt Lacey & S/Ldr Boyd 501 got one each . S/G Pearce last seen in a spin and he bailed out. S/G Newman wounded in the leg and back "the CO is missing". Organised search and nothing seen People were very pessimistic. Still nothing seen. Geoff, W/Cdr Roberts and self evidently passed over C/O. Nothing seen except a lifeboat. "At last" C/O found by S/G Fox. Jolly good show! C/O 10 hrs in water and paddled 10 miles. Was he tough: picked up fit as a fiddle."

A JG 2 Me 109 gets clobbered by Bertie, May 19th, 1941.

One week later, the squadron provided high escort during a Roadstead on shipping off Le Havre. The Spitfires engaged the attacking Bf 109s, with Flight Lieutenant Mortimer-Rose destroying one, and damaging another. Now with the rank of Flying Officer, Wootten destroyed another Bf 109: -

"I was Yellow 1, as high cover in Gudgeon III. When approaching target Perky Leader made an attack on one of two Me 109's. I attempted to attack after Perky Leader, but due to A/C was unable to turn tight enough. I broke away and attacked another 109 below. I closed to 30 yards and gave a short burst with a small amount of deflection. It peeled off to the right with black smoke pouring from his engine and glycol pouring from his port radiator, his hood flew off. At this point I was fired on by another 109 and took violent evasive action. The last sight of the 109 I attacked was he was going down vertically

for the sea, and due to evasive action I lost him. On asking pilots of the other squadrons if a 109 was seen to go in S/Ldr Howell 118 Squadron said he saw a big splash 1 mile north of the target area. This I claim as the Me 109 I attacked. Nothing to note except I experienced difficulty in doing tight turns."

An entry in his log book gives more information on the engagement: -

"Another very successful raid on Cherbourg. Morty had a bang at one Me 109 & knocked its oleo leg down and later pushed him into the sea. I had a bang at one Me 109 & it has since been confirmed. Got a bullet in the port wing and a bit of shrapnel on the engine cowling. Nothing lost. Bloody good show!"

Pilot Officer Masters destroyed a Do215 on July 16th, but the squadron lost Sergeant Martin the next day during an escort of M.G.Bs in a search for a missing Blenheim. Pilot Officer Masters claimed one Bf 109F destroyed, and Flying Officer Baynham destroyed three. Flying Officer Wootten: -

"Very many bandits about. S/G Martin shot down, S/L Blake chased home. Geoff Baynham got 3 109's. Good show. I had a 'squirt' missed 109."

On July 18th, Flying Officer Wootten assumed command of 'B' Flight and was promoted to Flight Lieutenant; and 12 days later Squadron Leader Blake left the squadron to take up a Wing Commanders post at Exeter. By now, 'Bertie' was a much liked and well respected squadron member. He was easily recognised in his white flying suit, with 'Poopdeck' his Bull Terrier, in tow. When operations permitted, he used to take 'Poopdeck' flying with him, cramming him into the cockpit for local flights. He also used to try to fly any type of aircraft he could. From his log book, he managed to fly Beaufighters, Defiants, and Whirlwinds, Hurricanes, and anything else he could get his hands on!

Their last main operation of the month was providing cover for Hampdens over Brest on July 24th. As part of 'Operation Sunrise' the bombers were part of the force detailed to attack the warships Prinz Eugen and Gneisnau. The entry in Flight Lieutenant Wootten's log book reads: -

"Daylight raid on Brest. Bomber A/C engaged 3 Boeings, 78 Wellingtons, 18 Hampdens, 15 Halifaxes, 20 Havocs. Very heavy flak but very little fighter opposition to Sqns in target area. 2 of our LR Sqns patrolled Brest for 15 mins and smoke screen seen, balloons at 2000'. 7 direct hits on Gneisnau. One on Scharnhorst, Prinz Eugen & a tanker straddled. 9 Wellingtons, 5 Halifaxes, 2

The Faithful Few

Hampdens missing. I was high cover at 33,000 feet with Bob Masters. One 109 seen but not engaged. Scharnhorst at La Pallice. Flak terrific. We escorted 2 Boeings home. Made landfall east of Plymouth. We flew high escort for the Hampdens. Flak!! Once seen, never forgotten. 109s..what the hell? Crossing too bloody far. We would do it again but we would not relish it. I hate water, especially when its salty!"

The first 10 days of August were taken up with convoy patrols and local flying. One section performed an endurance and fuel consumption trial to Norwich and back to Warmwell, while Squadron Leader Harborne Stephen arrived at 234 on August 6th to take command.

On August 11th, the squadron flew to Wattisham prior to operations the following day. They flew on to Martlesham Heath, and joined up with 66 and 152 Squadrons to cover the returning bomber force which had attacked the power stations at Knapsack and Quadrath. The engaged the enemy in the Antwerp area, and Squadron Leader Stephen damaged a Ju 88 (thought to be a night fighter) and Pilot Officer Masters damaged a Bf 109. 152 Squadron lost Sergeant White, and 66 lost Sergeant Stevens. Wootten recorded the mission as: -

"We took off as high escort to 152 and 66 Sqns. The sea crossing to the Dutch coast was carried out at sea level. On sighting the coast we climbed and made for Walhoorden where we orbited for about 10 mins. Me 109's sighted as we crossed the coast. After 5 mins the Me 109's gave a little trouble. On return with Blenheim, CO was attacked by 2 109's. I gave one a burst and missed but caused it to dive away. Later I was attacked by a Ju 88 night fighter but I avoided it and the CO put in a few good bursts and set the port engine on fire. Our navigational Blenheim with a section as escort was shot down on crossing the Dutch coast with one of the escorting Spits. Bad show! The operation a great success. Blenheims scored direct hits on turbine houses & boiler houses at the large power station. We returned without losing a person, the others not so lucky!!. Once again long sea crossing which caused me some misgivings. Flak not too bad but never the less bloody frightening. Whirlwinds escorted bombers to Dutch coast and straffed shipping on the way home."

The squadron returned to Martlesham Heath at 12.55, and got back to Warmwell later in the evening. Three days later it was announced that Flight Lieutenant Wootten had been awarded a well deserved DFC.

Four aircraft from 234 joined others from 501 and 118 Squadrons from the Ibsley Wing for a patrol over the Cherbourg Peninsula. A Bf 109 attacked Pilot

Officer Masters without effect, but managed to break up in mid air trying to recover from its initial attacking dive. First the tail came off, followed by one wing before dropping into the sea. The Spitfires lost height and returned to Ibsley. A further sweep of the area was flown the next day, this time from Warmwell, but nothing was seen.

On August 18th, the squadron flew to, and operated from Coltishall, acting as escort to Blenheims attacking shipping off the Dutch coast. One ship was sunk, and one Blenheim lost. The squadron returned to Warmwell during the evening. Eight days passed before their next operation over France - this time they were engaged on a low level attack on Maupertus Aerodrome. The squadron lost one pilot and Spitfire - Sergeant Cliff Jacka who was flying P8046, a presentation Spitfire titled 'City of Worcester I'. Flight Lieutenant Wootten wrote of the sortie: -

"Ground straffing is not my idea of fun!! Very intense light and heavy flak encountered. Sgt Jacka missing. Poor old Cliff! One or two people shot up, I hit a gun post and set fire to a Me 109. Steve set fire to a Ju 88. Whirlwinds also pranged a few A/C."

On September 4th, Flight Lieutenant Wootten took part in an uneventful wing sortie over Cherbourg, covering six Blenheims. Nothing was seen by the squadron and they made their way back home.

It was back to Ibsley on September 8th, to operate with 263, 118 and 501 Squadrons on an anti shipping strike on a convoy off Jersey. The ships and the barges they were towing were duly attacked, with immediate results. Four Bf 109's attacked 234, but without success, and the wing returned to base.

Flight Lieutenant Wootten next flew on a escort operation with 118 and 501 Squadrons, covering Blenheims to Cherbourg on September 20th: -

"We took off as meduim escort to 6 Blenheims to bomb a whale oil tanker in Cherbourg harbour. We approached the peninsula on the west and experienced a fair amount of accurate flak. We did the run from south to north and straight home. Landed at Ibsley and returned to Warmwell. Nothing seen!!"

The last sortie of the month was against enemy shipping off Cap de la Hague. All vessels were shot up, and one was left smoking, and another was seen to sink. The Squadron suffured no loss, with only one Spitfire returning with a single bullet hole in a port aileron.

The Faithful Few

The Squadron returned to Warmwell, and continued with its regular duties, covering the coast and convoys. Practice flying took place, using the camera gun, and later air firing. The next big sortie they participated occurred on October 13th. Listed as Circus 108A, and operating from Redhill, the formation consisted of the Kenley Wing flying close escort, high cover was provided by the Northolt Wing, target support was by the Tangmere Wing, and the rear support was provided by the Wittering Wing. 234, as part of the Porthreath Wing were engaged as the escort cover.

Light flak was encountered over Gravelines, and heavy over Boulogne. 30 Bf 109s intercepted the formation near St Omer, and two 109s were attacked bt Flight Lieutenant Mortimer-Rose and Sergeant Peter Fox. The latter's 109 was seen in a vertical dive and on fire.

A further operation was flown from Westhampnett on October 15th, proving cover for Blenheims attacking the dock yards at Le Havre. As opposed to earlier missions, the squadron were heavily engaged by Bf 109s, and a melee ensued. Pilot Officer Shepherd destroyed a Bf 109F and damaged a 109E, Flight Lieutenant Mortimer-Rose damaged two 109Fs and Squadron Leader Stephen and Pilot Officer Denville shared in the destruction of a 109F. Sadly, Sergeant Barnett was shot down during this engagement, and crashed into the Channel.

A Roadstead to Cap de la Hague was flown on October 17th, without result or loss, and a Rhubarb in the Cherbourg area on October 20th. Sergeant Peter Fox failed to return from this sortie. His Spitfire was hit by flak and was last seen by the squadron weaving, with flaps down and attempting a forced landing. He successfully got his stricken fighter to earth, and was rapidly taken prisoner.

NCO pilots of 234 Sqn. Centre is Cliff Jacka, killed in action flying the presentation Spitfire 'City of Worcester I'.

Three more sotries were flown up to the end of the month, without further loss. Weather caused the cancellation of a couple of missions, however they successfully undertook a shipping reconnaissance south of Barfluer, and attacked a ship of about 600 tons and a flak ship, both of which were sunk. All aircraft returned safely.

Four engagements were undertaken in the first eight days of November, including attacks on a radio station at Joburg which left the building badly damaged. Other stations at Point de Saire and Audeville were also hit. Pilot Officer Meyer developed engine trouble during the latter sortie, and had to force land on Alderney.

Flight Lieutenant Mortimer-Rose and Pilot Officer Bland surprised an E Boat during a shipping reconnaissance near the Channel Islands, and attacked it. After several passes, the E Boat was seen to sink north of Sark.

By now, Flight Lieutenant Wooten had been with 234 Squadron 14 months, and he was deemed as 'tour expired', and on November 10th 1941, he was posted out from operations, and given command of No 2 Delivery Flight, based at RAF Colerne. He stayed there until on January 14th 1942, he was post in to 10 Group, as Squadron Leader in the tactics role.

Nearly six months passed with Group, until he was posted out, and back onto operations to command his first squadron - 118 at Ibsely on June 8th. Their CO, Squadron Leader John Carver DFC had been killed in action two days earlier on a sortie to Maupertus.

The squadron were engaged in an identical role as 234 were - providing cover for the south coast, interceptions of enemy aircraft, and convoy cover, as well as joining in with wing operations over Europe. They also trained hard, covering low flying, dog fight practice, and local flights. During one practice interception, on June 13th, the Spitfire flown by Pilot Officer Klink crashed at Aldersholt Park, near Fordingbridge and was killed.

Four days later, a flight from the squadron engaged several FW 190s on a shipping reconnaissance, and Flight Lieutenant Newbery and Flying Officer Claude managed to damage one of their assailants. However, during Circus 193 from Redhill, the squadron suffered a disaster, losing four pilots and aircraft. Flying Officer Veen, Pilot Officer Stenger, Sergeant Van Houten, and Warrant Officer Noel. Veen, Stenger and Van Houten were Dutch and were all killed. Warrant Officer Noel (actually an alias for the French pilot Adjudant Nioloux) was taken prisoner.

Their next Circus operation was more successful, with only one Spitfire being damaged. Flying Officer Claude had to crash land at Redhill after a cannon shell had destroyed his hydraulic system. Claude was unhurt and the aircraft repairable. In early July, the squadron began participate in exercises to improve communications between forward units and fighter bases, along with co operation sorties with the Army, and they continued for one week. Unknown to them, it was part of the build up to Operation Jubilee, the Dieppe raid.

The regular routine continued until August 15th, when secret orders were received by the squadron. Officers on leave were recalled, and the fitters worked tirelessly to modify the Merlin engines to increase boost from 12 to 16lbs. The next day, 21 aircraft left for Tangmere, with in total 80 squadron members. The squadron operational dairy recorded: -

"On arrival at Tangmere we found that the old station headquarters had been handed over to us, with 4 other squadrons to sleep in, whilst our feeding was done in the officers and sergeants messes on the aerodrome. Food and service was excellent and particularly so considering the enormous inundation which had taken place at Tangmere. We were not told at this stage what it was all about and in view of the previous trip to Tangmere for a similar purpose, pilots were naturally a little apprehensive that arrangements might again fall through."

The pilots were somewhat crestfallen when they were told they would be going back to Ibsley on August 17th to take part in a Wing Sweep. This they successfully completed and returned to Tangmere later in the day. On August 18th, a meeting was convened of senior officers at Squadron Leader and Wing Commander level, plus intelligence officers. The secret orders were then handed over which explained 'Operation Jubilee' to all present, and that the operation was on for the early hours of the following morning.

118 were at readiness at 4 am, and put up six aircraft for station defence. In all the squadron flew four times during 'Operation Jubilee' Squadron Leader Wootten recorded the day in his log book. For the first sortie: -

"Shambles! 118 were last to withdraw. No action. Saw one 190 but did not attack."

His second entry reads: -

"Blackie (Flying Officer Blackburn) attacked a Mustang. Missed it thank Christ!"

Finally, the last entry reads: -

The Faithful Few

Bertie's personal insignia whilst commanding 118 Sqn.

"Cowlings and A/C falling through cloud. Hurricanes did their stuff and everything. Was a hell of a battle above cloud. The Commando withdrawal was 109s and 217s. My bloody radio faded and glycol temperature soared. Sqn got 2 217s - bloody good show! Bloody awful Jerrys around. 5 shot down. What a conclusion to a wonderful day. Sqn was wonderful, not a bloke lost. Minnie Blake missing. What a bloody shame!!"

The only damage to one of their Spitfires occurred when Sergeant Watson suffered a tyre blow out on Spitfire EN964 during take off on a sortie.

Ibsley briefing: 118, 501 & 66 Sqns formed the Wing there.

The Faithful Few

The morning after 'Jubilee' the pilots were interviewed by the press and had their photographs taken. As the squadron diary put it: -

"They described this ordeal as more terrifying that the Jubilee operation."

Bertie in white flying suit with other 118 Sqn pilots at Ibsley whilst participating in the 'First of the Few'

The squadron returned to Ibsley, and suffered an anti climax to the pervious few days. To make things worse, they were told that the wing were to leave Ibsley, with 501 Squadron going to Middle Wallop, and 118 and 66 to Zeals, as the Station was to be handed over to the Americans.. The 118 Squadron diary again: -

"The three squadrons had got on famously at Ibsley, and we were all very sorry at this move, and we were inclined to say harsh things about our gallant Allies the Americans who are taking over Ibsley, but a 'pep' talk from the C.O. put a stop to the rot."

118 Sqn pilots at Tangmere during 'Operation Jubilee' Sqn Ldr Bertie Wootten seated far left, in from of him the Ceylonese Sgt Jimmy Tallala; centre is Dick Salisbury, behind him Robbie Robson, with P/O Levinson & Sgt Buglas far right.

Over the next few days, they prepared for their move to Zeals which took place on August 24th. It was described as: -

"Zeals is an aerodrome. At present it lacks accomodation and is a seething mass of mud. We are all cramped into one dispersal hut and a few tents and the echelon is located in a commandeered piggery. The Officers Mess is a mere 6 miles from the dispersal. The Engineer Officer who has spent 18 months getting our equipment into tip top condition is walking about in a state of utter defection, seeing the self same equipment lying in a sea of mud. However the only possible arrangements have been made by the station staff for our reception. Food is excellent and everyone is helpful and sympathetic. We grouse, but grin and bear it."

Conditions gradually improved, and the squadron get down to its usual role, including escort duties over France and the Channel Islands. They also operated from Hawkinge on 'special duties' on October 8th and 9th, covering Dover and Gravesend, before returning to Zeals. A spell of bad weather hampered operations, before things got back to normal. Of note during this month was when Sergeant Hollingworth was returning from a cannon test out to sea, when he spotted a strange looking aircraft over Poole Harbour. Upon investigation, it turned out to be a Spitfire IX fitted with floats. Both Spitfires were shot at by the harbour defences, and Sergeant Hollingworth dived into cloud, while the float equipped Spitfire alighted in the harbour.

During November, the squadron did escort missions to American bombers, including one to Maupertus Aerodrome. 12 Fortresses bombed from 23,000 feet. Squadron Leader Wootten recalled: -

Press call: pilots of 118 Squadron, F/O Dick Salisbury reclining centre.

The Faithful Few

" One straggled over the target, and came out very slowly. One or two E/A were seen, and smoke trails."

The second sortie was not so successful: -

"Bloody awful Forts flew too slow. Turned left after bombing instead of right then penetrated into France SW. Quite a few Fw's about which made a few attacks. 118 overshot and eventually came back by doing a left hand orbit. We left them half way back due to lack of petrol."

More bomber escort missions were flown up to Christmas 1942, and Squadron Leader Wootten managed to get home on leave, but he was

W/C P Walker, Tangmere Wing Leader, S/L P Gibbs, S/L C Appleton, S/L EW Wootten, S/ L Yule; atop Hurricane is S/L D Du Vivier.

COs' de-brief, post 'Jubilee'.

back in action before the new year, escorting 12 Venturas over France. The squadron moved from Zeals to Wittering on January 3rd, and then to Coltishall on January 17th. On January 27th he escorted 12 Bostons to Flushing and called the operation a 'bit of a cock up' as the Bostons were intercepted on the way out. On January 29th, he was leading the squadron, covering Venturas from 2 Group to Ijmuiden, along with 167 Squadron.

During this sortie, 118 engaged FW 190s intent on attacking the bombers. Squadron Leader Wootten singled out the leading FW 190, and gave it three bursts, hitting the wings with De Wilde strikes, and later, two noticeable cannon strikes on the starboard wing. It turned inverted, did a half roll and dived down. Flight Lieutenant Shepherds section was attacked head on, resulting in his No

2, Flight Sergeant Cross being shot down. Sergeant Lack attacked the FW 190s which had assailed Yellow Section, closing to 300 yards and staying firmly on the tail of one 190, which by now had entered a dive. Sergeant Lack gave it an eight second burst and broke away, and Sergeant Hollingworth saw the 190 dive into the sea. Hollingworth also damaged an FW 190, but not before one had shot holes in his starboard wing.

Bertie's Spitfire NK-B.

Two more pilots were lost on operations on February 24th, with Flight Sergeant Croall being killed and Flight Sergeant Buglas coming down in the sea, and being rescued by an ASR Walrus.

The rest of the squadron made it back to Coltishall, and had prevented the enemy fighters getting to the Venturas, however the FW 190s were a powerful opponent, compared to the Spitfire Vb's flown by Squadron Leader Wootten. Several times he makes mention of 190s getting away, describing them as "too bloody fast!!"

118 flew their 100th sweep on March 19th, 1943, covering Venturas to Maasluis. The Wing Leader, Wing Commander Blatchford destroyed one FW 190 by shooting the tail off it, and damaged another. Flight Lieutenant Newbrey also destroyed a 190, with Squadron Leader Wootten seeing it crash into the sea. On the return journey, Sergeant Lack was hit by friendly fire from a sea fort off Harwich, and before he could bale out, plummeted into the water.

Squadron Leader Wootten made his final combat claims on April 4th 1943 during a Ramrod to Rotterdam when he encountered and damaged two Fw 190's. Pilots from 118 damaged a further four enemy aircraft, and destroyed another two during this mission, however, Flying Officer Levinson was shot down and killed.

Squadron leader Wootten led 118 Squadron until June 1st 1943, when he was promoted to Wing Commander and took command of flying at Fairwood Common. There then followed a short attachment to 257 Squadron at Warmwell where he got to grips with the Hawker Typhoon.

In January 1944 he was posted to the Mediterranean, spending nearly six months with HQ before joining 244 Wing as a supernumary wing leader under Wing Commander Hugh Dundas. Given command of his own wing, 322, he participated in the invasion of southern France, and stayed with 322 until it was disbanded in October 1944. He then took command of

A 118 Sqn Spitfire damaged by flak during a 'Rhubarb', 1942.

324 Wing at Florence. Posted back to the UK in December 1944, he was posted to Washington as RAF Liasion Officer to the USAF.

Returning to the UK in January 1946, he became Wing Commander Flying at 1 Ferry Unit, Persore, and later commanded RAF Station Newton. He later commanded 245 Squadron at Horsham St Faith, and established the first official RAF aerobatic team, with lineage which can be traced to the modern Red Arrows.

In the 1950's he took over 229 (F) Operational Conversion Unit at Chivenor, then to the Middle East at Deversoir and Kabrit, Canal Zone, before returning to Linton on Ouse. In 1959 he became Air Attache in Caracas, Venezuela with the rank of Group Captain. A move to Middleton St George followed in 1963 to the Lightening and Javelin Operational Conversion Unit, before on again to Leconfield with 19 and 92 Squadrons. Several high ranking staff postings followed between 1966 and 1971, and culminated in his post as a Aide de Campe to HM Queen Elizabeth.

His decorations included a Distinguished Flying Cross and Bar, an Air Force Cross in 1950, the Venezuelan Air Force Cross in 1963, and a Companion of the British Empire in 1971. He retired from the service in 1974 with the rank of Air Commodore, and became an aerospace consultant with British Aerospace. During his operational career, he had over 5,000 flying hours to his credit, and had flown over 60 different types of aircraft, from Tiger Moth to BAC Lightning (which he still flew aged 58), however all his operational flying was in Spitfires. He retired to Norfolk, and passed away in 1999 aged 81. Bertie was one of the kindest pilots the author has ever had the pleasure of meeting and it was easy to see why he had such a long and auspicious career.

The stained glass memorial window to Bertie Wootten
at St Nicholas Church, Blakeney. Designed & made by
Jane Grey ARCA, FMGP, & given by Bertie's brother
'Bunty'. Depicting both a Spitfire and the 234 Squadron
badge, it is a fitting tribute to 'One of the Few'.

Chapter Four

Dennis Conon Williams hailed from Bromsgrove and joined the RAF on a short service commission in 1938. His father was the Reverend Canon Harold Williams BA, a first world war veteran who had been awarded the Military Cross for his service.

On October 4th 1939, 141 Squadron reformed at RAF Turnhouse. 49 NCO's and airmen were the first to arrive, under the command of Squadron Leader W A Richardson. The first aircrew to arrive were Pilot Officer A W Smith and Pilot Officer R A Howley, soon followed by Flying Officers R E Orchard, D C Williams, and H T J Anderson. However the squadron had no aircraft whatsoever, and had to borrow several Avro Tutors and a Tiger Moth from 603 Squadron who were sharing the base. By the 24th, they had managed to purloin an Anson, but nothing else.

By the end of the month they were allocated a few Blenheim 1F's and began the job of collecting them and ferrying them back to Turnhouse. By the 28th, five were available for collection. Flying Officer Williams collected one of these from RAF Church Fenton, and more aircraft began to come on to the strength, with the process carrying on until late November. Despite the lack of Blenheims, the squadron had also received several Gloster Gladiators, which were used for formation flying, and local flying practice.

On the 1st December, 141 suffered their first fatalities of the war. A Blenheim detailed on a radar reconnaissance flight was seen to dive out of cloud at high speed and crash near Leuchars. The crew of four were all killed - Pilot Officer R M Williams from Monmouth, Pilot Officer H G Yelland from Winnipeg, Canada, and Aircraftsman 2nd Class L Dale. The other crew member was not listed.

The winter hit with a vengeance, with an exceedingly wet spell which caused the Blenheims to sink into the wet ground. Flying only took place during gaps in the weather, and more aircrew were posted in. Flying Officer Williams had a near miss on December 10th when he had to force land a Blenheim near Linlithgow. He had been returning to base after taking a pilot to Catterick to ferry a Spitfire back. The aircraft was destroyed, and Williams didn't escape unscathed, suffering arm and shoulder injuries, which hospitalised him.

The Faithful Few

The bad weather continued into January 1940, and the squadron had another Blenheim damaged when Pilot Officer Gard'ner force landed near Torphichen, before snow stopped flying entirely.

There then followed two changes of base - firstly 141 were posted to Prestwick, moving mid February, before going on to Grangemouth. By March 10th, five aircraft were ready to go to Northolt, but once again the weather changed, and prevented the move, so there they stayed. April opened with the rumour of new aircraft. Unlike most rumours, this turned out to be true - 141 were to be a Defiant squadron, and by April 8th they had received three, however, the Gladiators and Blenheims were still held, until the last were ferried out by the start of May.

The Defiant, was, in shape, not dissimilar to a cross between a Hurricane and a Spitfire. Large of build, and powered by a Merlin engine, it housed a crew of two - pilot and gunner. The gunner was housed in a large, four gun, electrically powered turret located behind the pilot's seat. However, the extra weight of the turret and gunner, was to prove a problem on day operations, affecting the manoeuvrability, especially compared to the Bf 109.

The Defiant was a throwback to the latter stages of the First World War, when the RAF were operating the Bristol Fighter, which employed the pilot and gunner arrangement. The Bristol Fighter was highly successful, and it was thought that the Defiant would be just so. However, the speeds of air combat were much higher this time around, and it would prove problematic for the pilot and gunner to act as one. Daylight operations were to prove this.

Familiarisation flights were flown, along with anti aircraft cooperation duties, and training for the radar stations. On May 25th, they suffered their first loss of a

P/O Geoffrey Pledger & F/O Dennis Williams, 141 Sqn.

Defiant and its crew, when Sergeant Keene and Aircraftsman Whitman crashed near the airfield. Both were killed instantly, and the aircraft burnt out.

June saw the flights divide - 'A' went to Leuchars for air firing practice at towed targets, while 'B' went to Acklington for theirs. On June 3ʳᵈ 1940, 141 were finally deemed operational. June saw little other that much flying practice, with the only incident of note being when for Pilot Officer Orchard and Pilot Officer Constantine who managed to run their Defiants into each other on the ground.

On July 9ᵗʰ, orders were received that the Squadron was to move to its HQ to Biggin Hill, and the aircraft were to operate from West Malling, with most of the aircrew having moved down within two days. Local flights were flown, and several Defiants were being upgraded with new constant speed airscrews. Flying Officer Williams flew an anti aircraft cooperation flight on July 17ᵗʰ, and the next day all aircraft flew to Hawkinge at 17.10 hours and patrolled base until 20.45 hours, before flying back to West Malling.

On July 19ᵗʰ, they left for West Malling at 08.45 hours, and were called to action just under two hours later. At 10.38 hrs 'A' Flight were ordered off to patrol 20 miles south of Folkestone. What happened then was disastrous.

The Flight of nine Defiants was 'bounced' by a superior force of Bf 109s. In the chaos that ensued, they were subjected to a concentrated attack, with the Germans knowing just how to deal with Defiants. During the Dunkirk operation, 264 Squadron had some real success in combat, as the Germans mistook their Defiants for Spitfires, and had made stern attacks, only to fly into directly into the fire of the gunners. By now, though, they knew how to avoid this 'sting in the tail'.

A section of Bf 109s attacked them head on, while a second section came in from astern, but below, coming in at a level where the gun turrets would never be able to reach them as they were unable to depress the guns that low.

Squadron Leader Richardson, leading the Defiants wrote:

"At 12.35 the order was received to sweep Cap Gris Nez at 5000 feet. The squadron was attacked out of the sun by 20-25 Me109's. I immediately turned to port, completing a steep turn of 360 deg. This proved ineffective, as A/C attacked from below and to the outside. I then carried out S turns, turning always to the attack, this proved effective. After 5 mins, Red 2 and myself Red

The Faithful Few

1 were the only two Defiants left, so decided to break off the combat and return to base."

Pilot Officer Halliwell, Squadron Leader Richardson's gunner, wrote: -

"Me 109s came out of the sun. As they came in to deliver attack, I had one in sights until well within range and opened fire whilst still astern (slight deflection). Tracer bullets were seen to hit e/a, which dived down and disappeared into the sea, leaving a large round patch of oil and foam."

But the Germans had the upper hand: four Defiants were shot down into the sea, taking with them 3 pilots and 5 air gunners. Only Pilot Officer Gardner, the pilot of Defiant L7016, was rescued. By now the aircraft had broken formation and were trying to head for home, using whatever cloud was available for cover. Pilot Officer Donald made it back, only to crash in Dover. His gunner, Pilot Officer Hamilton baled out but landed in the sea and was drowned.

Flight Lieutenant Loudon managed to make Hawkinge, but his gunner, Pilot Officer Farnes, returned by boat, having baled out into the channel. His aircraft, L7001, was a write off.

Pilot Officer MacDougall filed this report showing the ferocity of the attack:

"Owing to the fact that Green 1 and Yellow 2 did not take off, I assumed Yellow 2's position - I followed the squadron at 5,000 feet - I never saw any of the enemy planes at all, during the first two attacks, but bullets were being fired at me from all angles. After the 3rd attack my engine cut, and believing I had been shot down, ordered the Air Gunner to jump, but as I got no answer assumed him killed, and decided to come down to sea level to land. On my way the engine restarted, and I was able to proceed to my base, where I found the turret empty, the Air Gunner having obviously baled out previously."

Sergeant Wise, the unfortunate gunner, was never seen again.

The fact that three aircraft managed to get back to Hawkinge was due to the timely intervention of the Hurricanes of 111 Squadron, who had seen the attack unfold. The 111 Squadron ORB takes up the story: -

"At 10,000 feet, Green 2, Pilot Officer Copeman saw a formation of 20 enemy aircraft out to sea off Folkestone. Green section went in to attack and interceptions were made. Flight Lieutenant Connors DFC made a beam attack

on a Me 109 which he shot down in flames. He then made an attack on a further Me 109 which was carried on by Pilot Officer Copeman who chased it within 5 miles of the French coast and left it in a badly damaged condition. In the meantime. Pilot Officer Stimpson made attacks on several Me 109's, one of which was seen to crash into the sea by Green 1. 5 aircraft landed at Hawkinge 13.25 - 13.30 hours, and the remaining 7 aircraft landed at Croydon at 13.50 hours. The formation of Me 109's were attacking a squadron of Defiants from 141 Squadron when 111 made the interception. 10 aircraft in all were seen to fall into the sea, but out of that, 4 were probably Defiants."

The cost to 141 was much higher - four aircraft lost, two written off, and one damaged. But the human cost was four pilots and six air gunners. All in the space of a few minutes.

The Bf 109s were from JG51, whose pilots in turn over claimed a total of 11 Defiants. *Hauptmann* Trautloft, *Oberleutenant* Kath, *Leutnant* Wehelt claimed one each, while *Leutnant* Pinchon - Kalau v. Hofe claimed three. All were with *Stab* III/JG53. *Oberleutenant* Oseau of 7/JG51, *Feldwebel* Lausch and *Leutnant* Schmidt of 8/JG51, and *Oberleutenant* Lignitz of 9/JG51 all claimed one apiece.

It had been a terrible start to 141's Battle of Britain, and the following day, it was released from operations 'for a short period'. On July 21st, instructions were received that the unit was to move to Prestwick, and all aircraft based at West Malling, Biggin Hill and Hawkinge were to leave. At the same time, Flying Officer Williams, and Flying Officer Tamblyn were recommended as flight commanders, but soon after, Tamblyn was posted to 242 Squadron.

Back in Scotland, their flying duties resembled those of their pre operational days - sector flights, AA Cooperation duties and local patrols. In early August, Flight Lieutenant Fitzgerald DFC took command of 'B' Flight, and the flight detaches to Dyce. There then followed another move, this time back to Turnhouse, before Squadron Leader Wolfe takes command. At the end of August, 'B' Flight moved back south, taking detached flights to Gatwick and Biggin Hill. This time the Defiant wasn't to be committed to daylight operations, but it was to find a second wind, tackling the German bombers by night.

Lacking in airborne radar, they were to patrol until vectored onto a target by ground control, and then to search visually to try and locate their intended target. Those early days were very much hit and miss. However, Pilot Officer Robin Lucas remembered: -

"Several others and I were replacements when the squadron was posted to Prestwick to rest, re-form and train for operational night flying. When we came south to Gatwick and Gravesend we were mainly concerned with the defence of London at night. With primitive radar, the interception rate was low. My memories of Defiants are happy ones. Although slower than a Spitfire, but a shade faster than a Hurricane, it was a remarkably stable aircraft with no vices and therefore ideal for flying blind and at night. I think the Spitfire pilots were often surprised when we flew in atrocious conditions."

Les Smith was an Air Gunner with the squadron, and had been posted from 219 Squadron when they re equipped with Beaufighters. He joined 'B' Flight which was based at Biggin Hill. He recalled: -

"Our Squadron's task was to man a protective 'patrol line' south of London, which ran from Canterbury in Kent to Guildford in Surrey. We had to fly up and down this line for 1 ° to 2 hours, twice or sometimes even three times a night, trying to intercept German bombers either going to, or coming from London. In spite of our warm flying gear it was still freezing cold in the draughty turret up at 10,000 to 15,000 feet. Also it was no joke getting up to this favourite height of the bombers , for this side of London was thick with barrage balloons up to 5,000 feet, and then we had to put up with the trigger happy anti-aircraft gunners who were also thick on the ground in this area.

"The bombing increased in September and October, and when we were near the Canterbury end of our patrol line, I could see my home town of Gravesend. Sometimes I could see fires raging in the town from the bombing, and I knew my Mother, father and Brother were down there. The frustrating part about this was that we could never find the aircraft which dropped the bombs. The night sky was such a huge void, and one aircraft such a small dot in it, that the only way we could spot them was from the glow of their engine exhaust pipes."

The daytime battles of September 16th had been fought, and during the darkness the German bombers were again making their way to their intended targets. Defiants were airborne, and one crewed by Pilot Officer Waddingham and Sergeant Cumbers, was patrolling at 9,000 feet over the Kent and Sussex coast when at 23.59 hours, they caught a He 111. Pilot Officer Waddingham: -

"During a clear moonlight, with 20/25 miles visibility, on a patrol line Maidstone to Tunbridge at about 9,000 feet, I sighted an E/C which was illuminated by searchlights at about 5 miles away, and approaching me on the starboard side - I climbed at full throttle in order to intercept and when I got

within 1000 yards from the A/C, I flashed my letter of the day to the guns, which were at the time firing at least 1000 yards to the rear and about 300 feet below the target - the guns however did not cease fire. I started the attack, which started in a stern chase, the E/C heading towards the coast, and turning alternatively from port to starboard, presumably as an evasive tactic to escape the searchlights. This movement however, gave me an advantage, as it enabled me to gain ground by turning inside his turns. When I was 500 yards to his rear, and about 300 feet below him, I pulled my boost cut out control, and turned on his starboard beam and positioned myself thereon, slightly below at 400 yards distance. From this position I gradually closed in to approximately 30 to 50 yards, still on his starboard beam, when my gunner opened fire on my orders - after firing about 600 rounds which were seen by my gunner to hit the E/C directly from tail to head, the E/C turned over in a steep bank to starboard, past the vertical and fell headlong to earth, half on his back. During this violent manoeuvre, the E/C almost rammed me, and after recovering from my breakaway, the E/C had fallen so low that it was out of searchlights and out of my sight."

Pilot Officer Waddingham continued to patrol after the engagement, when he spotted another raider: -

"I caught sight of another E/C approximately 3000 feet above me, and about 5 miles away - straight ahead and heading S.E at 90 degrees to my course, which was approximately N.E from Tunbridge Wells. I climbed to intercept and head off the E/C, but when within 1000 yards I saw another aircraft which I presumed to be enemy, 300 yards to the rear of my original sighted plane. I climbed until I was positioned 1000 yards on the starboard beam of the leading A/C, and at this juncture I saw the following A/C open fire with his front gun on the leading A/C, at about 300 yards range. I then identified the pursuing plane as a friendly Blenheim fighter - (I had not been informed of the presence of this A/C in my vicinity). It is possible that the Blenheim hit the E/C in the tail, but the E/C was returning fire from its back blister gun. During this engagement I was rapidly closing the ground, and after approximately 5 seconds period, during which the two aircraft were firing at each other, I had closed in to within 400 yards of the E/C, still on his starboard side. Then the Blenheim appeared to cease fire and broke away - I decided to engage the E/C which was rapidly going away, and got to within 30 yards, still on his starboard beam, when my gunner opened fire with at first a very short burst of barely 1 second - this burst on account of our very close proximity went right over the E/C , my gunner then corrected his aim and let him have a long burst of approximately 8 seconds, which set his engine on fire and the plane appeared

The Faithful Few

to dive down. But during this engagement I presumably had slightly overshot my mark , and had placed myself slightly ahead of the E/C, and although I corrected my movement by throttling back hard, I did not avoid a short burst of incendiaries from his front gun into my turret. This caused me to break away to starboard. This A/C was seen by the Coastguard to be on fire, and RAF ceased plotting it, 8 miles from the French coast when it obviously fell into the sea - and although until confirmation had been received, this E/C was only claimed as 'probable as it only had one engine on fire."

With the turret out of action. Pilot Officer Waddingham returned to base. Les Smith recalled this combat: -

"…on the 16th September our luck changed, and we shot down a Heinkel 111, and by an amazing stroke of luck on the 18th we downed a Junkers 88, but these were our only two victories throughout the 24 weeks of the Battle of Britain, and the London Blitz. You might say this was a very poor effort, especially at this point of the battle, our day fighter companions, in their Spitfires and Hurricanes, in many cases had notched up double figure victories. The reason for this was that, in 1940, our Nightfighters, and the equipment in them, were out of date compared to the modern aircraft the Germans were operating. However, once the RAF received the modern Beaufighters and Mosquitoes, with cannons and air-to-air radar, the situation improved rapidly in our favour."

The Ju 88 shot down on the 18th was destroyed by Sergeants Laurence and Chard (though some other references suggest the 17th) during a patrol between Maidstone to Tunbridge. His combat report read: -

"I came across an E/C which although not illuminated by searchlights, shone in the brilliant moonlight about 150 yards away. He was coming on converging courses at the same height as myself. I quickly turned and gave chase and managed to keep him in sight, until I overtook him to about 50 to 60 yards away. My gunner gave him a short burst, which caused him to make a complete turn right over my own craft and at the same time he dropped, or rather jettisoned, two large bombs. He then proceeded S.E and sped off. I again turned and gave chase, and after pulling the plug, I overtook him in about 3 minutes and took up my position under the starboard main plane. My gunner then again proceeded to let him have another short burst which again caused him to turn over my aircraft, but during this evasive manoeuvre, my air gunner let him have another short burst from underneath , and as the enemy stared to dive, he let go one last burst right into his cockpit, which sent him crashing to

earth. In all, only 35 rounds were used from each gun."

The Ju 88 caught by Sergeants Laurence and Chard was a machine from 3/ KG54 heading to bomb London Docks. The aircraft broke up in the air over Maidstone, with the wreckage dropping into Tonbridge Road and St Andrews Close. The crew of four - *Leutnant* Ganzlmayr, *Oberfeldwebel* Fachinger, and *Unteroffiziers* Bauer and Schlossler all perished.

During operations from Gatwick, contacts were made with more enemy aircraft, but no further kills were made. Weather hampered operations, along with mechanical problems, and sometimes the unwanted attention of our own AA gunners. Pilot Officer Waddingham and Sergeant Cumbers, along with Sergeants Green and Bowman, found themselves on the receiving end during a patrol on October 16th.

Three days later, Williams and Pledger, operating out of Gatwick, spotted 2 enemy aircraft, and had managed to stalk them, closing to with 100 yards. However at the vital moment, the guns failed to fire, and they had to break away.

To bolster the night defence, 'A' Flight moved down from Drem to join the rest of the squadron at Gatwick, with them arriving on October 25th. Once again, circumstances prevented Williams engaging the enemy, when during a patrol two days later, he was forced to return to base after his instruments froze up.

During November, contact with the enemy was somewhat limited, however on November 11th, Sergeants Hamer and Hill engaged a Ju 88, opening fire on it, only for the German gunners to fight back, hitting and damaging the Defiant. The Ju 88 was in turn claimed as a 'probable'. Interestingly, some of the night operations took a couple of the Defiants over France. Pilot Officer Cuddie and Sergeant Creswell intruded over Boulogne on November 20th, and Pilot Officer Constantine and Sergeant Croxton ventured over Le Croto on November 22nd.

Only one success was recorded in December, when on the 22nd, Pilot Officer Benson and Pilot Officer Blain, flying as 'Creeper 35' spotted a He 111. Pilot Officer Benson wrote: -

"I started off on a dusk patrol at 17.15 hours, when the setting sun was still giving a bright red glow and the visibility above cloud, at the time 3000 feet,

90

was perfect up to 2000 yards. Over the coast, somewhere in the vicinity of Hastings, the controller vectored me on and E/A, which I was told was at 18,000 feet. At the time my height was 15,000 feet, and I started to climb at once. My gunner was the first one to spot the E/A in a rear position heading for London. I then caught sight of him myself at 16,500 feet, approximately 1500 to 2000 yards away. Climbing on a practically parallel course, I flew on and pulled the plug to climb and catch up. I estimate the aircraft was flying on a course of 350 degrees, at about 170 mph. I kept well out of his sight, underneath him, to get into a satisfactory position, and my gunner asked me to get as near to him as possible. We were able to close in to about 75 yards on hi port side, and slightly behind, my gunner gave him one burst of approximately 3 seconds which he followed up promptly with two more short bursts.

All the while I made full use and took all the advantage possible of the dark sky background, keeping well out of his sight, and taking him entirely by surprise. My gunner directed his initial burst of fire on the lower gun turret and port engine, and his last two bursts at the pilot, and I believe it must have been the rear gunner whom I saw fall from the bottom of the plane after the first burst. At the time it was getting too dark to observe the enemy aircraft markings or colour, but I felt fairly confident it was a Heinkel 111.

After the second and third bursts, I went round in front of him and flew forwards and backwards underneath him. He took no evasive action whatever, probably because of the complete surprise of the attack. I then saw smoke coming from both engines, and flames from the fuselage. To make certain that the E/A

Pilots of the Flight at Crawley's George Inn. L-R: F/O De La Torre (IO), F/Os Williams & McDougal. Seated L-R: F/O Constantine, F/L Fitzgerald, F/O Waddingham & P/O Pledger.

was quite destroyed my gunner and I watched it and saw it go down in a shallow spiral dive, and we saw it crash on the ground and appear to blow up. I am informed the E/A crashed at Etchingham."

Williams and Pledger were on patrol at the same time, and had a good view of the burning He 111 making its way earthward.

The Faithful Few

The He 111 was from 3/KG55, and on a mission to Manchester. It crashed at Underwood House, Etchingham, killing three of the crew. Only one of the crew survived, that being *Gefreiter* Wrobelewski who Benson had seen bale out.

Less than a month later, Benson narrowly avoided being killed when he crashed his Defiant on the aerodrome; it smashing into a sandbagged emplacement and bursting into flames.

January was a quiet month for 141, with only 25 night operations being flown, and only five enemy aircraft being spotted. Williams and Pledger had spotted one on January 16th, but it had dived away over the Channel. However, on the positive side, Flying Officer Waddingham and Sergeant Cumbers were awarded the DFC and DFM respectively for their successful engagement the previous September.

On March 24th 1941, Williams was to have yet another crash landing, however with this one, he was lucky to walk away from it. With Pledger on board, they had taken off from Gravesend to perform an air test in Defiant N1795 after it had received a 30 hour service. Upon getting airborne, the normally reliable Merlin engine failed. The Defiant rapidly lost height, skidded across a field, and crashed into an embankment on Watling Street, not far off the end of the runway. The wings were torn off, as was the propeller assembly, and the fuselage ended up on its port side, with the tail section twisted upside down. Luckily, it did not catch light, and they managed to extract themselves with very minor injuries.

The third time this happened to Flying Officer Williams, he was not to be so lucky. Two Defiants, N1725 piloted by Squadron Leader Wolfe with Pilot Officer Pairmain had taken off from Gravesend at 22.52 hours, with Williams and Pledger following eight minutes later. Squadron Leader Ted Wolfe DFC recalled: -

"I was also flying at the same time when Willy and Pledge were killed. We were both recalled to Gravesend by Biggin Hill, and he went into cloud at 1,000 feet about 10 minutes before I descended in circles. I recall that night the weather and the R/T was rather poor. I got back at 00.38 hours, but Willy didn't."

In reality, Williams' Defiant had nearly made it back, but in the bad weather, it had scattered itself across the ground at a place called Little Hermitage, just over two miles from Gravesend.It was suggested that the aircraft might have stalled on approach when they encountered very heavy rainfall. Williams and Pledger were killed instantly and their loss was instantly felt by the squadron. Geoffrey Pledger was buried back in his home town of Southend on Sea, while Dennis Williams was cremated at Perry Barr.

Pilot Officer Robin Lucas: -

"I particularly remember Williams because he was quiet, kind and charming man, completely opposite to the split arse gung-ho image of a fighter pilot which has sadly and inaccurately been fostered over the years. His charm and calmness have always stayed in my mind."

Defiant N7195 lies broken on an embankment at Watling Street. Both Williams & Pledger escaped with only minor injuries.
(Les Smith)

*S/L Ted Wolfe DFC, OC 141 Sqn;
he was flying on the night that
Williams & Pledger were killed.*

*P/O Robert Lucas,
who vividly recalls
Dennis Williams.*

Chapter Five

Nevil Everard Reeves was born on July 16th 1920, at Manor Farm, Naunton, near Upton upon Severn. Educated at Hanley Castle Grammar School, he became head boy, and excelled at sporting activities, in particular cricket.

He joined the RAF in 1939, and during his flying training, he was sent to fly twin engined aircraft, culminating in him attaining many flying hours on Blenheims. His natural ability with such aircraft ensured he was to hone his skills as a fledgling night fighter pilot, with his first operational posting to 604 Squadron in February 1941

Sgt Nevil Reeves airborne in a 604 Sqn Beaufighter over Wiltshire.

Along with his radar operator, Sergeant Moody, he joined 604 at Middle Wallop on February 15th, with their first flight with the squadron being in Blenheim L8681 on a sector recce, where they were able to familiarise themselves with the area. New to the squadron, Sergeant Reeves would have been able to have learnt an awful lot about night fighting from the crews there - for there were pilots in 604 who were to rapidly reach 'ace' status, and undoubtedly the stellar crew of that time was Flight Lieutenant John Cunningham DFC, and Sergeant Fred Rawnsley. On the very evening Sergeant Reeves arrived, Flight Lieutenant Cunningham destroyed a He 111 of 7/KG27, shooting it down at Harberton, in Devon.

Sqn Ldr John 'Catseyes' Cunningham's famous Beaufighter, R1201, at Middle Wallop. Reeves flew this machine several times.
(Allan White)

Reeves made his first solo trips in a Beaufighter on February 19th, when he took R2143 up on two separate flights to gain experience on the type. More training flights took place before he was able to become 'operational' - numerous air tests, AI (airborne interception) radar training, night flying training and Army Co-op flights. During this period, 604 were having a very successful time against the German bombers, being expertly guided to their interlopers by the ground control stations at Sopley and Exminster.

On March 4th, Squadron Leader Anderson destroyed a He 111 of 1/KG28, on the 12th Flying Officer Geddes destroyed a Ju 88 from 6/KG76 which crashed at Kingston Deverill in Wiltshire, and Flight Lieutenant Cunningham put in a probable claim for a He 111. The following night, Flying Officer Chisholm claimed two He111s destroyed, one of those being the 6/KG55 machine which crashed at Falfield in Gloucestershire with the loss of the entire crew. Flight Lieutenant Lawton claimed a Ju 88 destroyed and a He 111 damaged the same night. It must have been frustrating for Sergeant Reeves to see the other pilots in action, but it wasn't long before he was deemed operational and was joining in on the nightly hunts over the south west.

On April 4th, six patrols were flown, with Flying Officer Crew shooting down a He 111 of *Stab* III/KG26 at Hewish, Weston Super Mare. Three of the crew baled out to become POW's. Flight Lieutenant Lawton and Flight Lieutenant

The Faithful Few

Watson both claimed He 111's as probables, but in deteriorating weather, and low on fuel, Watson, and his radar operator, Sergeant Patson had to bale out of their Beaufighter, with both coming to earth safely.

By the end of the month, 604 had claimed a further 14 aircraft destroyed (of which six were claimed by the then Squadron Leader Cunningham DSO DFC) with two probables and two damaged. Only one Beaufighter had been damaged, when Flying Officer Crew's mount had been hit by our own anti aircraft fire.

On May 1st, an incident occurred which would prove in the long run to be beneficial to Sergeant Reeves. That evening, Flying Officer Joll, along with his radar operator, Sergeant O'Leary located, and engaged a He 111. However this was not prove as one sided as most of the combats had been, for the gunners on board the raider put up a stern defence, pouring accurate return fire into the Beaufighter. Sergeant O'Leary was hit and wounded in five places, and Flying Officer Joll had to break off the attack, leaving the He 111 damaged.

On the night of May 4th, Sergeant Reeves finally had his first encounter with the enemy, when he damaged a Ju 88, before he lost contact with it. However, the sortie was to prove even more eventful, for upon return to Middle Wallop, Reeves found that the undercarriage on his Beaufighter was totally jammed, and all attempts to lower it failed. There was no option but to make a belly landing on the airfield, which he safely did. His combat report read: -

"I took off from Middle Wallop at 02.30 hrs and went over to Sopley. At about 03.00 hrs we were put on to a raid going 150 degrees at about 16-17,000 ft. After several changes of course, contact was estimated about 1500 ft ahead and 1500 ft above.

After flying on 150 degrees for a few minutes, very heavy AA fire was experienced, presumably firing into the apex of about 20 to 30 searchlights. We were illuminated for about 5-6 minutes but the E/A was not seen to be illuminated. After establishing contact, we flew on 150 degrees at about 280-290 mph for about 20-25 minutes before visual was seen, at about 1500 ft above (about 70 degrees) and 500 ft in front, dead ahead, the exhausts being seen far in advance of the silhouette.

We pulled up level and fired a burst at about 200 yards from dead astern, and then a short one at extreme short range. Shells were seen to enter the port side of the fuselage and I saw a flash from the port engine. We came in too fast and had to break away to avoid a collision; as we did so the Op saw flames coming from the port engine. I throttled back and contact was immediately lost, but seen 5-10,000 ft below is diving to port. The contact was not maintained.

We then flew 330 degrees and picked up Sopley after 10-15 minutes, who continued to vector us on 330 degrees; eventually the fixed us to the west end of the Isle of Wight, and as they did so AA again came very close. Re Op fired a very cartridge and the guns immediately ceased fire."

Wing Commander Appleton had to belly in two nights later after return fire from a He 111 had damaged his aircraft, and 604 lost another aircraft on the 7th when Sergeant Wright engaged a He 111 off Portland, and shot it down into the sea, but upon their return, the port engine burst into flames. Sergeant Wright and Sergeant Vaughan had no option but to bale out, and they landed in the sea, but were safely picked up.

A near tragedy occurred on May 11th, when Flying Officer Crew engaged what was thought to be an enemy aircraft, only to actually shoot down a Hurricane. The pilot baled out and was admitted to hospital with minor injuries. It is proof that so called 'friendly fire' is not a new thing to the annals of warfare.

There then followed a lull between May 15th and the 25th, where the weather seemed to be limiting enemy operations over the south west. Wing Commander Appleton destroyed a He 111 near Liverpool on the 28th, this being a 7/KG27 machine which crashed at Buckley, Flintshire. That same day, 604 suffered a training accident when during air to ground firing practice near Swanage, the Beaufighter with Pilot Officer Jackson, Sergeant Boulton and Sergeant Hawke on board, flew into a hill, killing them all.

June 1941 was busy again, with more claims being made by Flying Officer Geddes, Flight Lieutenant Budd and Flight Lieutenant Watson. Despite fleeting contacts, Sergeant Reeves made no more engagements. New arrival Pilot Officer Gossland destroyed a He 111 (though he thought he had shot down a Ju 88) on only his third sortie, catching a machine from 1/KGr100, the German Pathfinder unit, and shooting it down at Maiden Bradley, Wiltshire. The entire crew were killed. However, 13 days later, Pilot Officer Gossland was seriously injured when his aircraft suffered engine failure and crashed eight miles from Middle Wallop. He was lucky that his radar operator, Sergeant Phillips, was able to drag him clear of the wreckage before it caught fire.

Within the first nine days of July, 604 claimed ten aircraft destroyed, plus two damaged, with Flight Lieutenant Speke, and Flight Lieutenant Chisholm accounting for three each. On July 17th, Flight Lieutenant Speke was awarded a DFC. Sadly, eight days later, Flight Lieutenant Speke and Sergeant Dawson went missing in Beaufighter X7548. Later that afternoon, reports came back to Middle Wallop about an aircraft which had crashed near the top of Oare Hill, near Pewsey. Upon investigation, it was confirmed that it was X7548 with Speke and Dawson on board. For some unknown reason, it had crashed into the hill at very high speed, hitting the ground at an angle of 80 degrees from the vertical.

During early August, a flight from 604 was detached to Coltishall in Norfolk, consisting of Wing Commander Appleton, Squadron Leader Cunningham, Flight Lieutenants Lawton, Lee and Patten, and Flying Officers Geddes and Edwards, along with Sergeant Phillips. The remainder of the squadron, including Sergeant Reeves, continued to operate out of Middle Wallop. The aim of the Coltishall flight was to counter the intrusions over the east coast, and on August 22nd, Squadron Leader Cunningham claimed their first kill, a He 111, and another on September 1st. The detached flight continued to operate from Coltishall until it returned to Middle Wallop on September 20th.

Sergeant Reeves continued to fly operationally, with his next encounter with the enemy coming on October 11th, where he picked up a target near Bath, and chased it at 3,000 feet, all the way to south London, before losing it. The following night, while operating from Colerne, he was aloft for a total of five hours and 30 minutes before coming back to base. He was also flying with the fit again Sergeant O'Leary. They would prove to be a formidable team, flying together until the end of November 1944.

Six days later, Sergeant Reeves was posted from 604, to a new squadron forming at Colerne - 89. A mixed bag of crews arrived from different squadrons, with the bulk coming in from 406 Squadron, and the task now in hand was to get all Beaufighters ready for the long flight overseas to North Africa. By October 25th, two flights were at Portreath ready for the move. Long range fuel tanks had been fitted, but the trip out was hampered by a spate of broken engine bearers, which in turn had to be investigated by Bristols.

1 Flight got away to Gibraltar on November 24th, 2 Flight followed on the 26th, and the 3 on the 30th. During the leg of Gibraltar to Malta, they lost one Beaufighter and crew - Pilot Officer Hodsmen and Sergeant Monger disappearing over the sea. 1 Flight had also been attacked by Cr 42s off Panatalleria, but all had evaded their assailants.

The Faithful Few

By January 1942, 89 were based at Abu Sueir, but began to send detached flights out to other locations, such as Idku. Sergeant Reeves was based there in February, along with Pilot Officers Nottage and Springin. Squadron Leader Pain and Flying Officer Fumerton claimed the squadron's first kills on March 3rd, when they destroyed a He 111 apiece. However, 'Moose' Fumerton was slightly injured by return fire, resulting in him having a short hospital stay. However, on his return to operations, he destroyed two He 111s of II/KG26 near Alexandria.

By the start of May, crews from 89 had claimed five more destroyed, two probables and two damaged. Pilot Officer Kinmonth and Sergeant Edgar destroyed the squadron's first Italian raider, an Sm 79, and damaged another on May 11th.

Still kill less, the recently commissioned Pilot Officer Reeves, was posted to Malta on June 22nd, with Flying Officers Fumerton and Mitchell, and Pilot Officers Shipard and Ross. This posting to Malta proved to be the turning point for him, enabling him to make his first kills of his service career.

First off the mark on July 1st were Flying Officer Fumerton and Sergeant Bing who destroyed a Ju 88 of III/KG77, while Pilot Officer Ross and Sergeant Thompson probably destroyed another. The following night, Reeves and O'Leary claimed a Ju 88 as well (which turned out to be an Italian Z1007), while Flying Officer Fumerton and Sergeant Bing brought down a Ju 88. Three days later, Pilot Officer Reeves destroyed a Ju 88 of 6/KG77, and then followed this up with yet another Ju 88 on July 17, this aircraft coming from KuFlGr606. This time he chased the aircraft back to Sicily, before shooting it down near Gela. Other crews had

Nevil Reeves at left with other aircrew of No 89 Sqn, Abu Suier; Ken Gray on Reeves's left.

success too, with Pilot Officer Shipard and Sergeant Oxby destroying three Ju 88s in three weeks. Reeves finished the month off with the destruction of a KGr 806 Ju 88 west of Gozo.

At 'Readiness': P/O Reeves in a Beaufighter cockpit.

Pilot Officer Reeves and Sergeant O'Leary claimed again in August, this time a Z1107 (actually an S84) on the night of the 14/15th, thus making him officially and 'ace'. The Malta detachment had indeed been a good move. Reeves also despatched a 7/KG54 Ju 88 on September 9th, but unlike the others, this was done in daylight, while acting as escort to an anti shipping strike. He had also been instrumental in the rescue of Moose Fumerton and his Radar Operator, after they had to bale out into the sea on August 10th after their Beaufighter suffered engine failure. After spotting them in the water and plotting their position, he called in a launch to pick them up.

However, September ended on a sad note, when Flight Lieutenant Waddingham DFC and Pilot Officer Cumbers in Beaufighter V8268 crashed after engine failure, with Flight Lieutenant Waddingham being fatally injured. The same fate befell Wing Commander Stainforth AFC and Pilot Officer Lawson in X7700 the following day, but in this case the crew bailed out too low. At 43 years old, Wing Commander George Hedley Stainforth AFC had an auspicious pre war flying career, and was a member of the Schneider Trophy teams of 1929 and 1930. In 1931, he set a new world airspeed record of 407.8 mph.

Squadron Leader Pain assumed command of the squadron, until he was lost during an intruder operation over Sicily on November 8th when his aircraft also suffered engine failure. Taken POW, he managed to escape and evade, making his way back to Allied lines. On November 24th, six aircraft and crews were despatched to Algiers, while 'B' Flight temporarily disbanded and the remainder was absorbed into 'A' Flight. The Algerian detachment saw success, and the Malta detachment continued to do so.

On January 8th, 1943, Pilot Officer Reeves destroyed a He 111 near Tripoli, resulting in him, and Warrant Officer O'Leary being awarded well earned DFC's. Eight days later, he was detached to Bersis, near Benghazi. While based at Castle Benito during February he made his last claims of the North African and Mediterranean campaign - A Ju 88 destroyed and one damaged during the night of 21/22nd, and a Ju 88 destroyed on the 26/27th. His combat report of

The Faithful Few

February 21st/22nd read: -

"Scrambled at 05.25 - told 320 degrees Angels 15,000 feet the 340 degrees on arriving at approximately 14,000 feet on this vector G.C.I took over and turned us to port on to 160 degrees - during the turn I saw two aircraft pass overhead going on this course - contact was held on two blips - one of which went off to one side at 7,000 feet - the other was held and jinking hard and a visual was obtained. We closed to 200 yards and fired a 5 second burst - many strikes were seen and pieces flew in all directions, one motor emitting clouds of white smoke and the E/A began to behave in a very drunken manner and the rear gunner ceased to fire. The 'innards' of my reflector sight fell into my lap - I replaced same and opened fire again at about 100 yards. Again burning pieces flew off and E/A went down glowing - we followed and the E/A was seen to crash onto the sea a few miles N.W of Tripoli and burned on the water for some minutes."

Nevil Reeves, F/O Doug Oxby and Merv Shipard with captured Kubelwagon. Oxby became the RAF's most successful radar operator, participating in 21 kills.

But the engagement was far from over as a second Ju 88 was encountered: -

"Shortly afterwards G.C.I again took us over, turning us from 360 degrees to 120 degrees - contact was held through extremely violent jinking - a visual was obtained and we closed to approximately 150-200 yards and fired a 5 second burst - the cannons only firing for a second or so when they failed - some H.E cannon strikes were seen on top of the fuselage and port wing between motor and fuselage and machine gun strikes seen on the wings. The rear gunner again soon ceased fire, but E/A turned very hard to port. I followed and was able to out turn E/A - I fired 3 or 4 more bursts allowing deflection and saw quite a lot of machine gun strikes - the cannons still not working - but the E/A dived away and was lost in the murky part of the sky."

The Faithful Few

His next victory came in the early hours of February 26th. Flying Beaufighter V8309 'W', he engaged another raiding Ju88, one from II/KG76: -

"Scrambled at 0400 hours on 320 degrees Angels 12. As we crossed the coast on this vector at approximately 4,500 feet the A.A started to come up. G.C.I took over and gave us 360 degrees 15,000 feet - they turned us shortly afterwards on to 160 degrees and a contact was obtained - we had only reached 11,000 feet by then. The E/A was then slightly above but climbing at a very slow speed and jinking hard - we followed climbing at between 100-110 mph and on arriving at the same height as the E/A, which was by then 16,000 feet a visual was obtained at 1,500 feet - E/A was still jinking violently. We closed to 100 yards and fired a 5-6 second burst - the port engine caught fire and other pieces flew off left and right - the E/A slowed right down and we passed by it doing only 120 mph. E/A was then seen banking vertically to port - two bomb flashes were seen underneath as E/A jettisoned, and the E/A dived away in a spiral turn towards the coast it seemed to flatten out still on fire and was seen to crash - owing to haze we could not tell if over land or sea - but anyway within a mile or so of the coast, 5-10 miles north of Tripoli. No return fire was experienced."

He became 'tour expired' in May 1943, and along with Warrant Officer O'Leary, was awarded a bar to their DFC's, before being posted back to the UK.

Ken Gray was a pilot with 89 Squadron in North Africa, and remembered him well: -

"Nevil bubbled over with joi de vivre and was affectionately known as 'Golden Bollocks' for his dashing good looks. He was a great favourite in the mess, and with the 'erks', for he seemed to get along with everyone. He was an exceptional pilot, who had an exceptional radar operator in Alexander O'Leary - now he was a real renegade but a delightful character. Quite a pair, Reeves and O'Leary."

Another member of 89 Squadron was Doug Oxby, who flew as radar operator to Flying Officer Merv Shipard. He recalled:

"I am happy to say I that I had the pleasure and privilege of knowing Nevil Reeves during his time with 89 Squadron. When I joined the squadron in February 1942 at Abu Suier, near Ismailia, in Egypt, Nevil had just been promoted from Sergeant to Pilot Officer. He and his Radar Operator, Sergeant Mike O'Leary were members of 'B' Flight while my pilot; Pilot Officer Mervyn

The Faithful Few

Shipard and I were in 'A' Flight. Since I lived in the Sergeants mess I had little contact with Nevil, either on or off duty at the time. It was not until June 1942 when he and Merv Shipard, Mike O'Leary and I, were members of a detachment sent to Malta that I came to know him well.

I recall that he was about 5ft 10 ins tall and was of a medium though muscular build. He had a mop of wavy, golden hair with fuzzy arms and legs which earned him the nickname 'Golden Balls'. He was extremely handsome without being the slightest bit vain. Operationally he quickly earned a reputation as a keen, courageous and competent night fighter pilot. He spoke with a somewhat clipped manner of speech and with a near Oxford accent. I enjoyed his friendly attitude to everyone and his quiet sense of humour. Although I never flew with him on operations, I did have the privilege of assisting him on several non operational sorties such as night flying tests and air firing exercises."

Doug Oxby finished the war with the rank of Wing Commander, and holds the DSO, DFC, and DFM. He also became the most successful Radar Operator in RAF history, having taken part in 21 victories.
John Ross was another 89 Squadron pilot: -

*F/Os Merv Shipard & Nevil Reeves in front of Beaufighter
'Slippery Ship II' whilst re-fuelling at Tobruk.*

"Nevil and Mike O'Leary made an exceptional crew, as shown from the results in Malta and North Africa. He as also an outstanding pilot as well as what we Aussies quote as a 'good bloke!' We both played cricket with the 89 Squadron team in the Middle East, which was incidentally, undefeated!"

It was a further nine months before Reeves returned to operational duties, again with Warrant Officer O'Leary in tow. 239 Squadron, based at West Raynham, were in the process of re equipping from Beaufighters to Mosquitos. The squadron were part of 100 Group, and were to provide night time bomber escort in an effort to counter the extremely effective German night fighters. These operations were coded 'Serrate'. However, with hardly any serviceable aircraft available, operations were few and far between in the early days of re equipping. They arrived at 239 on February 6th, 1944, and the squadron Operation Record Book recorded the following: -

"The Squadron has received a considerable amount of 'glamour' with the posting in of F/Lt N.E.Reeves DFC and Bar and W/O A A O'Leary DFC and Bar, DFM; both with 9 victories to their credit."

Nevil's Beaufighter at 'Readiness'.

Training commenced as of the 18 crews on the unit, only eight were deemed operational, and only six of those had done a full scale operation over enemy territory. The quality of the aircraft delivered from Fighter Command was somewhat suspect, and extra time was spent trying to get these into a suitable operational condition. Three sorties were flown on February 15th, but without result. On the 20th, things improved considerably, as numerous contacts were made, but no visual contact at all. The squadron diary concluded: -

"This is, no doubt, the result of lack of practice, a factor which will be eliminated gradually as weather (and the quality of the aircraft) improves."

Things did improve the following night, when Flying Officers 'Tex' Knight and 'Paddy' Doyle destroyed a Bf 110. Things were much different for Wing Commander Evans, who was chased by two enemy aircraft before getting away. By the end of the month, 239 had lost two crews: Flying Officers Knight and Doyle failed to return from a sortie on the 25th, and the last word from them was that they "were still being fired at." while Flying Officers Munroe and Hurley were returning to base, without radio, when they hit a tree, and crashed. The body of Flying Officer Knight was washed ashore at Ramsgate two days later.

Engine problems were becoming quite common, and a Mosquito was damaged due to an engine failure. The squadron diary noted: -

Nevil strikes a pose back at the family farm, 1944.

"This incident comes after a whole series of engine failures, and the aircrew have almost ceased to place any trust in the reliability of these old Merlin XXI engines. All the aircraft we received from Fighter Command were in a very bad condition and it has been a thankless task trying to keep them serviceable. The other two squadrons engaged on operation 'Serrate' have had exactly the same trouble, but we unfortunately have lost more crews than they have during the past two months. The aircrew, however, must be congratulated on refusing to be shaken by all these mishaps, and the news, two days ago, that all our operational aircraft are going to be re-engined with the new Merlin XXII's is a just reward for their continued fortitude and cheerfulness in the face of circumstances that would, undoubtedly, have shaken men with less moral fibre."

Flight Lieutenant Reeves had taken part in several bomber support missions, including sorties to Munchengladbach on March 11th, Frankfurt and the Ruhr on March 13th; and Nurnberg on March 31st. During the Munchengladbach sortie, he'd picked up several contacts and had a chase with a night fighter lasting some seven minutes, and over Nurnberg he had attacked an enemy aircraft only for it evade him.

By mid March, the squadron had a total of 22 crews on strength, but only 12 of those were fully operational. Sharing West Raynham were 141 Squadron, who certainly gave 239 an incentive to get the crews going, especially when two of their crews had returned with three kills each! This they duly did, when

The Faithful Few

Squadron Leader Kinchin and Flight Lieutenant Sellors destroyed a Bf 110 during the early hours of April 23rd.

Two more crews were lost in the next two days - Flight Lieutenant Butler and Flight Sergeant Robertson went missing on their first operation, while the popular crew of Flying Officers Armstrong and Mold failed to return. The squadron was issued a stand down order, but this was nothing to do with crew losses, but more to do with the inception of new policy. The squadron dairy recorded: -

"An operational squadron is a sensitive organism, and any reflection on its ability to 'take it' is quickly resented."

The Squadron were quickly back on operations, with seven aircraft and crews being available. Flight Sergeants Campbell and Phillips brought down a Ju 88 in the Ruhr area, but only after a protracted battle where the German night fighter was giving a good account of itself before it succumbed to the guns of the Mosquito. It inflicted heavy damage on the aircraft, and knocked out the starboard engine. Undaunted, they limped back to West Raynham. Flight Sergeant Campbell was recommended for the DFM for this feat of airmanship.

Despite his near misses to date, Flight Lieutenant Reeves opened his 239 account during a 'Serrate' operation north of Aachen. There they had picked up a contact, which in turn was identified as a Do 217. Closing to 150 yards, Reeves gave it a six second burst, which immediately sent it down in flames.

Two more sorties followed - the Swinemunde mission was cut short after their radar failed, and the Olligmes sortie near Paris was deemed as 'uneventful'. His next mission was a search for the acting squadron commander, Squadron Leader Kinchin and Flight Lieutenant Sellors, but nothing was found. With the death of Kinchin, who was also OC 'A' Flight, there arose a vacancy, to which Reeves was duly promoted. The squadron diary noted: -

"Nevil Reeves is a comparatively new member of the squadron, but he has already carved a niche for himself by his ability, by his early victory…and by his charm of manner."

He completed operations to Dusseldorf and Karlsruhe, and in both cases had numerous contacts, but on April 28th, he successfully engaged a Bf 110 near Moutzen, Aulnoye. Closing to 150 yards, he opened fire, hitting the starboard engine. Return fire was experienced, and Reeves gave it two more bursts, and sent it earthward. Flying Officers Depper and Follis downed a Bf 110 and a Ju 88 that night, thus making it 239's best night to date.

On May 1st, Reeves was promoted to the rank of acting Squadron Leader to cover his position as OC 'A' Flight and a commission was soon granted to O'Leary, who became a Pilot Officer.

Thanks to the much improved reliability of the Mosquitos, and the radar, more operations were flown and completed. More claims were made against the opposing night fighters - Flying Officer Bridges and Flight Sergeant Webb destroyed a Bf 110 on May 11th, with Flying Officers Breithaupt and Kennedy downing another Bf 110 on the 13th. The crew of Flying Officer Bridges and Flight Sergeant Webb scored their second kill the same night, this one being a Ju 88. Further claims followed on the May 25th sortie, with the crews of Flight Lieutenant Hughes and Flying Officer Perks, and Flight Lieutenant Raby and Flight Sergeant Flint both destroying Bf 110s. Flying Officers Breithaupt and Kennedy bagged a Ju 88 and damaged a Bf 109.

Towards the end of May, Squadron Leader Reeves flew three more operations - to the Friesans and Keil Bay on the 22nd, to Aachen on the 24th which resulted in him returning early with AI failure, and back to Aachen three days later. This second Aachen trip was to prove eventful, as the squadron diary noted: -

"S/L Reeves and P/O O'Leary in DD622 crossed into enemy coast at Egmond and was immediately engaged and held by 3 searchlights in turn tighter with a considerable amount of light flak and was only able to escape by taking the most violent evasive action. Shortly afterwards a weak Serrate contact was observed over Leeuwarden aerodrome. Target was either orbiting or patrolling the airfield. This contact was lost, but later an AI contact was picked up and during the ensuing chase the Serrate reappeared and married with AI and a second AI contact was observed. It was presumed that these tow contacts represented a pair of E/A doing a G.C.I. practice together. After a 12 minute chase a visual was obtained and easily recognised as a Me 110. Fire was opened at 120 yards range dead astern and after a 3 seconds burst E/A was seen to be on fire on both sides of the fuselage. The flames spread as the aircraft rolled over and over until it hit the ground and exploded."

The Bf 110 so expertly despatched by Squadron Leader Reeves, was one from 7/NJG1. The pilot, *Unteroffizier* Joachim Tank baled out, but the other two crewmen were killed. On the negative side, the squadron lost one of its original crews - Flying Officers Paddy Bailey and Chalkey White, and their loss was felt deeply. They had taken off at 23.45hrs in Mosquito HJ714, and nothing more was heard from them.

Two missions to Trappes were flown at the start of June; on the 1ˢᵗ two Bf 110s were claimed, and on the 2ⁿᵈ a Bf 110 was damaged. During the second Trappes sortie, Squadron Leader Reeves obtained a backward AI contact and turned to approach it head on. It was in fact a Ju 88 which was creeping up on them. As they closed head on, the Ju 88 opened fire. Reeves turned to give chase, but the enemy aircraft pulled off a vertical dive from 12,000 feet, and got away.

With the onset of D Day, the squadron flew missions over the beaches, with Flight Lieutenant Welfare and Flying Officer Bellis destroying a Bf 110 on D Day itself. No further claims were made over this period, with Squadron Leader Reeves flying four missions over the beaches and France. Flight Lieutenant Welfare and Flying Officer Bellis destroyed another Bf 110 on the 11ᵗʰ, in an eventful engagement: -

"Delivering the final burst from minimum range they flew right through the blazing plane as it lurched drunkenly before crashing in flames. The entire surface of the Mosquito was blistered and the fabric of the tail unit completely burnt away, but the crew brought the a/c some 300 miles safely back to base."

On June 19ᵗʰ, Squadron Leader Reeves and Pilot Officer O'Leary left for Buckingham Palace for the investiture of their DFC's, which had been awarded prior to them joining 239. After a very short spell of leave, they were back on the squadron, flying a sortie to Prouville on the 24ᵗʰ which was listed as 'uneventful'. Their Orleans sortie gave them their last kill with 239 when they destroyed yet another Bf 110. Attacking it from 200 yards, they set it ablaze, before it dived vertically into the ground. This was the squadron's 30ᵗʰ kill.

239 Had begun to have real success on operations. Between D Day, and the first week in July, they had accounted for four Bf110s, four Ju 88s, two Fw 190s, a Me 410, and a lone He 177 over the Ruhr. Squadron Leader Reeves finished July with missions to Wessling, Givors and Stuttgart.

Despite the inherent risks of combat operations, training was at times, almost as dangerous. During single engined flying practice near Peterborough on August 6ᵗʰ, Squadron Leader Reeves found that his starboard propeller refused to unfeather. Losing 1000 feet a minute, he managed to reach base and belly land in on the grass. He flew five more sorties to Northern France, Aire and the Forest de Lucheux, Givors and Brunswick, before he was taken off operations and posted to 100 Group on August 31ˢᵗ.

The Faithful Few

In October 1944, he was sent to the Bomber Support Development Unit at Foulsham, flying with them until mid December. This unit were continually testing forms of AI and warning systems, and the best way to do that was on operations. He flew 10 sorties with the BSDU, encompassing low level support flights, high level intruder flights, and freelance patrols. Awarded the DSO in October, he claimed his last kill (his 14th) while with the BSDU on December 10th when he destroyed a Bf 110 west of Giessen: -

"At 4 ° miles (our A.I set was stuck on 5 miles range - what a hardship!) the two contacts appeared on A.I, if anything slightly to starboard

F/L Nevil Reeves, a decorated 'ace' at home in 1944.

and still close together.. As the range closed the furthest contact turned starboard in a northerly direction and is thought to have gone down. The other contact was chased on a heading of approx 230° and was found to be well above, difficulty being experienced in closing range and gaining height as well. A visual was obtained on slightly green exhausts well above at 1, 200 ft. We were now between two layers of cloud and horizontal visibility was very bad, we closed in on exhausts and a blur or aircraft was seen 10° above at 200 ft. Mosquito started to go underneath to have a better look when at 50° below, still at about 200 ft range, aircraft started to turn gently to starboard two tails were clearly seen against the cloud above which together with the exhausts could make it none other than an Me 110.

Fire was opened from 10° behind to starboard allowing slight deflection. On exhausts, large flashes were seen around the starboard engine and due to intense darkness visual was lost. Visual was again picked up at about 500 yards by the glow from the starboard engine and range was closed and another burst fired - no exhaust was seen on the starboard side, again strikes were seen and a large white streak of flame shot back from the aircraft. About three more bursts were fired and many strikes seen before aircraft vanished into cloud at about 14,000 ft - combat starting at above 18,000 ft. About three minutes later a large explosion was seen just behind us beneath the clouds which glowed for several minutes. "

By now promoted to Wing Commander, he was posted to his first full command - 169 Squadron at Great Massingham. He arrived on January 17th 1945, and made his first operational flight with 169 on January 22nd, flying Mosquito

MM626 on a Serrate mission to Gelsenkirchen. One contact was made, but lost. His second flight was to Mannheim on February 1st, with no result.

By now, the dynamics of the war were changing. Whereas 169 had been performing Serrate duties as per 239, and other Special Duty Mosquito squadrons under Bomber Command, night time ranger patrols were also being flown. This entailed attacking any targets of opportunity - transport, factories, and airfields.

On February 25th, Wing Commander Reeves took off en route to Juivincourt, where they refuelled the aircraft, and proceeded over Germany on a Night Ranger sortie. Targets were plentiful, and Reeves destroyed three trucks near Salzburg, dropped two 500 lb bombs on a factory north east of Rurdorf, and damaged two trains before returning to base. Similar operations were flown between Hecht and Widder on the 28th.

During a Ranger to the Munich area on March 24th, Wing Commander Reeves had plenty to do. He attacked motor vehicles 10 miles north of Mergen airfield, dropped one bomb on a factory outside Erbring, attacked more vehicles at Altenthanket, hit a train at Bad Abling Station and more vehicles five miles east of Holzkirchen, shot up the railway south of Memmingen and more vehicles in the vicinity, before finishing off a train, and returning with the bomb doors jammed open.

Airfields were an important target, and the RAF began to use napalm as a suitable weapon. Along with 141 Squadron, 169 carried out such missions, with each Mosquito carrying two drop tanks each carrying 100 gallons of the mixture. The use of napalm was known as 'fire bashing', but it was not without its risks, as the drop tanks had a habit of failing to separate from the aircraft. This was due to the petroleum elements in the napalm affecting the release gear. Wing Commander Reeves flew his first 'fire bash' on April 19th when the squadron laid waste to Flushing airfield.

One of the pilots to have a near miss with a hung up napalm tank was Flying Officer Keith Miller. Upon return to base on May 2nd, the tank fell off on touchdown, but didn't ignite, with the same thing happening to Squadron Leader Wright upon his return. Of note is the fact that Keith Miller was the Australian international cricketer, who later became what is regarded as Australia's greatest all rounder. He represented Australia 55 times, scoring 2958 runs (including seven centuries), and took 170 test wickets.

Wing Commander Reeves led 12 Mosquitos on a low level attack on Jagel airfield on May 3rd, losing the crew of Flying Officer Catterall DFC and Flight Sergeant Beade. This mission turned out to be his last of the war. He continued to command 169 until it disbanded in August 1945, with most of the aircrew being posted to 627 Squadron ready for Pacific Operations, Posted to command 141 Squadron on August 24th, he stayed with them until they too were disbanded on September 7th.

Many years on, the surviving aircrew of 169 remembered Nevil Reeves fondly. John Beeching was a pilot on 169, and he recalled: -

"I was a pilot on 169 Squadron at Great Massingham for the entire time Nevil Reeves was the squadron commander there. As I never managed to climb above the rank of Warrant Officer, our social and professional activities generally moved in different orbits, with possible exceptions when we were invited to officers' mess parties and usually finished by chalking up a load of blacks, record of which is hardly the sort of chronicle you will be putting together!

My main recollection of Wing Commander Reeves was that he was a superb Mosquito pilot. He loaned us his aeroplane one, either NT228 or NT146 (I flew 57 different Mosquitos and can't remember all the fine details), to fly on a bomber affiliation exercise with a couple of Halifaxes which were at Fulsham. Before we took off, he pointed a finger and said 'Don't bend it..' We didn't, but we had to land at Fulsham to liaise with the Halifax crews. The aircraft carried Wing Commanders pennants painted on the nose, so when we drew up by the control tower, a couple of well disciplined erks came racing up with a ladder and stood expectantly by as the door opened. Two scruffy W/O's clambered out and ambled off, leaving the pair still waiting for the exalted being whose loge adorned the front of the plane, possible not knowing the complement making up a Mosquito's crew.

The other not very memorable occasion I had direct dealings with N R was when we were flying on a 'Haystack' exercise one night. Disastrously, from the time I turned on the aircraft's power (TA263, got that one right) the transmitter was broadcasting, unknown to us, our conversation to the world at large. After three hours of dragging ourselves through the valley of humiliation, including conjecture as to who had impregnated a WAAF control tower operator who happened to be on duty at that time, we arrived back on the circuit at Great Massingham. I was turning onto finals, with wheels down and most of the flaps when some rude person, flying a funny circuit, slid in from my right, and successfully precluded me from landing, a hazardous business at the best

P/O Brown (left) & F/O Keith Miller with their 169 Sqn Mosquito at Great Massingham. Miller is regarded by many as Australia's greatest all round cricketer, and was a close friend of Nevil's.

of times, so I had to g round again. Fred, my Nav/Rad, said, 'Who do you think that was?' and idiot replied, 'probably Reeves. He thinks he's Jesus Christ and can do what he likes.' We had barely regained the dispersal when the telephone rang and I answered it. A voice said, 'Jesus Christ would like to have a word with you first thing in the morning...' I don't recall I was severely chastised over the matter, but I do recall that most of the WAAFs crossed over to the other side of the road when they saw me approaching. I have a small notation written in my log book by Nevil Reeves regarding the matter generally. Like I said, I was good at chalking up blacks. And that, generally, was the sort of association I had with Nevil Reeves. Not the stuff to fill a book about heroes, but there we are.

Keith Miller knew Nevil very well indeed: -

"He was one of the finest men I met during the war, and one of the most handsome. He had film star looks, was easy to talk to and commanded respect. A true leader, he loved sport, cricket in particular, and since he lived near Worcester where Australian sides opened their tour we had much in common.

The Faithful Few

He even took me to Newmarket Races for the few times racing ran during the war. Racing was then on the July course where wartime derbies were run.

I also remember that we had a race up the long Newmarket straight in our Mossies, where I beat the Wingco by a nose! After the war he came to Australia lecturing to RAAF pilots on jet plane tactics. It was the last time I saw him."

After the cessation of hostilities, Wing Commander Reeves stayed in the RAF, serving overseas, later lecturing on jet fighter tactics. To ensure he was still able to continue flying, he dropped to the rank of Squadron Leader, but with the post war concerns over the Russian threat he was brought back from tactics lectures in Australia and New Zealand, and sent to the Air Fighting Development Unit at West Raynham. There, he took over at the Fighter Interception Development Squadron from Squadron Leader Lomas DFC in November 1948, and was under the command of Wing Commander Bob Braham DSO** DFC* AFC.

During a blind landing trial on January 27th 1949, using the now disused Great Massingham airfield, he crashed during an overshoot in very foggy weather, his Meteor IV, VW782 impacting one mile west of Massingham village, killing him instantly.

The FIDS Diary recorded his passing: -

"Squadron Leader Reeves had been with the unit only two months but during that time he was much respected by everyone, he was an efficient C/O, and his death is a sad loss to this unit."

But what happened on that fatal last sortie? Squadron Leader John (Andy) Anderson was on duty that day, and recalled the incident: -

"At the time of the extreme East/West tension (the Berlin Airlift Period) H.Q Fighter Command envisaged a situation whereby day fighter wings might have to be scrambled in marginal weather, with the consequent problem of getting them down safely at the end of the sortie. C.F.E. West Raynham was accordingly tasked with examining this aspect and devising a recovery system, hence the Rapid Landing Trials of 1949. The squadrons were currently equipped with Meteor IVs which had neither navigation nor approach instruments, so the automatic choice for the final approach element had to be Ground Control Approach (G.C.A.) which is where I became involved.

Nevil Reeves, in white slacks, with Mosquito TA263, crash-landed by Keith Miller near Great Massingham.
(Keith Miller)

G.C.As were then mobile self contained units and No.9 G.C.A was sent to C.F.E for the trials; the CO was S/Ldr Eddie Le Conte, also ex 604. G.C.A comprises two quite separate radar systems, one providing all round coverage for locating, identifying and marshalling aircraft to a position where the other, with precision equipment but coverage limited to the runway approach, can take it over for the final talkdown. The person doing the marshalling was termed the Director, and the one doing the talkdown, the Controller: for the trials F/Lt Jacks Spruce was the Controller and I was the Director.

For trial purposes the C.G.A operational element was positioned at Great Massingham, a disused wartime airfield some three miles west of Raynham, mainly to keep trials aircraft clear of the very busy Raynham circuit. Wing Commander Braham was in charge of the trials as O/C Night/All Weather Wing; other pilots regularly involved were Nevil Reeves, Cas Castagona, Red Armstrong, Duncan McIver and Jimmy Thomas - as distinguished and proficient bunch as anyone could have wished for. The aircraft used were again Meteor IV's which normally did touch and go landings at Massingham, and landed back at Raynham after each sortie.

The trial called for the landing rate of four aircraft a minute, which was wildly optimistic; one aircraft every four minutes was fairly normal for G.C.A. but obviously we would have to improve on that or most of a Wing of short endurance jets would end up flying gliders. Operating with the B29 (Superfortress Group) at Marham, we had achieved intervals of two minutes and I believe the Berlin Airlift got it down to this figure too, but this was only possible with crews arriving overhead beacons strictly to a pre arranged schedule. Controlling Meteors for the Rapid Landing Trial proved to be an altogether more exciting (stimulating?) experience!

When we though we had a viable system the Duxford or Horsham Wing would be 'borrowed' to try it out on that strange animal 'the average squadron pilot', after which it was usually 'back to the drawing board'. The best we achieved in the end was landing pairs of aircraft at around 1min 20 sec intervals, and that involved a much modified system and a lot of fast talking. By this time the N.A.W pilots and C.G.A. crews were working as a highly efficient team with complete confidence in each other; sadly events were to prove there was a degree of over confidence.

That then was the position one morning when Jack Spruce and I checked in at our Raynham admin office, with radiation fog limiting visibility to around 200 yards; a call to the Met office confirmed the obvious - no chance of improvement before early afternoon.

Definitely not flying weather, so we resigned ourselves to a morning in the rest caravan adjacent to the G.C.A. truck at Massingham, drinking tea, smoking and playing bridge; life could be pretty tough on G.C.A at times! First, however, a wander over to the N.A.W. crew room for a natter and a coffee, where Bob Braham's cheerful greeting 'What are you two buggers doing here? We're going flying!' got the answer it deserved. 'No, seriously though' said Bob, 'Nevil and I are going off shortly for a weather check followed by a Q.G.H to be overhead Raynham at 2,000 feet, 20 minutes after take off; you take over from there and talk us down to land at Massingham.' The realisation that he really meant it had a very sobering effect.

As the name implies C.G.A is only an approach as distinct from a landing system, normally terminating with 'half a mile to touchdown, look ahead and land,' the pilot having previously advised on overshoot procedure should the runway not be in sight at this point. Our protests that conditions were way below our minimum were smilingly brushed aside with 'stop worrying, you'll get us down alright; and make sure the kettle's boiling before we land'. Well, aircraft had been talked down in sub minimum conditions before - I'd been involved with some myself - but these had been emergencies which had to be got down somehow.

Deliberately taking off in short range jets in fog to land at a disused airfield with no approach lighting, and no possible diversion if things went wrong, was something else again, and I didn't like it one bit. However, to work and in spite of our misgivings everything went exactly as planned. Nevil landed first, Jack talking him down almost to touchdown and Bob followed again with no bother, calling, clear of the runway and shutting down. I was just beginning to relax and thinking how good that tea and cigarette would taste, when Nevil called me again to say he was taking off again on runway 10 (i.e. downwind) for another G.C.A. approach. The idea of taking off with at most 15 minutes fuel remaining really startled me. I hadn't been outside for some time, so perhaps conditions were better than I thought, and anyway, Nevil had just landed so knew exactly what conditions were like, so back to work.

Keeping the circuit as tight as possible I handed over to Jack for the talkdown and my part of the act was over, could lean over to watch proceedings. The approach was perfect, so no wind so no drift or turbulence to worry about, and reached the point 'On the centreline, on the glide path, approaching to touchdown, look ahead and land' when suddenly the aircraft response veered right and shot off the side of the radar display, followed by Nevil's call 'Overshooting'. We managed three more identical results - a perfect approach, the sudden turn to the right at the last moment and the overshoot. Obviously Nevil was seeing something he thought was the runway then realising his mistake. After the final call 'Overshooting' I went through the patter 'Roger, pull up, turn port to 120 and soon as possible level at 1,000 feet and call steady.' I never received the call.

The Meteor crashed near Massingham village and Nevil was killed instantly. I thought he must be out of fuel but the crash investigators said not, the engines were on full power when he went in. Presumably, he stalled in from a tight instrument turn at low level, trying to get another circuit before the fuel finally gave out.

The G.C.A. was completely exonerated at the subsequent enquiry, it had, after all, never been intended to cope with these conditions, but apart from the official verdict you always ask yourself if there was anything more that could have been done. In this case I could sadly and truthfully answer 'not a thing.'

On the demise of Nevil Reeves, Beaufighter and Mosquito 'ace', and the eighth top scoring RAF night fighter pilot, I leave it to Keith Miller to sum up: -

"In 1949 I was in the UK with Don Bradmans team, and I met Jim Wright, a S/ Ldr Flight Commander under Nevil. He knew NR very well and said Nevil was far too good a pilot to crash the way he did. I made an effort to visit his grave at Ripple. I adored this wonderful man. I looked up to him like God. I can still 'see' him. I'll never forget him. He was my idol. And I think on his grave it says he was 28 years old. What a tragedy!

The grave of S/L Nevil Reeves at Ripple Churchyard,
Upton-upon-Severn, Worcestershire.

Chapter Five

Edward Nigel Bunting was born in 1917, and lived in the St John's area of Worcester, where his father was a prominent local doctor. He was an active member of the Oxford University Air Squadron, and was called to full time service at the start of the war.

He joined 85 Squadron on April 2nd 1941, after completing his night fighter training with 54 Operational Training Unit. The squadron was based at Debden and had re equipped with Boston Havoc I's in February. Prior to that, they had been a Hurricane squadron, and had operated with distinction during the Battle of France and the Battle of Britain, with seven pilots being killed in the Battle of Britain alone. Now, they were re-deployed as a night fighter squadron, a much different role to the one some nine months before.

Without flying operationally, Pilot Officer Bunting was sent on a Blind Flying approach course at Watchfield, returning to the squadron in early May. He joined 'B' Flight, under experienced pilots such as Pilot Officer Geoffrey Howitt, Pilot Officer Geoffrey Goodman, Flying Officer James Marshall DFC, Flying Officer James Bailey, and Flying Officer Vivian Snell. All these pilots had amassed many day combat sorties to their credit, mainly during the Battle of Britain. By then the squadron had moved to Hunsdon, where they would stay until May 1943.

Pilot Officer Bunting's first listed flight was in Havoc I, coded VY-Y, on May 4th with Flying Officer Cordingly, undertaking an operational dawn patrol between 04.35 and 05.20 hours. He flew his second four days later, in VY-T, but with Sergeant Propert as his Radar Operator (R/O). Early May, was eventful, with the squadron claiming 11 aircraft destroyed or damaged, the first being when Flying Officer Hemingway damaged a He 111 on the 7th. Six days later, Flying Officer Hemingway had to bale out of his Havoc after it suffered complete instrument failure during a patrol. Bunting flew six more night/dawn patrols up to the end of May, in Havocs T, X, V, Y, Q, and P.

June started with Sergeants Grey and Franklin in VY-P attacking a Ju 88 and a Do17 on the 4th, however they submitted no claim. Pilot Officer Bunting and Sergeant Propert flew again on June 11th, but with no success. Flight Lieutenant Raphael and Aircraftsman First Class Addison (strangely, there were several AC1s flying as R/Os at this time, but without rank, or flying brevet. Addison

Boston Havoc night-fighter of 85 Sqn.

had flown operationally with 23 Squadron between August and early 1941 when he was posted to 85 Squadron) destroyed a He 111 over the Isle of Grain on June 13th. The machine, from 3/KG28 exploded in mid air killing the entire crew. They attacked a second He 111, and claimed it as probable. On a sad note, Sergeants Berkley and Carr failed to return. They had been engaged in two combats over the Thames Estuary, and it was thought they had been shot down, their Havoc 'K' crashing into Barrow Deep at 01.21 hours.

Pilot Officer Howitt damaged a Ju 88 the following night, and nine days later, Bunting had his first contact with the enemy near Bury St Edmunds: -

"Took off at 00.55 hours. Saw several blips and saw exhausts of an aircraft identified as a He 111. I gave a 5 second burst from dead behind and saw strikes on the port side of the fuselage , the port wing and port engine. Return fire was experienced from the top rear position with apparently two guns. E/A dived deeply with smoke, glycol fumes and sparks coming from the port engine, then pulled out of the dive and began flying in circles losing height slowly on one engine - no exhaust flame being seen from the port engine. The Heinkel was followed and closed, but twice overshot and the E/A was lost at about 7,000 feet when it was still diving."

July proved quiet - Flying Officer Arbon attacked a He 111 some 15 miles south of Clacton during the early hours of the 3rd, and Pilot Officer Howitt with Sergeant Reed as R/O claimed a He 111 destroyed 15 miles east of Clacton on the 14th. They hit it in the starboard engine and fuselage and it rolled over to port and fell away. Flight Lieutenant Raphael and Aircraftsman Addison attacked another He 111, despite experiencing return fire, they set it alight, and watched it crash into the sea.

During a patrol on July 24th, Pilot Officer Bunting's Havoc suffered technical problems, making him pull off a forced landing at Martlesham Heath. New models of the Havoc were delivered at the end of July, and start of August, with the Mark II coming onto front line service. They offered more hitting power for they were armed with 12 guns, but thanks to the increased armament, the operational endurance had decreased.

Despite increased patrols, it was mid August before any further action, for on the 17th Sergeant Grey damaged a Ju 88 , leaving it with a smoking engine. Three days later, one of the more experienced aircrew left - Pilot Officer Howitt was posted to instruct at 51 Operational Training Unit, Cranfield. More patrols followed, but still no success, however Pilot Officer Bunting, and the squadron CO, Wing Commander Sanders DFC undertook an air sea rescue sortie for a ditched bomber crew. They sighted them in their dinghy, and circled overhead, protecting them until a launch picked them up.

Havoc VY-Q. Note the 85 Sqn octagon insignia and the nose-mounted AI radar.

Pilot Officer Bunting only managed one more enemy contact during September, when during the night of the 16th, he responded to two radar contacts, and despite getting within visual range at one stage, he lost his intended target. The same night. Flight Lieutenant Raphael didn't let his target escape. He caught a Ju 88C-4 intruder from 1/NJG2 making its way up the edge of the Thames Estuary, and shot it down off Clacton. All the crew were taken POW.

During that September, the squadron recorded 53 attempted interceptions from 21 radar contacts. Only five raiders were visually spotted, and the only success was Flight Lieutenant Raphael's Ju 88.

October carried on with few actual engagements, however an incident arose on the 27th which would, indirectly, have a massive impact on Pilot Officer Bunting's combat career. Pilot Officer Phil Reed, who used to be Pilot Officer Howitt's R/O, fell off the back of a lorry on the airfield perimeter track, suffering a heavy concussion, thus making him temporarily unfit for flying.

The month closed with the loss of the squadron CO. During a night patrol, Wing Commander Sanders DFC, with Pilot Officer Austin DFM as R/O were engaged in combat some 20 miles north east of Deal. While tackling a raider who had apparently bombed some ships in the Channel, he was either hit by defensive fire from the German aircraft, or from AA sent up from the ships. Chillingly, the squadron diary records his last radio messages: -

"Put me over land, I will have to bale out. Have been rather badly hit."

"I'm going over. I can't make it - I can't make land."

Nothing more was heard, and despite the squadron, along with Hurricanes of No 3 squadron taking part in a search in the morning they were never seen again. Both crew are remembered on the Runnymede Memorial.

December saw the fit again Pilot Officer Reed return to operations, this time as R/O to Bunting. Their first sortie together was on December 17th, and they remained as a crew up until July 1944. In January 1942, both were promoted to Flying Officer. Engagements were proving unfruitful, and despite sorties where they managed radar contacts, they were unable to get results. At the end of April, they were posted to Central Flying School, Upavon on a four week course, returning in time on May 22nd to represent the squadron at the funeral of Flying Officer Henry Babington, ex 85 Squadron, who had been killed in a flying accident while serving with 157 Squadron.

At the start of June, they lost another aircraft, and one crewman, when on the 2nd, Flight Sergeant Gibbs and Sergeant Waller were shot down near Foulness point. Flight sergeant Gibbs was spotted in the water by Flight Lieutenant Tappin of No 3 Squadron during the subsequent search, and was picked by a rescue launch. Sadly, the body of Sergeant Maurice Waller was recovered from the mouth of the River Crouch.

On July 2nd, Flying Officer Bunting was promoted to deputy flight commander, and given the rank of acting Flight Lieutenant, backdated to week ending June 19th. On July 30th, they spotted a Ju 88 which in turn spotted them and got away - the Havocs were slow, and at a slight disadvantage when it came to chasing German raiders. The squadron only had one confirmed success in August, when Sergeants Sullivan and Skeel attacked a Ju 88, which then crashed trying to evade them. It came down at Burnham-on-Crouch, killing the crew of four.

Then, to much relief, the squadron replaced their Havocs with Mosquito II's in September, and now with a much better aircraft, maybe they would have more success. Bunting flew his first Mosquito sortie in VY-S on September 7th, taking off at 22.10 hours and coming back at 00.30 hours. The following month he damaged a Ju 88, hitting its port wing and engine, but it managed to get into cloud cover and get away. The next one wouldn't be so lucky.

No 85 Sqn, Hunsdon, 1942. Rear row, L-R: F/Os Townsin & House, F/L Snell, F/O Bunting, S/L Raphael, Sgt Mold, u/k, F/O Hall, F/O Reed, u/k, F/O Skelton. Front: Sgt Bray, F/O King, others u/k.

In January 1943, Wing Commander John Cunningham DSO* DFC* took command of the squadron. A highly successful night fighter pilot, he had 16 kills to his credit, and he set about leading from the front.

Inspired by their new CO, the pilots began to make kills in the new Mosquitos - Squadron Leader Green and Sergeant Grimstone destroyed a 4/KG40 Do 217 over the Thames Estuary on April 15th, while Flight Lieutenant Howitt DFC (who had rejoined the squadron from Cranfield that month) shot one down at Bockings Elm, Clacton-on-Sea, this machine coming from 5/KG40. One crewman was killed, and three taken POW. Five nights later Flying Officer Lintott and Sergeant Gilling-Lax shot down a Ju 88 from 8/KG6 over Bromley. It broke up in mid air, scattering itself over Homefield and Widmore Roads. One crewman baled out safely, with the remaining three being killed.

The same crew destroyed a FW 190 of 2/SKG10 the following month over the Thames Estuary. This German unit carried out day and time bombing raids, carrying one bomb on a central belly mounted hard point, operating in a not

The Faithful Few

dissimilar way to the bomb carrying '*Jabo*' Bf 109s at the tail end of the Battle of Britain. They were, however more active on daylight targets on the south and east coasts, and suffered a high loss rate.

They finished May with another victory, this time over a Ju 88S-1 from I/KG66. It broke up in the air and crashed at Isfield, Sussex, during the early hours of May 30th. All three crew managed to bale out successfully. Wing Commander Cunningham DSO* DFC* made his first kill with the squadron - a 3/SKG10 FW 190A-5 on June 14th, shooting it down at Borough Green, Kent. The pilot, *Leutnant* Ullrich baled out, and was taken prisoner with serious injuries. A second FW 190 fell to the guns of an 85 Squadron crew on June 22nd, when Flight Lieutenant Maguire and Flying Officer Jones shot down a 2/SKG10 machine into the River Medway, taking its pilot, *Leutnant* Klauer with it.

Despite the numerous night time engagements, 85 Squadron were also experimenting with high level interceptions. Flight Lieutenant Reg Bray was one aircrew member involved in such flights, and recalled: -

"I served with 85 Squadron as a night fighter radio observer/navigator from December 1941 to December 1943, followed by a period with T.R E. Malvern on research flying.

Nigel Bunting and his navigator joined 85 Squadron (he was a Pilot Officer) as their first fully trained night fighter crew when the squadron was re-equipped with the Douglas DB-7 Havoc II. I Occasionally flew with Nigel as his navigator in the absence of his regular partner, Phil Reed, but worked more closely with him when a small three crew unit was formed in May 1943 equipped withspecially built high altitude Mosquito XV's, to combat the Junkers 86 which was becoming a nuisance at the time.

It was in the prototype MF Mark XV, MP469, that Nigel Bunting attained a height of 44, 600 feet; the highest altitude ever flown in a Mosquito. Our Normal working height was 40, 000 feet so there was little room for manoeuvres!"

During the early hours of July 9th, the squadron lost a crew. The pairing of Flight Lieutenant Lintott and Sergeant Gilling-Lax had been successful, but while engaging a Do 217 from 6/KG2, they were either hit by return fire or collided with their intended victim. The crew of the Do 217 all died when their aircraft crashed at Detling, while Mosquito HK172 crashed not far away, killing

The Faithful Few

both airmen. Both were awarded DFCs after their deaths.

Then, during a patrol during July 13th/14th, Pilot Officer Bunting encountered an Me 410 off Felixstowe, and engaged it. The report submitted by Pilot Officer Robinson, the Intelligence Officer of 85 Squadron reads: -

"Contact was obtained to starboard and well below at three miles range. Pilot then saw a red airborne light below and to starboard crossing immediately below the Mosquito and slightly behind. He started to turn to port to regain contact or visual but Operator reported another contact at three miles range 25 degrees out at 2 o'clock. But suspecting that the lower lighted aircraft might be a decoy, Pilot chose to follow the contact down. It was crossing starboard to port and Operator brought Pilot in behind at about 10, 000 feet range. When the range was closed to 7, 000 feet a visual was obtained on the exhausts, but the e/a appeared to have gained height. Climbing at full boost and revs Pilot very gradually gained very slightly. When radiator flaps were opened on account of over heating, the e/a gained very slightly. When radiator flaps were closed however, the Mosquito decreased range. Tha cashe was continued in this manner for about 15 minutes at 220 mph IAS during which the e/a took no evasive action. Eventually a visual was obtained against the light northern sky at a range of 1,800 feet, the height being 25, 000 feet. The type was definitely no British and Pilot believed it to be an Me 410. He closed to 200 yards at attack but his aim was spoiled by getting into the slipstream of the e/a. He dived below and closed in again firing two short busts of 1 ° and 1 seconds at the fuselage which burst into flames immediately. The e/a seemed to go out of control and went down upon its back with the fuselage burning furiously, its dive becoming vertical. Pilot watched it until it nearly hit the sea and just after he lost his visual there was a very bright red flash. The burning aircraft and the explosion were seen by other members of the squadron and were also reported by the Royal Observer Corps at Felixstowe.

The e/a was recognised from stern as an Me 210 or Me 410, by the low wing position, the high fin, and distinctive position of the tail plane in relation to the wing. The four exhausts were bright blue and easily distinguishable from those of a Mosquito. When it was on fire the shape of the fin was clearly seen also the shape of the cockpit, both conforming to those of a Me 210. The wings, on which black crosses were visible, also seemed to be those of an Me 210. As the Me 410 is known to be on the western front now, pilot claims an Me 410 destroyed."

It had indeed, been an Me 410 from 16/KG2, and was the first of its type to be shot down over Britain. The crew were *Feldwebel* Franz Zwissler and *Oberfeldwebel* Leo Raida, and were both killed when the aircraft hit the sea. Bunting continued his success, damaging a FW 190 off Eastbourne on August 18th : -

"One Mosquito XII, A.I Mark VIII, 85 Squadron, F/L E.N Bunting (PILOT) with F/O C.P Reed DFC (OPERATOR), took off from West Malling 23.05 hours 17th August 1943 and landed there 02.00 hours 18th August 1943. Controlled by G.C.I. Wartling, Controller P/O Goodhill, Pilot was on patrol over the Channel at 20,000 feet when he was informed of a customer 23 miles away flying west. Pilot opened up, and after three to four vectors obtained contact on an aircraft crossing and slightly below. Using full revs and boost, pilot closed and obtained a visual on a Fw 190 at 250 yards range, height 17,500 feet. E/A, which was carrying a bomb and long range fuel tanks, was weaving and climbing and diving. Pilot fired a short burst from 150 yards, and saw a bright flash on the starboard side of the E/A, which jettisoned its bomb and tanks. At this moment the pilot was distracted by the glare of a searchlight. When next seen E/A was turning starboard. For the next few minutes E/A attempted to evade our A/C by tight turns and shallow diving turns and climbing. Our A/C, however, maintained contact, and frequent visuals. Pilot fired two bursts with deflection, without observing any result. Finally E/

A was followed down in a very steep dive to 3,000 feet and contact maintained in the pull out, but lost to port soon after."

Obfdwbl *Leo Raida, Bordfunker of Me 410 U5+KG of 16/KG 2, the first to be shot down over the UK.* (Brian Sadler).

The squadron destroyed a second Me 410 on August 23rd, when Squadron Leader Howitt DFC and Pilot Officer Medworth shot one down from 15/KG2 at Chelmondiston, Suffolk, killing one of the crew.

A double success followed on September 6th when a pair of I/SKG10 FW 190s were shot down. The first, approached by Flight Lieutenant Houghton and Flying Officer Patston dived away and crashed near Bury St Edmunds, killing *Hauptmann* Geisler, the *Gruppenkommandeur*; while Squadron Leader Howitt DFC and Flying Officer Irving DFC sent the other into the sea off Clacton.

Flight Lieutenant Bunting made his second

confirmed kill on September 16th. Flying Mosquito YV-T, he caught and destroyed a Ju 88A-14 of II/KG6 off Boulogne. Flying Officer Hedgecoe and Pilot Officer Witham engaged a Ju 88 near Dungeness, shooting it down into the sea as well. However, accurate return fire had severely damaged their Mosquito, and they had to bale out near Tenterden.

Compared to the comparitively lean days of 1941 and 1942, the Squadron were having great success - another Me 410 fell to the guns of Lieutenant Weisteen and Flying Officer French on October 7th, it being sent flaming into the sea killing both crew. There then followed a period between October 8th and 30th when 85 Squadron shot down no less than seven enemy aircraft - three Ju 88S-1's, three Ju 188E-1's, and an Me 410. Two of those were brought down by Flight Lieutenant Bunting and Flying Officer Reed - a Ju 88S-1 from 7/KG6 10 miles south of Dover on October 9th and on October 17th an Me 410 from 15/KG2 at West Horndon, Brentwood. His combat report states: -

"He was vectored out over the sea off Manston and put three miles behind a bandit reported at 17, 000 feet. Pilot used his excess height to gain speed, and at 18, 000 feet contact was obtained below and slightly starboard , range two miles. The range was reduced fairly rapidly to one mile, but by then all excess height had been used, and the Mosquito, full out, closed very slowly on the e/ a which was climbing gradually and weaving a little. The e/a turned west and Pilot obtained a visual at 2, 000 feet range, recognising the e/a as an Me 410. The S/L's several times illuminated the fighter, which closed to 150 yards to attack. When, at 21, 000 feet, pilot came up to the level of the e/a at attack, the latter dived sharply, but Pilot got in a short burst observing strikes on the starboard wing. E/a took violent evasive action and drew away to 6, 000 feet but continued westwards, Pilot following visually and by AI. By cutting the corners, the Mosquito closed in gradually to a position 100 yards astern 10 degrees below when e/a began a dive. Pilot allowed him to dive into his sights and held him there for about two seconds while he fired. Strikes were observed all along the fuselage of the e/a which went over on its back and fell away with the fuselage ablaze, and exploded on hitting the ground near Hornchurch 0225 hours approx."

The Me 410 exploded with such ferocity that it scattered itself over a wide area, with only small traces of both crew being found. In fact, *Oberfeldwebel* Bleich and *Unteroffizier* Greinecker are still listed as missing.

Squadron Leader Maguire and Flying Officer Jones also destroyed two of the seven, bringing both down on October 15th. One, a Ju 188 from 1/KG6, was shot down into the sea, and the second, from 3/KG6 (the first Ju 188 brought down in England) crashed at Hemley, near Ipswich, killing two of the crew. *Hauptmann* Waldecker, the *Staffelkapitain*, was taken POW along with *Obergefreiter* Haupt. It had been the squadrons most productive time since the heady days of the Battle of Britain.

The Me 410 destroyed by Flight Lieutenant Bunting was his fourth 'kill' and his last with 85 Squadron, for in November, he was awarded a DFC, along with Flying Officer Reed, and posted out to 488 Squadron at Bradwell Bay, joining them on November 27th, and making his first flight in Mosquito HK380. He took command of 'B' Flight, while Flight Lieutenant Watts DFC took command of 'A' Flight. Gordon King remembered Nigel Bunting : -

"He was an extremely popular member of the squadron, and used to cart us about in his MG as he was one of the few officers who had a car at that time! You might be interested to know I called my son Nigel after him."

Last kill of the year for 488 fell to Flying Officers Robinson and Clarke, when they shot down an Me 410 from 14/KG2 at Iden in Sussex. The pilot was killed in an attempt to crash land the stricken aircraft.

The year ended on a mixed note - the New Zealander crew of Flight Sergeants Ernest Behrent and Noel Breward were killed when their Mosquito crashed into the sea just 10 minutes after taking off for a night patrol on December 30th. Both still remain missing. The next day, the Squadron CO, Wing Commander Hamley DFC, was promoted to Group Captain, and deemed tour expired, and posted to 62 Operational Training Unit. Wing Commander Richard Haine took command of 488 on January 2nd 1944, and Flying Officer Bergmann gave him a 'welcoming present' by intercepting an Me 410 from 16/KG2, and sending it down into the straits of Dover. Flying Officer Bergmann's Mosquito was damaged by debris from the stricken Me 410, and had to land at Manston on one engine. The squadron diary said: -

"A good effort by a keen crew."

On January 21st, the Germans launched 'Operation Steinbock' sometimes referred to as the 'little blitz', and was the largest air attack on England since Birmingham was attacked in June 1942. During the first phase, the crew of Flight Lieutenant Hall and Flying Officer Cairns had some luck engaging the bombers. The 488 Squadron dairy recorded the sortie: -

"While on freelance patrol intercepted and destroyed a Do 217 which they shot down into the Channel south of Dungeness with just one burst. Returning to base they saw an aircraft illuminated by searchlights 4 miles ahead, followed and shot down a Ju 88 which crashed near Lympne. 1ˢᵗ 'Double'. The Sunday papers took photos, calling them the 'Flying Tigers' to much embarrassment!."

The double consisted of a Do 217 of 1/KG2, with two crew baling out into captivity, and the Ju 88 was from 6/KG54, crashing at Sellindge, Kent with one fatality.

No 488 Sqn, early 1944. F/L Bunting seated front row, sixth right. W/C Richard Haine to his immediate right.

Despite an increase in sorties and engagements, there was nothing as a routine patrol. Even training was fraught with danger. The squadron lost Flight Sergeants Keith Watson and Ernest Edwards from 'B' Flight on February 3ʳᵈ, when their Mosquito crashed near Bradwell Bay during an exercise with searchlights. It was though that it was due to momentary loss of control after they had been dazzled by the lights.

The next night, Flight Sergeant Vlotman and Sergeant Wood intercepted a Do 217, and after a long chase it was shot down into the sea off Foreness. This would be the first kill for the Dutch pilot during his stay with 488.

A second crew was lost on February 21ˢᵗ, and like Flight Sergeants Watson and Edwards, this one wasn't to enemy action either. Flying Officer Tohunga Riwai (a Maori New Zealander) and Flight Sergeant Ian Clark were killed instantly when their Mosquito ploughed into the invasion 'steelworks' (metal obstacles placed to prevent an invading force getting ashore) just after take off.

One more kill fell to a 488 Squadron crew before the month was over - with Flight Lieutenant Hall and Flying Officer Marriott shooting down an He 177 from 2/KG100 at Lamberhurst, in Kent. Two of the crew were killed, three were taken POW, while the sixth, *Feldwebel* Graf remains missing. Prior to the engagement with the He 177, they had attacked a Do 217 east of Brighton, and claimed it as probably destroyed.

Following the loss of two crews, replacement aircrew joined the squadron, including Flying Officer Jeffs in from 51 Operational Training Unit, and Pilot Officer Spedding in from 62 Operational Training Unit. Upon arriving they paired up to make a crew, and were soon to see action.

Squadron Leader Buntings next successful combat occurred during the evening of March 14th, when he engaged and destroyed a Ju 188 of 4/KG2. After being hit, it began to break up, with the main wreckage falling at Great Leighs, near Chelmsford, killing five of the crew. One baled out, landing near Bradwell Bay and was taken to the station sick quarters. The next day, the wreckage of the Ju 188 was inspected by an examiner from the Air Ministry who claimed that it was the best shooting he'd seen in his life! This was the fifth kill that made Bunting an 'ace'. His combat report detailed the engagement: -

"I climbed from 16,000 to 20/21,000 on making contact which was at 3 miles range, 25° above, 20° off and estimated the enemy aircraft to be travelling at 160/170 mph. During the chase I was lit by searchlights many times, but closed in and obtained a visual at 300 yards of a Ju 188 doing mild evasive. I opened fire from 120 yards, dead astern with a 2 ° second burst observing strikes on the starboard engine and a big fire started on the wing outboard of the starboard engine. The starboard engine began to burn, and the E/A went down vertically to starboard. The fire went out temporarily but shortly afterwards there was a large flash on the ground. I orbited and gave fix which Control confirm as M.1735 and this is now known to be the position at which a Ju 188 has been found near Great Leigh."

A week later, the squadron had the best, and most successful night in their history, when they destroyed no less that five enemy aircraft. A raid of 144 aircraft had been plotted coming in from the Dutch Islands, and the RAF had countered it. Flight Sergeant Vlotman claimed two Ju 88s, with the second being sent into the sea near Herne Bay. Wreckage flew off the target and hit

The Faithful Few

Vlotman's Mosquito, damaging the starboard engine, and forcing him back to base. II/KG54 lost two Ju 88s so these could well be the Vlotman's kills.

Flight Lieutenant Hall and Flying Officer Cairns surprised a Ju 88 of 8/KG6, and shot it down onto the airfield at Earls Colne, where it crashing into three Marauders operated by the American 9th Air Force. Three crew were killed, one baled out safely and was taken POW.

The final two kills fell to Squadron Leader Bunting - the first coming down at 12.45 am at Cavendish in Suffolk. This was one from 9/KG30, with three of the crew being killed. The second victory was a 2/KG6 Ju 188 which crashed at Shopland, Essex at 1.10am, with only one crewman baling out: -

"I was scrambled from Bradwell Bay at 2335 under North Weald Control for searchlight interception (Controller F/Lt Day). We went on to orbit 'D' at 18,000 ft, and after one unsuccessful gauntlet we investigated one to the east and obtained a contact at 1 ∫ miles, slightly above, which immediately went below. We throttled right back and closed rapidly to 2,000 ft with E/A 45° below. I lost height at 170 IAS and saw a searchlight flick over E/A which was 3000 ft ahead at the same level. We were then coned by S/Ls and E/A made a diving turn to starboard…visual maintained at 350 yards and 10° above and E/A steadied into mild weaving. Throughout the interception he had been dropping

Ju 88 4D+AT of 9/KG 30, shot down by Nigel Bunting on March 22nd, 1943, at Cavendish, Suffolk. L-R: Feldwebel Elmhorst (gunner), Oberfeldwebels Mayer (pilot) & Szyska (W/Op), Felwebel Maser (obs). Elmhorst & Maser baled out safely but Szyska's 'chute didn't open.
(Brian Sadler)

The Ju 88's crash site at Cavendish, L-R: F/L Reed DFC, S/L Nigel Bunting DFC (pointing), S/L Watts, AOC Sir Roderick Hill, W/C Richard Haine DFC, Sgt J Wood.
(G/C RC Haine)

Window. The E/A was identified as a Ju 88 or 188 and I opened fire from dead astern 200 yards range. Strikes seen on port engine and wing root, resulting in fire. I gave him another short burst from 300 yards 10° deflection, hitting the fuselage and starboard engine and increasing the fire. E/A fell over to port and I took a camera shot of him going down. He turned over on his back and went down blazing. Shortly afterwards we saw the reflection of the explosion on the ground where we saw the wreck burning."

The second engagement proved to be a harder affair: -

We returned to orbit and shortly afterwards we went south east. F/Lt Reed reported Window and eventually obtained contact on an aircraft dropping Window at 3 ° miles range . We closed fairly fast at 4000 feet range when we were illuminated by S/Ls. We obtained douse (searchlights off - author) but E/

A began very violent evasive action. We nearly overshot beneath him and saw his exhausts 80° above, our speed was then 130IAS. I saw him begin to peel off to port so turned hard port and regained contact at about 4000 feet, and followed him partly visually and partly on AI through a hard climbing turn to starboard. He steadied for a moment, then dived very steeply to port. I took a quick shot but could not get on enough deflection, 300 yards range; we followed him down and through another starboard turn and steep climb getting into position 250 yards astern. He began a turn to port and I opened fire 1 ° rings deflection 250 yards, observing no strikes. I therefore decreased deflection to one ring and saw many strikes on the port wing and cockpit. E/A, which was recognised from its pointed wings as a Ju 188 , immediately burst into flames and went down steeply to port burning very fiercely. An explosion was observed on the ground, and we saw a burning wreck."

Two crews claimed a Ju 88 apiece during operations on April 18th, but this was nothing compared to the excitement caused by a visiting Ju 88 from 3/KG54. Damaged by AA fire over London, with no compass and an engine out, the crew had mistakenly thought they were over Holland, only to find that they had in fact landed at Bradwell Bay!

No training was complete without dinghy drill, and bearing in mind that 488 operated so near to the coast, it was certainly worth doing. Squadron Leader Bunting DFC organised such a exercise on April 21st , and as the squadron diary put it: -

" 'B' Flight dinghy drill at Westcliffe Baths and a good time was had by all!"

The squadron moved to Colerne on May 3rd, and then to Zeals on May 12th. They operated from there, until their return to Colerne on July 29th.

On May 15th, the crew of Flying Officer Jeffs and Pilot Officer Spedding shot down a Do 217 from 7/KG2 near Yeovilton, and later a Ju 188 of 2/KG6 at Henstridge. Four of the Dornier's crew were killed, while two were lost from the Ju 188. It is likely that the Ju 188 was also attacked at one stage by Flight Lieutenant Hall and Flying Officer Cairns. The Do 217 was credited to Jeffs and Spedding, but the Ju 188 was given to Hall and Cairns.

Throughout this period, Squadron Leader Bunting DFC led 'B' Flight, and took part in many night patrols. His efforts were duly recognised, by the award of the bar to his DFC on May 21st, with Flight Lieutenant Reed DFC also receiving a bar to his. At the end of the month, Bunting had to attend a Court of

Enquiry at RAF Ossington where he had to hold a 'watching brief' in the case of the shooting down of two Wellingtons by one of the 488 Squadron crews.

He returned on June 3rd, and went on seven days leave, and missed out on the early D Day operations. However, three days after his return, he was in action over the beach heads, and made 488's first post D Day kill by destroying a Ju 88. His combat report read: -

"I took off from RAF Station Zeals at 00.25 hrs and reported to Pool 2 who handed me over to G.C.I 82 control, who during the patrol, put me onto two bogies which were recognised as friendly. The first, a Mosquito, the second, a Mitchell. Another contact was obtained but showed a friendly response. The above took place over an area between Caen and St. Lo.

At approximately 04.10 hrs control began an interception on a Bogey coming east, and after several changes of vector, whilst at 8,000 ft we obtained contact 3 miles range at 4 o'clock 45 degs. Target was jinking violently, and dropping window, while flying in an easterly direction. We throttled right back, but overshot. We weaved to starboard losing height, and while turning back asked for further information. We were given vector of 350 degs and regained contact 2 ° miles range, 8 o'clock. Target turned east again and losing height we closed rapidly in the turn and obtained visual at 350 yds as we got below target at 4,500 ft. Target, which was silhouetted against the dawn, was flying straight, but changing height and using the little cloud cover available. Using night glasses, we identified it as a Ju 88, with external bombs on. At 150 yds range, I pulled up dead astern and fired three short bursts, closing to 100 yds. The first set his port engine on fire, the second blew up his starboard engine, and the third went into the fuselage. Pieces flew off, one piece seemed to be part of the Perspex cockpit cover. As I broke to starboard, we could see the E/ A had normal mottled camouflage and enemy markings. After flying level for a few seconds, with the fires increasing, it did a diving turn to the right and went vertically into the ground from 4,500 ft altitude. Burning wreckage was scattered over the ground when it crashed. Combat took place in a Caen/ Bayeux area. A pilot of another squadron reported over the R/T that he saw the burning aircraft go down. His call number was 42. On landing back at base at 03.55 hrs, Mosquito was found to have superficial damage from wreckage. An unused bullet was found in the starboard wing."

Five days later, Flight Lieutenant Hall destroyed a Ju 88 south of St Lo after a long weaving chase, and Squadron Leader Bunting DFC* destroyed a FW 190 near St Lo on June 17th, damaging his Mosquito during the engagement : -

The Faithful Few

"I was given a vector of 340 degs and on the turn at 0416 hrs contact was obtained. Range 2 miles, position 11 o'clock and well above. I climbed to 9000 ft holding Bogey who gained on us during the climb. My observer reported what appeared to be Window and at the same time I saw a flash in the sky which I now think was an anti-personnel bomb container opening. The E/A almost immediately turned hard port and I followed. A visual was obtained 250/350 yds ahead and above.

I saw part of the exhausts and identified the A/C as a Fw 190 and my observer confirmed it, using his night glasses. I positioned myself dead astern and below when I saw the whole of the exhausts which confirmed the identity. I closed in to 100 yds range slightly to port and below. I opened fire and gave him a one second burst. He exploded in front of me and though I pulled up to avoid flying debris, I was hit by it. The E/A was well alight and glowing and went down through the cloud, out of control. I made orbit and saw the reflection of a flash through the cloud which was, I think, when the E/A hit the ground. The combat position was south of St Lo area. The debris damaged my starboard radiator and caused my starboard engine to fail. I feathered, and returned to base on one engine."

By the end of June, the squadron had destroyed three Ju 88's, two more Fw 190's and a Me 410. On July 14th, Squadron Leader Bunting DFC* , along with Flight Lieutenant Reed DFC*; Flight Lieutenant Hall and Flying Officer Cairns, were all despatched to Buckingham Palace for their investiture by HM the King. Returning to operations, they continued to fly over Normandy, with other crews making more kills in the process, with four being made on July 29th near Vire. By then, only one Mosquito crew had been lost, that being Flight Sergeant Howard Scott and Flying Officer Colin Duncan who were killed when their Mosquito crashed into a wood north east of Holmsley South on July 15th when returning from operations.

F/O Spedding, a two-kill 'wizard'.
(Connie Storr)

On July 30th, 1944, Squadron Leader Bunting DFC flew his last operation, taking off from Colerne in his regular Mosquito, MM476, coded ME-V. With him was Flying Officer Edward Spedding, who had come in on the mission at the last moment due to Flight Lieutenant Reed DFC* suffering from the flu. The 488 Squadron diary takes up the story: -

"Operational sorties were flown during the night produced mixed feelings of jubilation and sorrow....Probable tragedy marked the sortie flown by S/Ldr E.N.Bunting DFC & Bar. Pilot and F/O E Spedding N/R. They were chasing fast flying FW 190s at a low altitude when they ran into flak. S/Ldr Bunting reported that he had been hit, and fifteen seconds later an explosion was seen on the ground. This crew are reported missing, believed killed. S/Ldr Bunting was Flight Commander of 'B' Flight and the squadron has suffered a severe blow in the loss of this able and popular leader."

In reality, they had indeed been killed when MM476 ploughed into a field near St Remy, south west of Thury Harcourt. Their bodies were recovered, and interred at the local church in a joint grave, where they rest to this day.

Group Captain Peter Townsend also remembered Nigel Bunting: -

"Very pleasant memories of a quiet young chap, lightish red hair; an excellent and reliable pilot. I left 85 Squadron but a month after his arrival so did not get to know him well. But he came back one day (can't remember where I was) in a Mosquito and gave me a ride in it, so that I was both impressed by his handling of the aircraft and the qualities of the latter."

Group Captain Richard Haine remembered when Squadron Leader Bunting was killed: -

"His death was a great loss to the squadron, and of great sadness to me personally. He was an excellent Flight Commander and a first rate pilot and one of the nicest men with a full measure of loyalty and integrity. He would have gone far I'm sure."

Chapter Seven

ernard Peter Klee was born in India, where his father was a serving army officer, and later returned with the family to England. He commenced his education at Plymouth Catholic College, and later at Worcester Royal Grammar School. A natural sportsman, during his time at WRGS he won the Allen Cup for shooting. A keen tennis player, he also excelled at cricket, and had county trials.

After leaving school, he joined the company of H W Ward & Co Ltd to pursue a career in engineering. He was soon to become an extremely popular member of staff, proving his ability to the company. By now war was looming, and Klee volunteered for service in the RAF in April 1939. After passing the necessary tests and medicals, he was put on the reserve list.

With the outbreak of war in September of that year, he was called to full time service, and began his pilot training. At the time when the Battle of Britain was at its height, the then Sergeant Klee was based at 6 Elementary Flying Training School, Little Rissington. He wrote to his family after literally passing his final exams: -

"Just a quick note during the morning break to let you know the exam results, I passed with 71.5%. We now have about 14 days to wait until the Air Ministry award us our wings, so I'll let you know when to cable Dad."

After progressing through advanced training, and being deemed suitable as a prospective fighter pilot, Klee would have faced posting to a fighter Operational Training Unit. Here the embryonic fighter pilot came to grips with the Hurricane and Spitfire for the first time. Here they learnt the rudimentary tactics employed in aerial combat, followed by dog fighting practice and gunnery exercises. He easily reached the required standard and received his first posting to an operational squadron, 222 (Natal), in December 1940. His first listed sortie was on December 21st 1940 in Spitfire X4246, during which he undertook a patrol of the Coltishall area.

222 Squadron were based at RAF Coltishall in Norfolk, and were engaged in patrols off the east coast, providing air cover for the fishing fleets from Yarmouth and Cromer, and dealing with the German aircraft that continually probed the eastern defences. This was a much different scene to the one they faced just

four months before, when deployed at RAF Hornchurch. There, they had fought a hard campaign in the Battle of Britain, losing 25 Spitfires, and nine pilots, with a further 10 being wounded.

Pilots of No 222 Sqn at Hornchurch, 1940; Norman Ramsay first left.

The squadron compliment now consisted of a mix of experienced men and new pilots, while others had been posted in from other squadrons. January 1941 saw Klee undertake more familiarisation flights, and short patrols. He rapidly became a very popular member of the squadron, flying as No 2 to the commanding officer, Squadron Leader Love, and later to Flight Lieutenant Brian van Mentz, his flight commander. While at Coltishall, he became great friends with the then Sergeant Rainford (Ray) Marland, a pilot who had been with 222 since September 1940, and had destroyed at least six enemy aircraft. Friends on the ground, they also became an effective team in the air.

German night intruder operations were also starting to make themselves known, and Coltishall was to become a regular target in later weeks. On February 10th, Sergeant Marland, and Sergeant Barnes from 257 Squadron, attacked and drove off what was thought to me a Bf 110, but not before it had dropped incendiaries over the airfield, damaging two hangars.

After what seemed like endless convoy patrols, Klee finally went into combat for the first time. Squadron Leader Love had attacked an He 111 on January 18th, and Flight Lieutenant van Mentz had caught another on January 31st ; and now it was his turn. While on patrol with Squadron Leader Love on the afternoon of February 15th, he engaged a He 111 15 miles east of Yarmouth. His combat report read: -

The Faithful Few

"Course of enemy aircraft due east, camouflage dark grey. After sighting bandit I approached down sun, and he did not sight me until I was 350 yards astern. He operated his boost cut out (mine already being operated) and then a few bullets were fired at me, all going below me. I gave 4 bursts; after the first burst at 300 yards the enemy fire was silenced. Then I just got closer and closer until approx 100 yards behind, after 2nd and 3rd bursts engines were smoking and the enemy aircraft was diving for the sea. I broke away to deliver another attack. I looked for the aircraft, but it was not to be seen, and on investigation saw a huge splash in the sea approx where I had lost sight of it."

The elated victor wrote to his family that night, giving further details: -

"Just a short note, as I'm going out to celebrate. I shot down my first jerry today. At 4 o'clock I was on patrol, when Ops told my section leader S/Ldr Love there was a jerry near us. I saw him and told him where it was, and still he could not see it. After that he told me to chase it and he would follow. He followed ok, but when he got there I had given it 2300 bullets and was deep in the ocean 15 miles east of Yarmouth. Well cheerio; I'm off to the party now. "

February 17th was a busy day for 222: Squadron Leader Love and Sergeant Christie engaged at Do 17 and left it smoking before it disappeared into cloud. During the afternoon, Sergeants Ferraby and Davies caught a Ju 88 of 6/KG 76 off Sheringham, forcing it to ditch. 45 minutes later, Squadron Leader Love and Sergeant Marland located another Ju 88, this time a 8/KG 1 machine, off Yarmouth, and after numerous attacks, it was last seen flying very near to the water. This aircraft disappeared off the radar at 15.19 hours and it was assumed it had dropped into the sea. It had in fact ditched, but the pilot, *Unteroffizier* Stebetack and the rest of the crew were never found.

Coltishall, 1941: P/O Klee & his close friend P/O Rainford 'Ray' Marland.

After a short spell of leave, during which Coltishall had been shrouded in mist and fog, more and less grounding all the squadrons on the airfield, Klee returned. On the days when the mist actually cleared, low cloud hampered any flying. However, on March 6th, Squadron Leader Love and Sergeant Marland damaged a Do 17, and with the weather becoming much clearer, Klee, flying with Ray

Marland, caught a Ju 88 of KG30 west of Yarmouth on March 8th: -

"Type of enemy aircraft Ju 88, camouflage dark green n. On proceeding on last vector of 270 degrees, I was about 80 yards to the rear and 30 yards out, when a twin engined plane dived through cloud between us. I saw 2 bombs dropping, so I broke away and attacked, having already informed Sergeant Marland, Yellow 1. E/A started climbing, then dived for the sea. I got in several deflection shots which appeared to hit, and an astern attack when E/A was diving for the sea. A thin trail of black smoke left the exhaust ports, but this was due to him operating boost cut out. Slight return fire was experienced from top rear for about 1 second then it ceased. I broke away at about 3,000 feet and Sgt Marland carried on attack as I had expended all my ammunition."

Ray Marland finished off the damaged Ju 88, sending into the sea. When being interviewed by the squadron intelligence officer after, he made a

No 222 Sqn Crew Room: pilots seated, L-R: S/L Love, F/L Thomas, P/Os Klee, Carpenter, u/k, Marland, next three u/k. Standing & writing is F/L Van Mentz.

point regarding the coastal guns in his combat report, stating: -

"AA were firing at E/A whilst we were attacking. Decidedly unpleasant as shells were bursting around us."

Another letter soon was winging its way to Worcester: -

"On my first flip since leave Sgt Marland and I saw a Ju 88 bombing Yarmouth. I engaged it first and put paid to the rear gunner. I fired all the rest of the ammo during the dive from 8000 feet. Marland whistled in and gave it the 'coup de grace' and the E/A finally crashed 10 miles SE of Yarmouth, no survivors being found by launches that went to investigate. Well, I must be off to bed, as I'm on dawn readiness which necessitates rising at 05.30."

Patrols and more spells of bad weather interspersed the days. On the afternoon of March 18th, Klee, flying as wingman to Flight Lieutenant van Mentz on a 'Kipper Patrol' (a fishing fleet protection flight) was vectored onto a raider coming in at 30,000feet. Starting a climb from 2000 feet, they soon spotted a Do 17, which in turn spotted them and dived away. Showing his experience, van Mentz pulled away from Klee and began his attack. Klee caught up, only to find out his leader had seriously damaged the Do 17. Klee later said: -

"When I opened fire from 250 yards, E/A's starboard oleo leg was hanging down and the aircraft itself was flying about five feet above the water."

It flew on, with one engine on fire, before ditching in the sea. Later that evening, the BBC mentioned this action during their evening bulletin.

Back at base, Klee wrote again: -

"Just another of my notes. The Do 17Z you heard on the radio that had been shot down on the Norfolk coast was the work of F/Lt van Mentz (my flight commander) and I, thus bringing my bag up to 2. 'Jeep' van Mentz did quarter and beam attacks , and I whistled up astern, opening fire from 250 yards, and closing to about 10 feet. Boy, it's the closest I've been to a jerry; I almost chewed his tail off with my prop. It's a good job I didn't as we were about 35 m out to sea. The jerry landed on the sea, and 2 blokes started swimming. Just after this the Dornier sank. The lifeboat was sent out but I don't believe anyone was found. It's estimated that you can only be conscious for 15 minutes in the sea in this weather."

The enemy aircraft was actually a reconnaissance Bf 110 of 3 (F)/ 122 piloted by *Oberleutnant* Frexer. Neither crewman was found.

Morale was high in the squadron; and Klee was one of few new pilots to engage the enemy. However, all were dealt a blow on March 24th when Sergeant Cockram was killed when he crashed after losing contact with Flight Lieutenant van Mentz in cloud. Tragedy struck again when on the 27th, Pilot Officer Logan and Sergeant Wilson collided near Easton. The loss of three pilots in as many days was a severe blow, but the loss of Pilot Officer Logan, a Battle of Britain veteran, and a highly experienced pilot, left a gap that was hard to fill.

Sergeant Scott was also killed on April 3rd after his Spitfire apparently broke up in flight over Southborough. It seemed they were having a rather bad spell indeed.

Further engagements took place during 'kipper patrols' with Flight Lieutenant Thomas and Pilot Officer Ramsay seriously damaged a Ju 88 on the 4th, and P/O Ramsay claiming a Do 17 the next day.

With the improvement of the weather, especially at night, German intruder aircraft were beginning to become more than a nuisance to the RAF. Equipped with converted Ju 88's and Do 17's, they followed aircraft back to their bases, often circling near airfields trying to catch them as they came into land - and at their most vulnerable. The Wellingtons and Hampdens of Bomber Command represented an easy kill, especially when the crews though they were more or less home and safe. Training bases were also targeted, and the intruder pilots began to make frequent claims.

It reached the stage that the evening appearance of an intruder in the circuit became so regular that the pilots christened him 'Coltishall Karl'. Treating it with humour tended to take the edge off things, but they were all in no doubt that if you encountered 'Karl' he would do his best to kill you.

One pilot on 222 had his own close encounter with the intruder menace. Pilot Officer Norman Ramsay was an experienced pilot, having first become operational in May 1940 with 92 Squadron. In June he was then posted to 610 (County of Chester) Squadron, before then going to 222 on September 15th 1940, and was commissioned in March 1941.

He was in the Coltishall circuit when Sergeants Marsland and Barnes had driven an intruder off in February and had to land with the airfield in total darkness. However, his encounter of March 12th whilst returning from a patrol of Cromer and Norwich proved to be a bit too close for comfort, as Norman Ramsay recalled: -

"Well, 'Coltishall Karl' nearly got me one night! He fired at me when I was on finals for landing. By the time I had realised what was happening, with tracer going by, he had to break off the attack, overshooting me and dropping incendiaries down my landing path. I touched down though these burning incendiaries turned off into the darkness and switched the engine off. As soon as I stopped rolling I leapt out and ran, expecting a strafing attack. Fortunately none came."

He added: -

The Faithful Few

"We did not fly every night, but I clearly remember the odd bombing the intruder inflicted. We and the other squadrons rigged up a machine gun outside dispersal in a vain attempt to get him. It made us feel better I suppose!"

By now, Klee was enjoying life with 222. In a letter home dated April 16th, he briefly described a little unofficial low flying: -

"I've spent an hour shooting up people on the Broads and got quite a kick out of it!"

On April 26th, he wrote what was to be his last letter home: -

"At present I'm having the car overhauled in Coltishall, so that it will be ok for my leave. The leave starts on 18th May, and I shall be bringing Ray along with me, we shall be arriving in the early evening. The Duke of Kent visited this station about a week ago, and we shook hands with him. His two stock questions seemed to be "How long have you been with the squadron?" and "How many have you shot down?"."

The same night, tragedy again struck the squadron. The Ferry Inn at nearby Horning was a popular haunt for airmen from Colitshall, and locals alike. During the evening, it was struck by two bombs, totally destroying it and killing 21 people. Of the dead, three were servicemen from 222 - Flying Officer Roberts, the squadron adjutant; Flying Officer Atwill, the squadron medical officer; and Flight Lieutenant van Mentz who by then had become 'B' Flight commander.

At just after 1 am on May 4th, Klee took off for a night patrol, with Sergeant John Burgess (another Battle of Britain veteran) following a few minutes later. The report filed by Flying Officer Raymond, the squadron intelligence officer, detailed the events that followed: -

"One Spitfire Mk2 P/O B P Klee (British) took off from Coltishall at 0110 hours, and one Spitfire Mk2 Sgt J H Burgess (British) took of at 0119 hours to patrol base. Later control warned both pilots, who were patrolling independently, than an enemy aircraft was orbiting them, and observers on the aerodrome also saw the enemy aircraft manoeuvring to get on their tails. Enemy aircraft believed to be a Ju 88, was constantly weaving, making steep turns, and otherwise evading our aircraft. Sgt Burgess managed to get the enemy aircraft in his sights and was about to fire when the enemy aircraft fired a two star cartridge (two reds) which dazzled him and caused him to lose

The Faithful Few

the enemy aircraft. He next saw two bursts of tracer flash past his aircraft, without however doing any damage.

At 0329 hours BST, observers on the ground saw a Spitfire (now know to be P/O Klee) fly straight across the aerodrome from north to south followed by the enemy aircraft, who fired a burst of cannon shell into the Spitfire, which crashed in flames to the south east of the aerodrome and burnt out. P/O Klee killed.

The exhausts from the Spitfires showed up very plainly, whereas the enemy aircrafts exhaust was not visible. The speed and manoeuvrability of the enemy aircraft was truly remarkable. Sgt Burgess did not succeed in making contact and the enemy aircraft must have left the scene of the action immediately after shooting down P/O Klee."

To add insult to injury, the intruder had also managed to bomb the airfield, narrowly missing the Officers Mess.

Unknown to those on the ground, Klee had fallen to the guns of *Leutnant* Hans Hahn of 3/NJG2, flying a Ju 88C-4. The downing of Klee was Hahn's ninth victory, though he had mistaken the Spitfire for a Fairey Fulmar. He was the most successful intruder pilot at that time, opening his scoring in October 1940 when he destroyed a 102 squadron Whitley that was taking off from Linton on Ouse. The night after Klee was killed, he returned to the area, and in similar fashion, shot down a Hurricane from 257 Squadron. The pilot, Sergeant Parrott was killed. On four occasions he had to return to his base at Glize-Rijen on one engine, one of those being when his Ju 88 had been damaged from debris from the destruction of a Wellington. He was awarded the Ritterkreuze on the 9th July 1941 for reaching 11 victories, becoming the first night fighter pilot to receive this honour.

But in the early hours of the 10th November 1941, his luck ran out. While operating over Lincolnshire, he had spotted an easy target - an Oxford training aircraft from 12 FTS. Pulling the Ju 88 in to attack, it seems he misjudged his approach, and both aircraft collided. Sergeant Graham and one other on board the Oxford were killed. The Ju 88 spiralled to earth, crashing near Grantham, killing Hahn and his crew.

Of those who served with 222 during this period, most did not survive the war. Klee's great friend Ray Marland attended the funeral at Astwood Cemetery in Worcester but he too was dead before the end of the year, being killed serving with 229 Squadron in Egypt on December 17th. 222 moved south in June and

P/O Klee seated in the Spitfire in which he was killed: 'Zanzibar III', ZD-T.
(Dilip Sarkar)

Lt Hans Hahn of 3/NJ 2, who shot down & killed P/O Klee over Coltishall during the early hours of May 4th, 1941.
(John Foreman)

by July was based at Manston, ready to participate in the fighter sweeps that were to take the lives of so many talented pilots. Norman Ramsey left 222 in October 1941 and went on to instruct at 61 Operational Training Unit at Rednal, spending nearly a year in that role. He was posted overseas, eventually joining 1435 Squadron at Luqa, Malta, spending seven months with them before coming back to the UK for another instructional post. He was awarded a well deserved DFC in September 1943. He retired from the RAF in July 1962.

Norman Ramsey concludes: -

"I remember Peter, and although he was in another flight, he was keen, and very good pilot indeed. Looking back, I really don't like to think of those who were lost, as it upsets me so. And there were so many of them."

The grave of P/O Bernard Peter Klee at Astwood Cemetery, Worcester.

Chapter Eight

E rnest George Boucher was born on December 30th 1922, at Enville, the second son of Cyril Benjamin Boucher and Margaret Anne Boucher, and educated at the King Edward VI Grammar School, Stourbridge. There, he excelled at Rugby, Boxing, athletics, and was a member of the Shooting VIII. It is fair to say he was exceedingly popular with pupils and masters alike. During the early stages of the war, he worked for the Air Ministry at Adastral House in London, later enlisting in the RAFVR and began his initial training in February 1941.

George Boucher pictured on leave with his parents, Uncle Alec &
'Rita' the dog!
(Mike Boucher)

Posted to No 3 BFTS at Miami, Oklahoma, USA for pilot training he later gained his wings, and was deemed suitable as a prospective fighter pilot. He returned to England the following year, joining 59 Operational Training Unit at Crosby-on-Eden, flying Hurricanes, prior to his first operational posting.

That came in August 1942, when he joined 174 Squadron. Based at Manston, they had re-formed only five months earlier, with the nucleus of the flying cadre being taken from 607 Squadron. Equipped with Hurricane IIB bombers, they were tasked with attacking ground targets in Europe. Sergeant Boucher made his first truly operational sorties on August 19th 1942, and if there was ever a case of a 'baptism by fire' this was it, for he found himself taking part in 'Operation Jubilee' - the Dieppe Raid.

The first flight of 12 Hurricanes took off at 04.40 hours, led by Squadron Leader Fayolle DFC. In the darkness, the squadron were unable to link up, and the sections had to make their way to the target separately, a gun emplacement codenamed 'Hitler', located on a hilltop. All pilots hit the target, and turned back for home. Light flak was encountered all the way, apart from when they strayed too close

George poses proudly with a training aircraft at Oklahoma.
(Mike Boucher)

Pilots of 174 Sqn just before Sgt Boucher joined them for Operation Jubilee; centre is the CO, S/L Fayolle.
(Mike Boucher)

to St Aubin aerodrome, and the flak units opened up, making it uncomfortable for them. On landing at base, it was found that Squadron Leader Fayolle DFC was missing. He had been seen crossing the Channel at high speed, and later observed engaging an Fw 190, aided by two Spitfires off Littlehampton. It is thought he rammed the Fw 190 when out of ammunition.

A second sortie, again with 12 Hurricanes, departed base at 10.25 hours, with Sergeant Boucher participating. The target this time was the eastern heights of Dieppe, but upon flying over the town, no target could be seen. The squadron made a steep turn and returned over the heights, but in doing so, the Hurricane flown by Pilot Officer Van Wymeersch was hit by flak and lost its starboard wing. The remaining aircraft dive bombed some woods east of Dieppe where troops were reported to have been seen, and headed back. Two more Hurricanes were missing, BE505 and Flight Sergeant Watson, and BP649 with Sergeant James, and it was thought that they most likely fell to flak.

One more sortie was flown during the afternoon to attack a gun emplacement codenamed 'Rommel' to the east of the town. All 10 pilots attacked the target, with the loss of Pilot Officer du Fretay in HL705, who was last seen going in to bomb 'Rommel'. The remainder of the squadron machine gunned German transport, headed for the coast, and returned at low level.

What a start it had been for Sergeant Boucher. 174 had flown 34 sorties in all, two by Sergeant Boucher, but in turn had lost five pilots and aircraft. To anyone new to operational missions, it would certainly made them wonder just how long it would be before they too were lost.

Apart from patrols, no major engagements were flown after Jubilee by 174, and in September 1st, they departed to Warmwell for deployment overseas. This was put on temporary hold on September 18th, and three days later they all returned to Manston, taking up their old role of flying offensive patrols, some against enemy shipping off the French coast.

Later in the year, numerous targets were hit by Sergeant Boucher and 174 Squadron: German hutted camps at Stadehillebrugge and Blankenburg aerodrome; shipping in the Ostend Bruges canal; railways at Le Treport, Abbeville, Furnes and Dixmunde, and naval craft off Dunkirk. Sergeant

Pilots of 174 Sqn eat 'al fresco' at RAF Manston.
(Mike Boucher)

The Faithful Few

Boucher also flew a night anti-shipping patrol with Flight Sergeant Wetere on November 21st.

In December, the squadron moved again, this time to Odiham, where they stayed until March 1943. They undertook a busy training regime, with as the squadron diary put it: -

"Firing practice - lots of!"

In February, they took part in Exercise Spartan, one of the largest military endeavours seen in this country. After the Dieppe debacle, it was designed to produce an offensive exercise, with the opposing forces of Eastland and Westland. It would simulate the establishing and forcing of a bridgehead in Europe, with massive amounts of troops deployed.

174 Squadron were on the Allied side, along with three other 'Army Support' squadrons, and a further seven fighter squadrons. Allied deployment was a total 19 squadrons, while the 'German' side had 13 in total. The squadron diary recorded it's involvement in Spartan: -

"Wrexham and Zeals parties have left on Spartan attachments. For this relief much thanks. These attachments have been more troublesome than a movement of the entire squadron. We await further instructions, meantime the squadron aircraft are all receiving hearty treatment in the shape of fresh camo. The new maguillage is extremely chic!"

Spartan continued into March, and the squadron moved to Chilbolton. The aerodrome was described as " *unsanitary toilets, poor communications. Bad time had by all.*" They endured these conditions until April, when they moved again, this time to Gravesend. More good news came in the form that the they were to lose their Hurricanes, and become a Typhoon squadron. On April 8th, 14 Typhoons were ferried in, with a 'fanfare of trumpets' as the squadron diary put enthusiastically!

Six days later, Sergeant Boucher, along with Jack Cobbett, Jimmie Reynolds and Stan Minnall made their first Typhoon flights. The next few weeks were taken up with getting to grips with this seven ton brute, and air to air, and air to ground practice firing. Air to ground firing could be hazardous, as seen on April 25th, when two Typhoons were damaged over Leysdown Range after debris had bounced back up, hitting the aircraft.

174 Squadron pilots 'roughing it' during Operation Spartan. W/O D Oram 3rd left, F/L F Grantham (OC 'B' Flt) far right.
(Mike Boucher)

May started with the squadron's first flying loss of a Typhoon and pilot. Flying Officer Jimmie Reynolds DFC crashed near Redhill during a practice flight. It appeared the tail unit snapped off, along with one aileron, and the Typhoon dived into the ground. This was to be repeated many times, as the early Typhoons had an inherent weakness around the tail transportation joint, and when put under heavy load, they would break off. This was remedied by the fixing of strengthening 'fish plates' around the tail and fuselage joint. Flying Officer Reynolds' death was keenly felt, for he had been one of the original squadron members upon its re forming. To make matters worse, the funeral on May 7th was handled poorly, and a complaint was made about the chaplain. The Squadron was rightly angry.

After more training throughout June, the unit moved to 121 Airfield, Lydd, and on July 4th, they were deemed operational. Four days later, Sergeant Boucher had a close call, but not in a Typhoon, but a Tiger Moth, when detailed along with Flight Sergeant Rowley to ferry a Typhoon from Detling.

Flight Sergeant Rowley took off cross wind, and ended up colliding with one of 175 Squadrons Typhoons, with the result that the Tiger Moth was so badly damaged it was written off, and Sergeant Boucher was admitted to the Military Field Hospital Tenterden, with cuts and bruises. His injuries were sufficient for him to be kept in for nine days, before being released and sent home on 10 days leave.

Returning to flying, he participated in more missions over France. Two pilots were lost on July 30th after a raid on Cortrai. Flying Officers Marky and Dunning collided crossing the French coast on the turn trip. One Typhoon was seen spinning down with the fuselage broken behind the cockpit, while the other dived away more or less intact. The loss of Flying Officer Dunning caused a stir at the time, as his father was Charles Dunning, the Canadian Minister of Finance. However, both pilots survived to be take POW.

The Faithful Few

Further targets were attacked in August, such as Merville, Amiens-Glisy and Woenschecht, with the loss of one pilot. During the Amiens-Glisy sortie, Sergeant Bouchers' Typhoon, JP444 suffered a technical fault just after entering its dive onto the target. However, Boucher managed to bring it back, landing at 125 Airfield.

174 Sqn, 1943. Sgt George Boucher 4th left.
(Mike Boucher)

The end of August finished with a several fighter sweeps and escorts, along with 175 and 245 Squadrons with two being led by the wing leader, Wing Commander Dennis Crowley Milling. Pilot Officer O'Callaghan had to be rescued from the sea after his aircraft, JP550 suffered an engine failure on the 19th, and Flying Officer Burney was injured on 25th after crashing his Typhoon on return to base. He stalled on approach in EK369, crashing onto the end of the runway, destroying the aircraft.

In September, they flew anti shipping sorties and several escorts, one to Lille, and bombed St Omer Aerodrome, with no losses and only one Typhoon being damaged.

By now with the rank of Flight Sergeant, George Boucher had become an experienced Typhoon pilot, but the sortie of October 5th, proved to be a bit more than anyone had bargained for.

Flight Sergeant Boucher, flying JP547, and acting as No 2 to Flight Lieutenant Grantham in EK175, took off from Lydd on a low level train busting sortie. They crossed the French coast three miles south of Le Touquet, shooting up a gun post on the way in. A train was sighted two miles ahead, and attacked first by Flight Lieutenant Grantham, with Flight Sergeant Boucher crossing it right to left. The train was hit, and stopped, but after the pair had picked up the railway line at Montrueil, Flight Sergeant Boucher radioed up that he was going to have to make a forced landing as the engine was running rough. This he did, jettisoning the door, before making a wheels up landing in a large open field.

The Faithful Few

The cause had been that when Flight Sergeant Boucher had hit the train engine, tender and the forward area of the cab with cannon fire, a chunk of the train had flown up, hitting the Typhoon in the engine, setting it alight. He flew on for about six miles before crash landing.

His report into what happened after his crash landing read: -

"I hid my map and mae west in the soft ground under a hedge. My parachute I left in the aircraft. I ran onto a road , on which was a Frenchman and a cart. I had learnt French at school and spoke to him. He said he could not help me, but told me to hide in the hedge. There was a pile of brushwood about 200 yards from the aircraft, and I got under that.

About an hour after the crash three German soldiers arrived and mounted guard over the aircraft, and I learned afterwards that two lorries loaded with soldiers went round the roads in the district. I remained in the brushwood until 06.00 hrs the next day (6 Oct). During that time two Frenchmen brought me food and wine. The three German guards went off for a drink after dark, and some Frenchmen took 140 gallons of petrol from the aircraft. The men who visited me told me not to move during the night, but just to walk out in the morning. They did not appear to know of any organisation.

In the morning left the brushwood, still in uniform, but with the badges removed. I passed within about 100 yards of the aircraft. I picked up a basket and walked through an orchard, picking apples from the tree as I went past the wreckage. A man and a woman were also picking apples at the time, so I did not attract any attention from the Germans.

My helpers had not made any arrangements for meeting me, and I started SW, with the idea of making towards Paris. At the first village at which I stopped, a German motor cycle patrol came through. I dived into a house, and the patrol passed without seeing me. I walked into the village of Bois Jean where I had been told there were no Germans. I asked help from a man working in the fields. He proved to be a Pole, and directed me to a large farm. After observing the house for some time, I went in and asked for food and civilian clothing. I was given a meal and told to go away and return at 17.00 hrs.

I walked into the fields until I met some children. I spent the day with them, helping them to tend their cows. At first the children would not talk to me, as they thought I was a German. When I produced some pennies they became friendly and shared their food with me. There were three of them - a girl of about 12 and two boys of eight and nine. They wanted to know why we had not invaded France and if the invasion would be delayed for more than a month or so now, as they were sure we would be in France by the end of the year. At lunch time the girl went for food for me. I gave her 100 Francs. She came back with the food - and the 100 Francs.

At 17.00 hrs I returned to the farm. Helpers were awaiting me there who put me in touch with an organisation which arranged my journey to the Spanish frontier."

Flight Sergeant Boucher was kept in hiding, moving him quietly, step by step to the frontier. Near the end of the month, he was ready to get to Spain: -

"I left France on 24 Oct in a party, mostly French, of 34, which included Sgt Thomas, RAF and two Americans. At midday on Oct 26 we arrived at a point north of La Munia mountain, still in France. Here the guides left us, giving directions to one of the Frenchmen, who forgot what they had told him. The majority of the party decided to spend the night in a hut on the frontier. With three Frenchmen and three Poles I decided to push on. We climbed La Munia (which took three hours) and as darkness was falling made our way into a valley on the other side. I was by this time suffering from snow blindness. We followed the valley and carried on until we came to Parxan which had been destroyed in the Spanish Civil War and was still in ruins. I went on from here with the three Poles and followed the river to the neighbourhood of Bielsa. At Bielsa, the Poles and I were arrested by the Spanish frontier police…They took us into the town police station, where personal particulars of us were taken and we were searched. As advised in lectures, I said I was an escaped P/W and the Poles corroborated the story. We were three nights in Bielsa. One of the Poles stole 3 lbs of chocolate from the police office, otherwise we should have starved. Here I had a chance of talking to a Spanish woman who talked French , and she agreed to post a letter to the British Counsel. It got through.

From Bielsa we were taken by car to Barbastro, where I was 14 days in prison. Here I received good treatment, though the governor is anti-British, anti-Polish, and pro-German. I got no palliase to sleep on. The consulate got in touch with me on 10 Nov. On 12 Nov a representative of the Spanish Air Force took me via Saragossa (two nights in a hotel) to Alhama de Ragon where I was interned for eight days in a hotel. I was two nights in Madrid, on the way to Gibraltar (arrived 27 Nov).

On November 30th, he arrived back in England at Whitchurch. The Squadron noted: -

"We have heard that Flight Sergeant Boucher is home, safe and well."

After a de-brief by MI9 and MI6, he returned home on leave, before re-joining the squadron at Westhampnett.

1944 opened with a change in direction for squadron operations. Despite taking part in missions over France, the training regime stepped up a gear. Low flying was encouraged to a degree, with the pilots conducting low level cross country flights, and various excercises with the Army, and Navy. The Typhoons had been equipped with rocket rails, allowing each one to carry eight 60 lb armour piercing projectiles, and many practice rocket firing flights were undertaken. However, the squadron stayed on operational readiness, and completed escort sorties, and ranger patrols. Such operations, performed at either squadron, or wing level, could cause real damage and disruption to the German war effort.

March 1944 saw a real increase in cross service exercises, practicing numerous dummy attack sorties on Army motor transport. The pilots accuracy with the 60 lb rockets increased, with great results on the targets at Pagham Range. A notable 'Long Range Rodeo' was flown on March 16th, along the route St Valery - Beauvais- Lagny- Mellin- Fontainbleau- Etampes- Dreux- Le Trait.15 Typhoons (with four from 174 Squadron) attacked the airfield at Melun/ Villaroche, shooting up several Ju 88's. The section from 174 Squadron, led by Flight Lieutenant Grantham attacked four Arado AR 96 aircraft near Etampes, with Flight Lieutenant Grantham and Warrant Officer Hayes destroying one each. Pilot Officer Cross from 175 Squadron destroyed a Ju 88, and Flight Lieutenant Davies DFC shot down a Bf 108 towing a target on an air firing exercise. Other aircraft on the ground were also destroyed, but it was not all one sided. Pilot Officer Cross had to force land his damaged Typhoon, Flying Officer Austin was missing, and Warrant Officer Scott was wounded, with all three taking hits from flak.

The last mission of March was undertaken on the 26th, when eight Typhoons attacked a 'Noball' target south east of Abbeville, with all pilots returning safely.

On April 1st, the squadron packed up, and moved to Holmsley South, getting it all done in a few hours. At readiness from the 2nd, they suffered several days of bad weather, which limited operations and training. This training was put to good measure, when in May, the squadron began targeting essential sites prior to D Day. They struck railways, sidings and rolling stock. Gun emplacements and radar stations were attacked with rockets and cannons, and any German transport was fair game. They, along with many other squadrons, began to do their best to disrupt the transport and communications infrastructure ready for the invasion. But the first part of the year hadn't been easy, for the squadron had lost seven pilots to date. In January, Flying Officer Cobbett and Flight Sergeant Smith had collided on a sortie to Bethune, with Cobbett being killed and Smith taken POW. In February, Squadron Leader McConnell DFC was shot down by flak near Percy, along with Flying Officer Proddow, who evaded capture. Four days after their loss, Flying Officer Reynaud and Flight Sergeant Brown were shot down by Fw 190s of JG26, with Brown being killed. The last fatality was Flying Officer Irwin on March 6th when his Typhoon suffered engine failure and crashed into the sea.

During May, Boucher flew 12 operational sorties; performing rocket attacks on radar sites at North Rouen, Cherbourg, and Levy, as well as armed recces, rocket attacks on transport at Villiers and west of Caen, and long range armed recces. It was all part of the attempt to disrupt communications and transport links prior to D Day.

Between June 2nd and June 5th, 174 flew sorties against radar stations at Cherbourg, Oudonville and Andonville, and flew three on D Day itself as part of 121 Wing. The first was a rocket attack on gun positions at Revier during the morning, followed by an armed recce south west of Caen, where they destroyed a vehicle, and a similar sortie covering the line of Balleroy-Bretteville-Mezidon, destroying a car, and a bridge.

Three long range armed recces were flown on the 7th, destroying lorries at Mesnil Vin, and damaging a tank at Hamars. Total for the day was 11 lorries, plus the tank, for no loss. A train was attacked the next day, but was heavily defended by flak guns, keeping the Typhoons at bay. Pilot Officer Boucher flew his next mission on June 10th as part of the Wing, against an enemy troop formation hiding in a wood west of Caen, and followed that up two days later with an armed recce to the west of Cherbourg. During that operation, Typhoon MM968, piloted by Flight Lieutenant McNeill, was badly hit by flak, resulting in him baling out into the Channel, but sadly, he was not found.

The following day the squadron performed their first sorties from advanced landing ground in Normandy. Operating as part of 121 Wing, they undertook an armed recce of the Barent area, and later attacked transport at Moult, before flying back to England. Three sorties were flown from Normandy on June 14th, all against enemy positions in and around Villiers Bocage, and a further three on the 15th. During the second mission, an armed recce of the Dozule area, Pilot Officer Boucher had to belly land Typhoon MM594 near the landing strip. It had been hit by flak during the recce and it had just managed to get him back to the vicinity of the strip. The rest of the squadron flew back to Britain after their last mission of the day, leaving Pilot Officer Boucher to spend his first night in Normandy.

The squadron soon returned to Normandy, but were to operate from B5/Camilly for two days, before going to B2/Bazenville. The advanced landing grounds were well within reach of German gunners, and B5 was heavily shelled on June 17th and 18th. A three ton lorry was burnt out, and tents were damaged, but there were no casualties. During this time, the squadron had deployed against targets at Fenquerolles, and attacked the brick works at Troaun with rockets. Due to bad weather, no more sorties were flown until the 22nd, when attacks were launched on German mortar posts at Tilly sur Seulles and an identified HQ at Cagny. The following day, the squadron had its most successful sortie in Normandy.

Two of the many targets attacked by 174 Sqn during the lead up to D-Day.
(Mike Boucher)

The Faithful Few

The morning had started with a rocket attack on targets in the village of Demouville, and a wood at Couverville. The second sortie was to a target at Giberville, and a strongpoint at Demouville, but it was the final mission that was to prove just how deadly rocket firing Typhoons could be.

German armoured vehicles and tanks had been seen near Couverville, and eight Typhoons of 174 were ordered in to attack. Caught out with limited cover, the squadron fell on them, using their rockets to good effect, leaving a number burning. The army later confirmed that the squadron had actually destroyed 20 tanks during this attack. Pilot Officer Boucher was one of those eight pilots who had efficiently devastated that armoured formation.

The month finished with sorties against enemy concentrations at La Folie, woods at Esquay, and mortar positions south west of Caen. The airport at Caen had become a major obstacle during early July, as the soldiers of the 12th SS 'Hitlerjugend' held on fanatically. 174 hit strongpoints and mortar positions, and managed to hit a stockpile of stored ammunition which exploded in a spectacular fashion. Tanks coming forward to bolster the German defenders were picked off, and any enemy vehicle had to proceed with caution, as the allies had more or less total air superiority.

However, every time the Typhoon pilots lined up to attack a target, they would be confronted with flak and return fire of all calibres, and they flew through this maelstrom each time to deliver their attacks. So far during the Normandy campaign, only one pilot from 174 had been killed, but as the ferocity of the battles increased, the squadron were to have more fatalities.

Fifteen more sorties were flown by the end of July 17th, with the main targets being in the Esquay and St Martin areas. On the 18th, the squadron flew seven sorties in support of the army as they pushed around the eastern edges of Caen. They hit flak guns at Bretteville-sur-Laize, attacked around 30 tanks at Frenouville, leaving three on fire. As the army encountered the Bourgebous Ridge south east of Caen, they ran into well organised armoured formations, which began to take its toll on the British tanks. Two sorties were flown against German tanks at Bourgebus, one of those dealing with some that had been deployed in dug out positions.

Only two sorties were flown on July 19th, before bad weather hit again, keeping the squadron grounded until July 24th. It had been a near miss for the pilots who had flown the first mission of the 19th, as during their recce they had been attacked by American Thunderbolts. Luckily, they had inflicted no damage to the Typhoons and pilots. As soon as the weather cleared, the squadron were back on the offensive, flying six sorties on July 25th and 26th. Flying Officer Boucher flew two sorties on July 26th, against motor transport and tanks near Conteville, and attacked German troops forming up for a counter attack near Fontenay Le Mancion. Flying Officer Walter Vatcher DFC was shot down by flak and killed during the second sortie. Popular with the squadron, his loss was felt keenly.

Boucher flew another two sorties on July 29th, the second being a rocket attack against tanks at Gavray. During the first Gavray sortie, Flight Sergeant James Sommerville in Typhoon JP671, was hit by flak and the aircraft was set alight. It flew into a line of trees, tearing the wings off and burst into flames killing the pilot instantly.

The squadron finished the month off attacking troops and vehicles in the Caumont, Aunay -sur-Odon and Beny Bocage areas, without further loss. The squadron diary entry for July 30th said: -

"The squadron had a second great day of strafing the hun."

S/L Frederick Grantham DFC, George's Flt Cdr & frequent leader of the Squadron over Normandy.

Between August 1st and 4th, 12 sorties were flown, with seven of those being undertaken on August 2nd, where they continually hit targets near Vire, taking out targets on roads, in fields and orchards. On August 3rd, Pilot Officer Boucher flew his last successful mission, against tanks hiding in a wood in the Falaise area. His final sortie was flown two days later.

During the evening of the 5th, six Typhoons left the airstrip for an armed recce of the Thury Harcourt area. They climbed to 11,500 feet over allied lines, and intense light flak was encountered south of Vire. Pilot Officer Boucher (Yellow 1) in Typhoon JP500, was hit. The remaining five aircraft covered him as he flew west to the allied lines, before he bailed out, his Typhoon crashing at Mont de Cerise. All this time they were still being fired upon.

Pilot Officer George Boucher fell dead not far from the wreckage of his Typhoon, and became one of the 151 Typhoon pilots lost in Normandy in 1944. He wasn't the last from 174 to die in Normandy - Flight Sergeant Eric Taylor was killed on August 10th, and Squadron Leader Frederick Grantham DFC, a great friend of George Boucher, was shot down on August 14th, and baled out, but was tragically killed by troops while attempting to regain Allied lines two days later. He was a highly experienced pilot, with hundreds of flying hours and dozens of missions to his credit. He had led the squadron on many occasions on the run up to the invasion, and into the campaign. He also had several 'kills' to his credit, downing enemy aircraft on long range sorties earlier in the year.

News of his death reached the family, and his old school, who wrote about him in glowing terms, describing him as one *"who gave as much to the school as much as he took from it - and more."* They went on to describe him *as " somewhat reserved in temperament, but always sound, unhurried and reasonable - qualities which, together with calm courage he displayed with such marked success during his flying days…He always worked and played hard, giving his best : during the war he was engaged on dangerous tasks. He had many adventures, he was shot down and made good his escape through occupied country, but he spoke lightly of theses things, taking them as they came as he had always done - and now, though we shall not see his square solid figure again or hear his quiet voice, I'm sure he would not want any fuss. He was an most enjoyable boy and a fellow upon whom you could always rely."*

In January 1946, a letter was received by the Boucher Family, from one Claude Pailleux, who had been very close to the place where Pilot Officer Boucher came down. The letter gave details of the final moments of Pilot Officer Boucher. He wrote: -

" A few days ago the Mayor of Caligny secretary gave me your address. I write to you on the subject of the death of your relative, who fell with his aeroplane quite near our home. Pardon my not having written sooner, but I have just been demobilised. I now give you all the details about the events which happened on the day of the crash of your relative's aeroplane.

On Saturday 5th August 1944 towards 8.30 in the evening the machine fell in flames in a field of beetroot. The pilot however had time to jump by parachute, but without doubt too near the ground, for it had hardly opened. Living about 500 metres from the place of the crash I went immediately within 100 metres or so of the plane and saw the body of the pilot which was surrounded by a number of Germans, who were searching for his papers.

I succeeded in obtaining the name of your relative, but they would not give me his address. The Germans, as they usually do, took his ring.

At last, after much speaking I obtained his identity disc which I still possess, giving name and number of your relative. When night came the Germans left, leaving the pilots body. I carried him in a hand cart, and brought him to my parents house. The moment he jumped in the parachute he must have been already wounded, for he had one wound under the throat, and around it he had fixed a white silk scarf, but besides that he was not badly shattered. We were able to arrange his hands in a cross since they had not yet stiffened.

On the morrow - Sunday - we were able to make him a coffin of oak by a local carpenter to bury him worthily. We placed him at the foot of a little shrine at the edge of a highway in the hamlet of Caligny. A number of people were present at the funeral at 3.0 in the afternoon. He was buried in a shroud, and a score or so of wreaths were placed there; some by the fighting services, and some by the local members of the resistance. The little wooden cross had also been given, which bore his name, and at the other end of the grave one of the propeller shafts of his plane. He was therefore buried with all the respect due to his courage.

At that time the battle was raging in the neighbourhood, and several days later we had to leave the district, and we returned a fortnight later.

I also send you two photographs taken on the day of the funeral. You will see that your relative lies honourably. Also I send a piece of his parachute, which I was able to snatch from under the nose of the Germans, and also a stripe which he was wearing on his shoulder, and a little forgotten paper in one of his pockets. All the rest had been stolen by the Germans. I have also got his identity disc....I did not send it in this letter, for fear it might get lost.

A few months ago some British army officials came to identify your relatives grave; but as I was then mobilised, they were not able to have the papers of his which I kept.

My parents are looking after the grave, which is always beautiful and tidy. We will take care of it with all the respect due to a man who fell far from his country."

The Pallieux family continued to look after the grave, even after Claude Pallieux passed away. It was continued by his widow and sister up until the late 1990's, when the Mayor of Caligny took over the duties, and ensured the grave is still cared for by the locals.

In May 2002 the Boucher Family were present at the unveiling of a framed photo in the chapel at Caligny, depicting the Typhoon pilots of 174 Squadron, and a small plaque giving the details of the life and death of George Boucher. Amongst the crowd were three of his ex squadron members - Doug Oram, Jack Hodges, and Frank Wheeler, there to remember George, one of the many Typhoon pilots who never left Normandy.

P/O George Boucher's grave, marked by a propeller blade from his Typhoon, the day after his death. 60 years on appreciative locals still maintain the grave.
(Mike Boucher)

Chapter Nine

Born end educated in Hereford, he worked pre-war for the well known cider maker, Bulmers, prior to the outbreak of the war. He enlisted in the RAF in 1939, and was selected for pilot training. He successfully completed his courses, and had his first operational posting, flying Spitfires with 602 Squadron in late 1940.

He served with the squadron until early May 1941, when he was then posted to join 213 Squadron, who were in the process of preparing for a move overseas. Sergeant Henderson was one of the 28 pilots of 213 who embarked on the aircraft carrier HMS Furious at Liverpool docks on May 11th, destined for North Africa.

10 Days later, the Hurricanes took off from HMS Furious at dawn, led by a crew in a Fairey Fulmar, acting as navigator. The flight went via Malta, with the aircraft eventually landing at Mersa Matruh.

Logan Briggs recalled the Hurricanes the squadron were equipped with: -

"We had Hurricane Is from May 1941 until March 1942; on the carrier we had long range tanks otherwise we couldn't have flown from it to Luqa = 3 ° hours, or Luqa to Egypt = 5 ° hours. In the June 1941 desert campaign all aircraft had 2 x 45 gallon long range tanks."

The following day, six Hurricanes left for Abu Suier, with another detached flight sent to Bagoush, comprising of Flying Officer Temlett DFC, Pilot Officer Douthwaite, and Sergeants White DFM, Wilson, Lack and Henderson. They arrived in the middle of a blinding sandstorm, and Sergeant Henderson had to land some miles away to allow the storm to blow itself out. This flight was referred to as 'C' Flight, and was soon attached to 73 Squadron at Sidi Haneish, with the addition of Flying Officer Sowrey, and Sergeant Pound.

However, this attachment soon became a temporary posting to help out 73 Squadron. The first engagements took place in June, when on the 15th, Flying Officers Sowrey and Temlett DFC each destroyed a Bf 109, with the latter also claiming a Bf 110. Sergeant Wilson also bagged a Bf 109, but Pilot Officer Pound was reported missing.

The Faithful Few

He turned up two days later in Mersa Matruh Hospital suffering from leg wounds inflicted by our own anti aircraft batteries. Further missions were undertaken, strafing German troops and transport, but without additional loss to 213 Squadron.

After a short time in Egypt, news was received that the squadron were to be pulled out and sent out of the delta. On July 3rd they went to Haifa, with a detachment in Nicosia, and were engaged in a ground attack role over the next few days. Along with 260 Squadron, they attacked Meskine, Talia, Ryack, Fah and Aleppo over a period of three days.

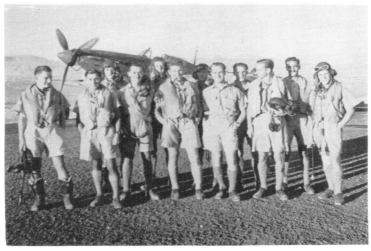

NCO pilots of 213 Sqn, Nicosia, August 1941. L-R: Sgts Edwards, Hancock, Marshall, PP Wilson, FA Wilson, Henderson, Lack, Stephenson, Ritchie, u/k, Sissons, F/S Wallace.

On July 20th, nine Hurricanes were despatched to Cyprus, and arrived with a ceremonial beat up of the area! Five of those aircraft were later used to form a flight at Famagusta for local air defence. Despite numerous patrols and scrambles, it wasn't until August 26th that Pilot Officer George Westlake destroyed an Italian Z1107 over the island, generating much press coverage into the bargain! While in Cyprus, the squadron still maintained detached flights from such places as Ismailia, Abu Zemina, Shandur and El Khanka.

During this time, many co-operation missions were flown with the Army, and airfield defences. Gunnery practice was frequently carried out in the form of 'shadow firing' where the shadow of an aircraft cast on the sea or ground was used as a target.

*Pilots at Nicosia, L-R: S/L MacDonald DFC, OC 213 Sqn, Sgt
Ritchie, P/O Douthwaite, F/L Lockhart, F/O Briggs, P/O
Westlake, Sgts Henderson, Stephenson, Hancock, Marshall, P/O
Pain; on wing: F/L Temlett; in cockpit: F/O Sowry.*

At the end of December 1941, the detachments were broken up, and the
squadron moved to LG 90, and detaching two flights - 'A' (with Sergeant
Henderson) to Khanka, and 'B' to Dekhelia. January 1942 saw 'A' Flight the
most active, flying numerous patrols, while Sergeant Henderson was scrambled
after an intruder on January 4th, but was unable to engage. During this period,
the conditions at LG90 were deemed as unsafe, as the airfield was covered in
areas of soft sand making manoeuvring, and take offs and landing dangerous,
so on January 14th, the squadron HQ moved to Idku.

*Sgt Henderson, El
Khanka, Egypt, March
1942.*

George Westlake recalled: -

*"Before going up to the desert though, we were
based at RAF Idku , just outside Alexandria
being used to try to intercept high flying recce
planes; Ju 86's specially modified to fly higher
than anything we had got. Their target was the
fleet in Alexandria Harbour."*

The Faithful Few

Logan Briggs again: -

"Those ops commenced at 15,000 feet, and gradually increased by increments of 2,000 feet until by early May we were stooging around at 29,000 feet (during the patrols over Alex we removed the long range tanks otherwise it would have taken 25 minutes to reach Angels 29!) I doubt if the ops room realised this because their radar was rather feeble. More success in shooting down marauding Ju 88's (from Crete) was achieved at the higher altitudes. I'm inclined to conclude that Hindoo claimed one destroyed shared with his No 1, one probable and one damaged."

Towards the end of January, the sorties flown by the squadron included practice bomber attacks on American B17's, night flying co-ordination with searchlights, and the usual scrambles, which were generally proving fruitless. The biggest problem the squadron faced was the amount of times the locals had tried to steal squadron property, including tents while the personnel were still in them! A raid by Military Police on a nearby village uncovered some of the missing property, and resulted in several arrests.

Weather conditions proved problematic, as did the effect of the desert environment on the Hurricanes - serviceability was at times poor, with the ground crews doing their very best to keep the aircraft running.

On January 28th, five Hurricanes flew to Port Said to relive 73 Squadron, who were in turn moving to the western desert, leaving only seven pilots at Khanka, with six aircraft. Things didn't improve, as interception exercises turned in near farces, and the locals stepped up their campaign of attempted thefts, getting away with at least one parachute. When scrambled against intruders, no contacts were made. It must have been a rather depressing time for the squadron. This theme, unfortunately, continued way into March.

While at Khanka, a captured Bf 109F paid them a visit, and was used in practice interceptions. There the pilots found out that although it was greatly superior in speed and climb, it wasn't so good in turns.

Despite no confrontations with the *Luftwaffe*, the squadron still lost two pilots in March. Sergeant Lee disappeared during a flight from Port Said to Idku on March 4th, and was last plotted at the eastern end of Lake Burrillas. Four days later Sergeant Howell crashed his Hurricane through the roof of the airmen's canteen during an air test, killing him instantly.

A second accident occurred on March 12th, when Pilot Officer Wilson collided with Sergeant Edwards during an exercise over Idku. Wilson had to bale out at 3,000 feet, and landed safely, only to be set upon by the locals who mistook him for a German pilot, but luckily, he was able to convince them of his nationality before they went too far.

On the plus side, the squadron were about to receive Hurricane IIs with the changeover to be completed by March 19th, with the pilots flying to the airstrip known as 'Kilo 8', to collect their aircraft and bring them back. At the same time a new patrol system was brought in, making it two aircraft on patrol as opposed to only one. The squadron maintained standing patrols over the coast, Alexandria Harbour, and Bar.

May opened with a change in fortunes for the pilots of 213. Sergeant Stevenson engaged a Ju 88 off Alexandria Harbour on May 4th, but was forced to break off after his guns jammed. Sergeant Hancock got better results on May 7th, damaging another Ju 88, before it got away. The next day, Flight Sergeant Horn intercepted a Ju 88 over Alexandria Harbour, and shot it down into the sea. Sergeant McKay damaged another Ju 88, aided by Pilot Officer Houle. From a period of frustration, the squadron were now having some success.

A second Ju 88 was shot down over the sea on May 11th, by Warrant Officer Wallace and Sergeant Hancock, it crashing into the sea 25 miles north west of Alexandria Harbour. Sadly, Flight Sergeant Horn, who had destroyed a Ju 88 only two days before, crashed into the edge of the lake on the southern boundary of the aerodrome, after his Hurricane had suffered engine problems. It had turned over in five feet of water and mud, and while he was extracted alive, he unfortunately died.

By the end of the month, the Squadron had flown a total of 833 hours during patrols over Alexandria Harbour, and had damaged two more Ju 88s, and destroyed another, having one Hurricane damaged.

Good news came the way of Sergeant Henderson, for on May 2nd, it was announced that after his interviews at HQ Middle East, he was to be granted a commission, rising to the rank of Pilot Officer. Also commissioned were Sergeants Hancock, McKay, and Ray Henderson's great friend, Ken Sissons.

For the first time since March 30th, the Squadron had to cancel its standing patrols due to serviceability hitting a new low, as the Hurricanes were taking a beating. While non operational, the Germans managed to bomb an ex Italian hospital ship, hitting the stern and causing damage. When the aircraft were serviceable, the squadron undertook several convoy protection sorties, but the enemy stayed well away on these occasions.

The squadron provided escorts for Field Marshal Smuts to Fuka on May 13th, and escorted him back on May 15th. He presented the flight commander with three bottles of whisky after landing, and as the squadron diary commented: "More of this will not be amiss."

By mid May, a return was requested of all pilots with over 200 hours of operational flying. Six pilots had over the required 200 hours, and they were given the option of going to instruct. Two pilots were said to be thinking about it, but in the end, they all stayed with the squadron, such was the need for experienced fighter pilots. Also, there was a change in leadership at 213, with Squadron Leader Kettlewell going to Ismailia, and command being taken by Squadron Leader Young DFC, from 73 Squadron, on May 20th.

During the morning of May 21st, Pilot Officer Henderson was scrambled to intercept a raider heading for the harbour. This was to be his first full engagement with an enemy aircraft, and he performed two attacks on the bomber, damaging it, before it dived away to escape. Sergeant Stephenson and Flying Officer Sowrey went one better, by destroying another Ju 88 south west of Burg-el-Arab during the afternoon. The following day, Ray Henderson and John Sowrey were, as the squadron diary put it: -

"...whisked off to the Egyptian State Broadcasting Co's studio to be 'third-degree-ed' re their combat yesterday. "Well, actually..."

Back at the Squadron, Flying Officer Sowrey and Sergeant Stephenson destroyed another Ju 88 during the evening of May 23rd. This time, the aircraft crashed into the sea, killing all on board. This was to be 213's last combat from Edku, as Squadron Leader Young DFC announced that a move was on the cards, this was confirmed on May 28th, when an advance party was scheduled to move to LG12. The move was carried out over the next three days, and went more or less to plan, apart from when their ground convoy was strafed by an enemy aircraft between Fuka and Daba. Last to move from Edku were the Hurricanes, leaving at 08.00 hours, and arriving at LG12 just under two hours later.

The Squadron later took over the North West corner of Gambut West, with the majority of the Hurricanes arriving there on June 4th. Despite several attacks

The Faithful Few

by German aircraft, including their regular pre-dawn strafe, they inflicted no damage. Three days later they flew their forst offensive sweep at between Acroma and Gazala. The formation was jumped by five Bf 109's, but suffered no losses. A similar action was flown on the following day, and once again the squadron was jumped by Bf 109's, with identical results.

213 scored a kill on June 9th, when acting as top cover for 73 Squadron over Bir Hacheim. 12 Bf 109s, with a few Macci 202s attacked the formation, with the result that they destroyed one Bf 109 and damaged a Macchi 202, again without loss. The following morning, they engaged a formation of Ju 87s over Bir Hacheim. The escorting Bf 109s attacked the Hurricanes, and in the melee that followed, Sergeant Jackson was shot down and taken prisoner, with Pilot Officer Hancock, hit in the arm by an explosive bullet, managed to land at El Gubbi. Despite the injury, and the loss of blood, he still managed a perfect landing. Pilot Officer Sowrey had his Hurricane badly damaged and had to force land. Upon doing so, he was strafed by three Bf 109s. After they departed, he began to walk back, and had to make his way through a minefield before he returned to our lines. The squadron claimed three Ju 87s damaged, and a Bf 109 probably destroyed.

A later encounter with Bf 109s resulted in damage to one of the Hurricanes, and left the Germans with at least three damaged aircraft.

By June 12th, the German forces were beginning to push forward, and the number of sorties flown by the squadron started to rise. Four were flown on the 12th, with the last one of the day resulting in the loss of two Hurricanes and pilots. Pilot Officer Peter Wilson was shot down into the sea the next morning during a sortie over the Tobruk - Gazala road, and Flight Sergeant Halvorsen was forced to bale out of his aircraft, and ended up in hospital suffering from burns. They had run into Bf 109s from 2/JG27, with *Leutnants* Friedrich Korner and Arnold Stahlschmidt claiming the stricken Hurricanes.

More sweeps followed, the Army holding the line at El Adem, the Squadron continuing to support troops in Tobruk and the surrounding area. However, German troop and vehicle movements were increasing, especially towards Tobruk. Gambut West was also attacked several more times, with Bf 109s bombing the base on June 15th, inflicting casualties on 33 Squadron. Earlier, 'B' Flight had been despatched to operate from the satellite airfield to LG 75. The situation was beginning the deteriorate, but the squadron flew operationally, with Flight Lieutenant George Westlake and Flying Officer Logan Briggs each destroying a Bf 109 between Gambut West and El Adem on June 16th.

The Faithful Few

On June 17th, an emergency order was issued withdrawing the squadron to Sidi Azziz, for the Germans were beginning to make real headway, with sections of the front line collapsing, they were then sent to Sidi Barrani South, before going to LG 75. This was the start of the squadron's nomadic North African campaign, for they were to move many more times before it was all over. By the time Tobruk fell on June 21st, the squadron was operating from LG 12 and LG 76, before moving yet again to LG 07. During the move, the column of vehicles were attacked by German aircraft. They only operated there for a day, before having to return to LG 12 as an enemy force had advanced some 18 miles to the west, and a withdrawal was ordered. The next day, LG 07 was in enemy hands, and the squadron escorted the bombers to attack their old temporary base.

During a patrol on June 26th, with 12 Hurricanes, they encountered a flight of eight Bf 109s. Flying at 19,000 feet, the 109s were a good 5,000 feet below. This made a real change, for it was not often the Hurricanes were able to get into such a position, for it was always the German fighters who held the height advantage. Not this time, for the squadron made full use of their position, and bounced the unsuspecting fighters, destroying five and damaging one.

Logan Briggs had his opinion when it came to flying Hurricanes in combat: -

"Dicing in a 2c (invariably clapped out) with 109s cruising around 6,000 ft above you was an exhausting and demoralising experience".

During the early evening, they were again in action, this time against Ju 87s over Matruh, destroying three and damaging four, making it their most successful day of their campaign.

This was tainted by the fact the Germans had broken through at Matruh, and 'B' Flight was ordered to LG 05, with the rest of the squadron to follow on. They stayed there until the evacuation of Mersa Matruh caused the urgent move to LG 154. The pilots clashed with Bf 109s again over Mersah, and despite four putting in a determined attack on the flight, Pilot Officer Beedham and Flight Lieutenant Olver destroyed one each.

At the end of June, a new front line was established at El Alamein, with the squadron deploying the pilots in a pattern of alternate 24 hours of duty, allowing some to have time in Alexandria.

July opened with more sorties over the El Alamein line, providing escorts for bombers and sweeps of the battle area, but engagements of July 3rd proved to be a disaster for the squadron. During a morning scramble, five Hurricanes were attacked by 12 Bf 109s. Pilot Officer Henderson flying Hurricane BM972, suffered serious damage. Pilot Officer Boucher was shot down and wounded, baling out of BN128. Sergeants Aitken and Jones, along with Flying Officer Briggs, managed to get back, but Pilot Officer Henderson had to belly land in the desert some 30 miles west of Burg el Arab, suffering a blow to his head in doing so. Despite this, Henderson began the long trek back to safety, before running into the army many miles from where he came down. For this, he became a member of the 'Late Arrivals Club' (founded in 1941) which enrolled pilots and aircrew who had been shot down and walked back. He was awarded a certificate of membership, and a badge depicting a pair of silver flying boots with wings attached!

While he was in the desert, the squadron flew a late afternoon sortie, and were mauled by a flight of six Bf 109s. Flight Lieutenant Cyril Temlett DFC and Sergeants Gordon Boulton and John Ritchie were killed, and Pilot Officer Ken Sissons was wounded. Only Pilot Officer Avise got away unscathed. Further fatalities were incurred on July 4th, with the loss of Pilot Officer Don Rehill and William Thomlinson.

Ken Sissons wrote to John Sowrey from hospital about that afternoon engagement: -

"About a week ago a young F/O Walsh of 92 was admitted to the ward in which Boucher and myself are gracefully recovering from a 109 complex. He told me that you had to bale out again, so I thought I would drop you a line to say how pleased I am that you fooled the Hun. As you know, Temmy, Ritchie and Bolton were killed on the same show as me. Avise was the only one to get back. I was wounded in the leg but managed to crash land. Butch was put into the same ambulance as me (he had been shot down earlier in the day along with Hindoo) and we have been together since then. Today I got a letter from Hindoo who is suffering from concussion in RAF Annassia Hospital. We hope to go to the convalescent centre together. Thomlinson was killed the day after Tem, and Don Rehill is also dead. Bally was missing when Slater wrote me on the 16th. I am so sorry about Tem, just before he got it I was chatting to him on the blower and we were dealing very effectively with the Huns (originally they were 25+ to our five). Someone straggled and was attacked, I turned to poop at the attacker and unfortunately ran through the bullet stream which was not intended for me. Tem rallied the boys and the last words I heard him say was "cover Siss!, cover Siss!". Bolton crashed almost on top of me , and the other two were about half a mile away, flamers. Would like to hear from you John.

The Faithful Few

Butch sends his very best wishes and that goes for me too."

Logan Briggs summed up that time with 213 Squadron: -

"June, July and August were desperate months; we destroyed many aircraft but also lost many pilots. An entry in my Form 414 for July 3rd reads: 'Me 109's trail us for 20 minutes; P/O Boucher and P/O Henderson attacked twice; both shot up, both ok'."

Pilot Officer Henderson eventually made his was back to 213 Squadron, but was deemed 'tour expired' and posted away in August to operate as a ferry pilot, and later having a short spell on ground duties lecturing the RAF Regiment on health matters. This must have been difficult for a pilot who had been flying fighters since 1940, and now found himself warning others of the perils of venereal disease!

However, in mid 1943, he returned to flying, with a refresher course on fighters, with him getting to grips with the Spitfire once again. During this course, he came across his great friend and ex 213 Squadron member Ken Sissons, and upon completion, they were both posted to 92 Squadron at Lentini West on August 28th 1943. By now they had both been promoted to the rank of Flying Officer. Henderson made his first squadron flight the same day, in Spitfire JL213.

September saw the squadron begin to re equip with Spitfire VIII's, and it began its supportive role during the invasion of Italy. They became the first squadron of 244 Wing to operate in Italy, when they joined components of 239 Wing at Grottaglie, and there began to fly its first of many escort sorties. Missions were flown covering Kittyhawks to targets such as Avellino, Bari, Pangrazio and Foggia, and when permitted they flew fighter sweeps, though axis fighters were yet to engage with 92 Squadron.

Their first success in Italy came on September 19th, when Flight Lieutenant Hards and Second Lieutenant Gasson damaged a Bf 109. FW 190s were observed, but not engaged during a sortie to Bovino on September 21st, but by the end of the month there was no further combat. 'B' Flight had been despatched to Gioia Del Colle on the 22nd, with the remainder of the squadron following. They rounded off the month with Ken Sissons leading a party into Bari, where he managed to locate and purchase no less than 300 bottles of beer. That evening they celebrated Squadron Leader Humphreys' award of the DFC by getting stuck into the bottles. As the squadron diary put it:

The Faithful Few

"No difficulty was experienced in sinking available supplies of liquor."

A second trip was despatched to the brewery in Bari, only to find the NAFFI had got there, and taken over the place, thus preventing more beer coming their way!

Abandoned Bf 109F on an Axis airfield.

October opened with patrols over Brindisi, with a further 22 sorties being flown over Lake Verno and San Severo on the 3rd. Flight Sergeant Savill had to belly land his Spitfire due to mechanical problems, and returned to Gioia via

Wrecked Ju 88s, He 111s & an Italian Z1107.

mule and Jeep. The front line was extremely active near Temoli, and over a period of seven days, numerous escort flights were undertaken, covering Kittyhawks and Balitimores. Four Spitfires from the squadron caught a Do 217 near Termoli on October 10th, and shot it down into the sea, but before it had crashed, one of its gunners had managed to shoot down Flight Sergeant McKay.

Further flights were made over Bojano and Foggia, before the Squadron engaged again: Flying Officers Hazel and Dibden damaged an Me 210. The month closed on a sad note, when on the 28th, four Spitfires were sent off in bad weather to undertake a shipping recce. The flight

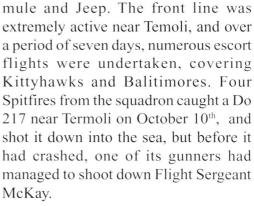

A 92 Squadron Spitfire prior to take-off.

got separated and only two landed safely. Flight Sergeant Askey and Flying Officer Sayle were missing. It was confirmed that Sayle had been killed when he crashed near Campobasso. Flight Sergeant Askey remains missing.

As the ground offensive ploughed on, the squadron continued escort duties, in particular numerous flights over the forward positions of the Sangro River. Enemy aircraft were pretty elusive during this period, with only two Bf 109's engaged on November 4th, without result. It wasn't until the end of the month that the first of the FW 190s were fully engaged, with Flight Sergeant Buchanan getting the drop on two FW 190s, destroying one. Although he only claimed it as probable, the army confirmed it had crashed. On November 28th, four Spitfires clashed with a mixed flight of Bf 109s and FW 190s over Torino de Sago, with Flight Lieutenant Nicholls destroying an FW 190, and with Flying Officer Dibden and Sergeant Peacock damaging one each. Warrant Officer Warren destroyed one of the accompanying Bf 109s.. Two days later, Lieutenant

Sachs destroyed an FW 190, during a morning sortie, and Flight Sergeant Buchanan and Flight Sergeant Brister diced with six FW 190s over Casoli. Flight Sergeant Brister was shot down and safely baled out, but not before he had despatched one of the FW 190s.

Ray Henderson's best friend, Ken Sissons.

More success followed during the first three days of December: Warrant Officer Warren damaged a Bf 109 on the 2nd; Squadron Leader Humphreys and Sergeant Hanson destroyed a Bf 109 each near Casoli on the 3rd, and Lieutenant Sachs destroyed two Fw 190s and probably destroyed another on the 5th. He closed to 150 yards, shooting one down, then spotted another on the tail of a Spitfire. Closing to near point blank range, he opened fire, with the result that the enemy aircraft blew up in front of him, debris smashing his windscreen and damaging his starboard wing. By now he had become the centre of attention for the remaining FW 190s who were opening up on him. They hit his Spitfire, blowing off the starboard elevator from his tail, and when he turned to counter another attack, he collided with one of the assailants, taking its tail and rudder off. With useless controls, Lieutenant Sachs parachuted clear. Squadron Leader Mackie also destroyed a Bf 109, making the squadrons score 11 aircraft in 11 days, without losing a single pilot.

Compared to the start of the Italian campaign where hardly enemy aircraft were encountered, it was certain that the Luftwaffe pilots were more than keen on joining combat as opposed to taking flight. On December 9th, eight Spitfires engaged 25 FW 190s and Bf 109s over Ortona, but they only resulted in managing to damage one FW 190. Similar clashes occurred twice on December 16th, with the enemy formations being excess of 20 each time. The Squadron claimed one Bf 109 destroyed, and two damaged, with a further three FW 190s damaged, with no loss in return.

These turned out to be the last combats for the squadron in 1943. By the end of December, they had flown 501 sorties, for a total of 819 hours airborne, plus a further 34 non operational flights.

The squadron was part of 244 Wing, and they were sharing Canne airfield with other Wing squadrons. The position of a flight commander had come up with 601 Squadron, and on January 5th 1944, Flying Officer Henderson was posted across the airfield to take up his new post. He also was promoted to the rank of Flight Lieutenant. 92 Squadron noted: -

"Hindoo to 601 Squadron. Very best wishes for future success."

The weather, and the poor condition of the airfield prevented 601 from operational flying until January 8th, when they sent aircraft over Yugoslavia, and later in the day, patrols over Ortona and Casoli. These locations were regularly patrolled up until January 16th, when the squadron began to move to Marchianese airfield, with 'A' Party setting off first. When at Marchainese, the squadron were now in the Fifth Army area, and were scheduled to assist with forthcoming special operations. 12 Spitfires flew in to Marchainese, with the remainder of the squadron, as 'B' Party, following on the 17th.

Only four patrols were flown in the period of January 18th - January 20th , plus a search for a crashed B17 and crew 60 miles off Naples, and a bomber escort to the marshalling yards at Avezzano on the 21st.

On January 22nd, the allies landed troops on the beaches at Nettuno, near Anzio. The Squadron flew cover for the shipping, and the landing forces, from dawn to dusk. Not one enemy aircraft was seen by the pilots, but it seemed that some had been seen in the Gaeta area, but no contact was made. Only one patrol was flown the following day, once again due to bad weather, but this had cleared up considerably by the 23rd, allowing sorties to be flown. The Squadron also took part in strafing targets, attacking vehicles, trains, and troops, with reasonable success.

The Faithful Few

The day got off to a bad start, when the Spitfires of Flying Officer Ibbotson DFC and Sergeant Henderson (yet another Henderson!) collided on take off, with Flying Officer Ibbotson's (JF754) being a total write off. Luckily both pilots were shaken, but unhurt. A second sortie during the early afternoon engaged 12 plus Bf 109s which were intent on attacking the shipping close to the Nettuno beaches.

Flight Sergeant Cooper closed on a Bf 109, and opened fire from 100 yards. Pieces flew off it, before it began to smoke and fall away. The pilot was seen to bale out, but his parachute failed to open. The flight leader, Flying Officer Blumer, also destroyed a Bf 109, before finding himself separated from the rest of the flight. He was then attacked by three Bf 109s, but succeeded in damaging one. A further three enemy aircraft joined in the attack. This time his Spitfire was hit hard: a cannon shell exploded in the throttle quadrant, severely injuring his hand, while both radiators were riddled and the engine temperature went off the clock. He broke away, making for the beaches at Anzio. When over the area, he baled out safely. Later admitted to an American Field Hospital, he had his third and fourth fingers of his left hand amputated.

Alex Blumer DFC recalled: -

"We were, at the time, a little disorganised having just moved over from the Adriatic and also had for a short while had a servicing and rearming unit on Anzio itself. I was evacuated from a field hospital in Anzio by destroyer, and finally hospital ship to the UK without rejoining the squadron."

601 Squadron continued to provide air cover over Nettuno, with the majority of sorties were carried out without any further incident. They lost another Spitfire on January 26th, but this was due to engine failure as opposed to enemy action. The pilot, Sergeant George baled out successfully. Beach head patrols continued until January 30th, when they escorted Mitchell bombers to targets at Cori.

By the end of January, they had destroyed 23 vehicles, three locomotives, and an ammo dump, and damaged a further 13 vehicles, 10 locomotives and four wagons. In the air, they had accounted for two Bf 109s and damaged another. As February opened, the squadron were back covering the beaches at Nettuno, but without direct contact with the enemy until February 7th. During an afternoon patrol, up to 15 FW 190s were seen to dive on shipping off Nettuno. Flight Lieutenant Henderson was leading a formation of eight Spitfire during this sortie, and he turned in to attack, getting within 60 yards of one of the FW 190s. He blew chunks off the target, before it fell away, and then engaged a second 190, hitting this one in the fuselage and wing roots. Flight Lieutenant Yarnall and Flying Officer Ibbotson DFC both claimed an FW 190 damaged apiece. The first Fw 190 attacked by Henderson was seen by the army to crash, confirming its destruction.

Flight Lieutenant Henderson continued to lead sections over the beach heads, and on escort and strafing sorties. The number of sorties had increased as the allies were trying to force inland, but were coming across stubborn resistance. Axis troops close to the coast were being dealt with by naval destroyers who had come in close to the beach, and who were shelling the Anzio to Genzano road. Despite the chaos on the ground, the skies over Nettuno were, for the main, enemy free.

On February 15th, the squadron CO, Major Osler destroyed a Bf 109 near Rome, and fought off another. He made three attacks on the second Bf 109, only for the pilot to bale out when put under pressure. The next day was eventful for Major Osler, for he had to return to base with engine trouble, and while making a dead stick landing the airfield was shelled. One shell dropped in front of his Spitfire, and it ran into the shell hole and somersaulted twice, before coming to rest in a crumpled heap. Luckily, Major Osler only suffered cuts and bruises and was soon fit for duty. The Spitfire, JF772 was a write off.

The next main engagement for 601 Squadron occurred on February 19th, while escorting Mitchells to Genzanoa. Fighters attacked the bomber formation, and at the same time, up to 15 FW 190s and Bf 109s attacked the Spitfires. Flying Officer Ibbotson engaged an FW 190, and then was attacked by three Macchi Mc 202's before dropping away from the dogfight. He rejoined the fray, and managed to get on the tail of a Bf 109 and shoot it down, it crashing into the woods north west of Anzio. Sergeant Henderson damaged a Bf 109 as well, leaving it diving away trailing black smoke.

They clashed with bomb carrying FW 190s over Nettuno the next day, without success. However, when the FW 190s were dived on, they jettisoned their bombs, and it appeared that in their haste, they had inadvertently dropped them on their own troops. Flight Sergeant Niven's Spitfire was hit by anti aircraft fire, forcing him to bale out, and land in the sea. He took to his dinghy, and was rapidly picked up by launch just off Felice Point. He was later admitted to hospital with shrapnel injuries to his chest and lags.

A second squadron pilot ended up being rescued from the sea just three days later on February 24th, when Lieutenant Pote's Spitfire suffered an engine failure,

The Faithful Few

177

and Sergeant Parker was caught off guard by a strong crosswind back at base, resulting in the undercarriage collapsing. By the end of February, the squadron had destroyed four enemy aircraft, and damaged four, but their strafing score had risen sharply: six aircraft on the ground, 29 locomotives, 51 wagons, 125 vehicles plus a fuel and ammo dump, all destroyed.

March began with more sorties over the Nettuno area, and the Anzio beach head, before the next dogfight on March 7th. Flight Lieutenant Henderson was leading eight Spitfires to patrol Anzio, when a mixed formation of Bf 109s and FW 190s were spotted flying line astern, and then dived under the Spitfire formation, heading for the beaches. Flight Lieutenant Henderson turned the formation to chase the enemy aircraft, and soon engaged them.

Flying Officer Ibbotson hit a Bf 109, which fell away and blew up in the air, and then he attacked another leaving it spinning away trailing smoke. Lieutenant Pote set another Bf 109 alight, hitting it in the engine and wing roots, and Flight Sergeant Eid attacked another, which blew up right in front of him, but the pilot managed to get out. Flight Lieutenant Henderson, with his No 2 Flying Officer Thomas half rolled down onto a pair of FW 190s, but he hadn't seen a pair of FW 190s which had appeared behind him. Flying Officer Thomas gave a warning, and Flight Lieutenant Henderson took violent evasive action, and made a steep climbing turn, and got separated from Flying Officer Thomas, who was in turn attacked by two enemy aircraft and was forced to defend himself. About three minutes later, Flight Lieutenant Henderson called up on the radio that he was over the Anzio area and that he had destroyed an enemy aircraft.

A second engagement ensued, and after that was fought off, the flight found that Flight Lieutenant Henderson was missing. He had in fact been shot down near Cori, and killed. He remained missing until 1947, when his body was located and exhumed, and he now lies in the Anzio War Cemetery.

Wing Commander John Nicholls was a Flight Commander with 92 Squadron, and later took command of 601 Squadron after Major Osler, before becoming the leader of 244 Wing. He remembered Ray Henderson: -

As far as I can remember, I first met Hindoo when I was sent on rest as a F/Lt to run a small training flight - more like a familiarisation unit for pilots on their way up to allocation to the squadrons along the North African coast at the end of April 1943. I think the place was called Sorman.

The Faithful Few

Hindoo, along with Curly Henderson, Jack Woollet and Ken Sissons joined us there, and they were already experienced pilots They were excellent pilots, and Hindoo was always a happy and exuberant type. Should I ever try to denigrate the cider industry, he would always threaten to take me down the Kings Cellar at Bulmers after the war. It was not to be."

F/L Ray Henderson & Bill Hayes of 601 Sqn, Casserta, Naples, 1944.

F/L Ray Henderson and groundcrew, February 1944.

Ray Henderon's grave at Anzio.

Chapter Ten

Originally born in Bewdley, his family moved to Rubery in later years, where his mother worked at the Longbridge Works. When he was 14, he took an apprenticeship at Longbridge, later volunteering for the RAF when he was 19. Called up aged 20, he began the process as a fledgling pilot.

"We had to do 12 hours flying at Cambridge to see if we had the aptitude or not. After that it was up to Manchester, where I was selected for single engined training out in South Africa. I went out there for 12 months, on Tiger Moths and Harvards, and got my wings, but I didn't do operational training until I got posted to Egypt, on 73 Operational Training Unit, and I flew my first Spitfire there."

Terry recalled his first flight in a Spitfire: -

"The first time I took off I pulled the hood up, and as I pulled it, it came off the runners. There I was about 500 feet up in the air , with my hand on the handle of this hood, and my other hand on the stick , and the aircraft is going up and down! I didn't know what to do, and I let the hood go. They never found it and when I landed, nothing was said."

Sgt Terry O'Reilly, 32 Sqn.

Upon completion of his operational training, Terry was posted to join 32 Squadron, based at Foggia, in Italy. It was equipped with Spitfire VCs and VIIIs, allowing the unit to fly ground attack missions, and escort duties when required. Warrant Officer O'Reilly arrived at the squadron in early July 1944, and soon was on operations. The squadron were operating as part of the Balkan Air Force, and were engaged in sorties over the Adriatic and into Yugoslavia.

Not long after joining 32, the squadron moved to Canne, near Termoli, flying its first sortie from there on July 17th 1944 - a sweep over Yugoslavia of Singe to Split, via Livno. Vehicles were spotted, and attacked, with a patrol bowser, a half track and a staff car being destroyed. The next day the squadron went on its first bombing mission, attacking the bridge at Prejidor, and a second flight sweep, destroying more vehicles.

32 Squadron: Sgt O'Reilley 4th left, sat on wing.

On July 21st, Spitfires were supplied for escort duties: -

"Six Spits from 'B' Flight were detailed for a special op. We flew to the Isle of Vis, refuelled with 90 gallon overload tanks and took off to link up with DC3's. My log book showed we escorted them to Tito's headquarters for them to take off several hundred wounded partisans. When we got there we just circled the emergency landing strip flying in pairs at different heights. I was at the lowest height, virtually low flying amongst the mountains. We escorted them back; whether Tito was aboard, going or coming - I don't know."

The Squadron suffered its first loss since the move to Canne. Flight Lieutenant Peter Quine had failed to return from a sortie over Knin. Heavy flak was encountered, and his Spitfire was hit in the engine. Attempting to force land, he crashed, tearing the wings off the aircraft, turning the aircraft over. The other pilots circled for a while, but did not see him get out. Sadly, he had been killed in the impact. A second Spitfire was lost the next day during a sortie to strafe and dive bomb Gospic Harbour, when hit by flak near Liuno. Flying Officer Wall, flying as No 2 to Squadron Leader Silvester, had his aircraft hit by small arms fire, and force landed near Prolog. He was seen to leave the Spitfire, and run to cover. The Squadron hoped that he might make it into the hands of the partisans. Warrant Officer O'Reilly participated on this mission, with his log book showing a flight time of 2 hours 25 minutes.

The Faithful Few

Two days later he flew down to Grottaglie, refuelled and swept the Montenegro area of Southern Yugoslavia, where he attacked and destroyed a truck. Up to the end of the month, the squadron attacked troops, vehicles and trains, without further loss. Good news came through that Flying Officer Wall had indeed made it into the care of the partisans, and that he would soon be back on the squadron.

Spitfire Mk VC of 32 Squadron kicks up dust as it taxis by.

Terry O'Reilly recalled: -

"Looking at my log book I noticed I had booked 40 minutes as the flying time from Italy to Vis. So we are talking about 10 miles across the Adriatic. My first operation from the Isle of Vis was shooting up German goods and troop trains which were usually armed with 20 mm and 40 mm ack ack. The targets were in the Mostar - Rastovicar - Jablanic areas. At 2000 feet or so a 40mm or 88 mm shell exploded behind my armoured seat, the kite was full of bits and dust, and the controls were all sloppy. I frequently think and wonder at the timing of the release of that particular shell, travelling that distance at a fair speed with the Spit moving at 240 mph, that minute fraction of a second made all the difference between talking for the rest of my life in a more or less ordinary voice, or a very high pitched one.

I put the Spit down on the island, taxied to the rank, got out and one of the lads said "Welcome to Vis, you have got over 30 holes in your kite, but we will soon patch it up for you. It will be ready late this afternoon. By the way the partisan Chief would like you to have lunch with him." The lunch consisted mainly of beans with 'Red Biddy'. I vaguely recollected climbing back into the Spit and landing back in Italy. By the way, if you ever got to Yugoslavia, don't be tempted to drink the local cheap wine!"

The Faithful Few

Warrant Officer O'Reilly flew again on August 2nd and 3rd, firstly on a combined operation on the Island of Korcula, some 40 miles South of Spilt, and then to Vis in preparation for a sweep on the Nebljusi - Knin area. The squadron strafed two targets setting light to German petrol storage areas. Terry remembered: -

A Spitfire VIII, note the external 'slipper' tank holding extra fuel to increase range.

"When I landed back at Vis, I found I had got a number of holes in my rudder, the flak had been fairly light, so they must have been fairly accurate."

For three consecutive days, the pilots attacked targets at the Humac Monastry, before taking part in bombing sorties to targets at Rogozinca. Trains were attacked on the line between Kauoth and Vitez, and the engine sheds at Kruseica were shot up, destroying one locomotive, and damaging another. Two Spitfires were also despatched to search the nearby islands for two German POWs who had escaped from the camp at Bisevo. They were spotted in a boat off Solta, and on the approach, both jumped overboard and scrambled ashore, so the pilots strafed and sank the boat.

By August 11th, Terry was regularly flying as No 2 to Flight Lieutenant Sylvester, (who took command on August 25th) and he had decided to go and dive bomb the German Headquarters at Kitstanje. It proved to be an eventful sortie for Terry: -

"As I pulled out of the dive and pressed the release button, my seat broke. I blacked myself out, injured my back and was virtually sitting on the floor of the cockpit and what made matters worse, I could not see out of the canopy. What happened to the kite whilst I was blacked out I don't know. When I came to I was automatically pumping the stick backwards and forwards and the kite was full of dust.

I turned the aircraft on its side and spotted a large lake, calling the CO on the R/T. I told him the problem and said I would meet him above the lake, the pair of us made our way back to Italy. The normal landings at our base at Termoli were always a bit dicey. You had to come in over a road and a hedge, and land on one of these short distance steel mesh runways. We used to come in 'hanging' on the prop at 80/85 mph. The kite normally stalled at 76 mph. Trusting my guardian angel I half side slipped it in with a bit more throttle than usual, then flattened out letting it drop onto the runway. The lads came out and helped guide me back to the rank. They had to lift me out of the kite."

August 15th was a busy day. A section bombed Kistarje, others bombed a saw mill at Nova Kasaba, and strafed a lorry at Han Pijesak. Other pilots took part in escorting rocket firing Hurricanes of 6 Squadron over the Northern Channel to Paj Harbour, where they sunk two schooners.

On August 21st, Terry took part in a different sortie other than attacking targets in the Maonski Channel: -

"I was detailed to be No 2 to Group Captain Selby who had been given the responsibility of finding an emergency landing strip in the heart of Yugoslavia for DC3's to land on. The actual strip would be cleared by the partisans. We would ensure that an approach and take off could be achieved. The duty of a No 2 is to protect at all costs the attack from the rear of your No 1. I am afraid on this occasion that duty was stretched beyond my interpretation of loyalty. The Groupy flew straight over Split, a major port at around 2000 feet and, of course they threw everything up at him, most of it exploding just to his rear, but he calmly continued even after I had called him up on the R/T, so I took evasive action, guided by my guardian angel and climbed up a further 1000 feet and watched from a safe distance. After what seemed time standing still, we were beyond their range and he had not been hit.

We found the area in amongst the mountains, a flat plateau near Polte, and it gave me quite a thrill to see bods on the ground waving vigorously. We did a couple of dummy runs to see if the approach was ok. However my admiration

A rocket-armed Hurricane of No 6 Sqn. No 32 Sqn's Spitfire provided escort for them over the Adriatic on numerous occasions.

went out to the crews of the DC3's - if they got it wrong, there was no running off the end of the runway, the end was a sheer drop of a couple of thousand feet. We flew back to Vis and I found myself down for Hurricane rocket escort the next day."

If ground attack operations were hazardous for the Spitfire pilots at the best of times, it could be worse for those flying the Hurricanes: -

"Our first job was to go in first to try and silence the 20mm and 40mm. We were in and out as quickly as we could but the poor old Hurricanes, because they were a bit ancient and leaded with rockets, used to stooge in around 160-180 mph. It was rumoured that no 'Peelo' ever completed a tour on their squadron. This may well have been an exaggeration, but in three days ops, three of the six got hit."

On the run up to the end of August, Warrant Officer 'Chop' Lamb was forced to bale out of his Spitfire after it had been hit on operations on August 25th. He was seen to bale out and land in a tree, but did not move. Pilot Officer Reginald Stringer, who had only joined the squadron on August 18th, died in hospital from Pneumonia on August 29th, and Flight Sergeant Peter Bignell was killed on operations on August 31st during a sweep in the Sjenica - Ivanjica -Pozaga area. Terry again: -

"Towards the end of August 1944, F/Sgt Pete Bignall, a New Zealander and my great friend, failed to return from Yugoslavia. I had the unenviable task of

writing to his parents. W/O Chop Lamb had also been shot down and we all assumed that he had bought it; however about a week later after one of our usual evening get togethers in our home made bar, stocked and operated by the Sergeant armourers, we retired to our tents. I slept in the same tent as Smithy, the squadron Chief Engineer Officer. Around 1 am Smithy was woken up by someone shaking him and saying "Smithy, 'Q' is U/S". After a few seconds it dawned upon us that 'Q' was the kite that Chop Lamb had been shot down in. Within moments everyone was awake and celebrations started with half a dozen of us sitting on top of a haystack, singing, in harmony (at least we thought that we were) . The others reacted by attacking us with water driven stirrup pumps, forcing us to retreat. It appeared the partisans had smuggled Chop Lamb to the coast, then he had come across the Adriatic, and had hitch hiked and walked back to the camp."

A B-17 takes-off behind Spitfires of 32 Sqn in Italy.

As September opened, there was a decided upturn in the number of sorties flown. Ground attack missions began to result in more targets engaged and destroyed. Hurricane escorts were again undertaken, with 6 Squadron revisiting Paj Harbour, hitting a barge, and later leaflet drops over Dugi. Terry undertook a leaflet drop, that didn't go to plan: -

"The CO asked me to do a quick recce for shipping in the Maonski Channel and to drop a large bundle of leaflets near Zadar.

I opened the hood, grabbed the leaflets and threw them out of the cockpit, well at least that was the intention; the leaflets flew back into the cockpit and down the fuselage. I quickly closed the hood and made my way back to Vis. Coming in to land, I slid back the hood and having done so, the leaflets rose from the cockpit floor and fluttered amongst the grapes and partisans; needless to say we did no more leaflet 'raids'"

The Faithful Few

The squadron lost no pilots on operations, and only suffered a handful of aircraft with minor damage, prior to the move to Brindisi. While based there, the squadron would later have two detachments at Metokhi and Araxos in Greece. Leaving on September 24th, the first operation from Greece was flown on September 26th by Wing Commander Woodruff and Pilot Officer Oates, performing a routine convoy patrol. However, upon return to base, rain had turned the airfield into a lake, and the pair had to land in fields some miles away. It became apparent their chosen landing ground would be under water during the winter season, so they moved what aircraft they could, and set about finding, and clearing a new strip.

On October 4th, a Ju 88 flew over the aerodrome, but got away into cloud before any aircraft could be got off. A second came over the following afternoon, and Terry was scrambled after it: -

"While sitting in the cockpit on readiness, a Ju 88 flew over the drome at about 1000 feet. I was first off the deck, but the kite I was flying was clapped out. Hal Oates in the other Spit kept losing sight of it, so on two occasions he had to line himself up with my kite. Eventually they both vanished, so I decided

A 'prang'!

to cut across country working it out that the Ju 88 needed to get back to Athens. After a few more minutes of flying, the 88 and I almost collided head on. I swung round in a tight turn, fired at it, knocking the odd piece off its wing, then it flew into the cloud. I followed, still firing, in the vain hope that I would hit it. I was still firing when I broke cloud, but instead of the 88 in front of me it was my chum Hal Oates in his Spit. Where he had come from Lord only knows. How he escaped the firing I don't know. Perhaps my aim was a bit ropey. The 88, we were told later, was shot down by some naval aircraft."

11 days later, the squadron lost its first two pilots while operating from Greece. While on convoy patrol, the Spitfire flown by Sergeant Jack Gooch suffered engine problems and the glycol temperature spiralled. He attempted to perform a force landing, and span in from 20 feet, killing him instantly. Sergeant Trevor Green was killed a few hours later when his Spitfire had fuel problems, causing the engine to cut. He attempted to ditch in the sea, but the aircraft went straight down, leaving only a patch of oil and a long range tank floating in the surface.

The Faithful Few

Further operations were undertaken over Athens, along with escort duties of DC3's, and once again, transport was targeted. On October 22nd, another pilot was killed, this time it was Sergeant 'Chat Chu' James, who was shot down attacking a train, that turned out to be heavily armed with flak guns. No trace of him was found, and it was assumed that he had crashed into the mountains. Terry was on that sortie and remembered: -

"I was on that particular operation on October 22nd that Nobby Clarke and I took on the South West part of the 50 mile stretch of railway line in the Larissa area. We spotted two trains pulling a large number of coaches a couple of miles apart, chugging towards Salonika. As I was in the better position to take the first train I shouted to over the R/T to Nobby to take the second. The train had pulled to a halt in flat countryside when I hit it with the 20mm.

To my astonishment as I drew rapidly close, in a brief fraction of a second I saw hundreds of German troops all standing in the open ground with nowhere to go, as if in a surrender position. Some people will not understand my next actions, but I am proud of what I did. I could have sprayed them all, but instead, continued the dive flattening out a couple of hundred feet above their heads, waggling the wings as I did so. It would have been slaughter, but I was not prepared to do this. Mind you, I did not go back to assess the damage to the train. When we all met up again two were missing: Chat Chu James and Gwyn Evans.

A number of lads got shot down near Larissa in Northern Greece, one of them being my room mate Gwyn Evans. The policy agreed amongst ourselves was that if you did not return, your chum had all of your clothing, etc, even the 48 Dollars from your escape pack. Because it was assumed after a week that Gwyn had 'bought it', I took the 48 Dollars with me to the Kitkat Nightclub for the lads to have a good night out. Just before we were due to leave, who should appear on the cabaret floor? It was none other than Taffy Evan. He had ridden all the was down from Larissa on the back of a donkey. He got his shirts and pyjamas back, but not the Dollars!"

On November 13th, the Squadron moved to Sedes, not far from Salonika. There the returned to flying sweeps onto Yugoslavia, attacking the German withdrawals. The day before, Terry was again airborne: -

"On November 12th I was detailed to go find the latest position of the German withdrawal. My No 2 was an Australian named Bill Cross. After flying for 20-30 minutes above fragmented cloud, with complete faith in my navigation and

map reading, I dived down through a hole in the clouds to about 2000 feet and found that I had not a clue as to where I was. But just at that moment all hell was let loose, which should not be happening because we were nowhere near the German withdrawal. Whilst all this was going on, Bill Cross called me up on the R/T to tell me his engine was over heating with a suspected glycol leak, so I told him to return. Still more puzzled by the heavy ack ack, I soon discovered that I was miles off track and to the South East of Skopje. I got back on to track North of Skopje into the area occupied by the Germans, and proceeded to my target area.

I was fired upon by 88mm guns, the great puffs of black and grey smoke on my starboard side. I felt elated because although they were spot on for height they were a few hundred yards short of their target. This continued for about a minute, until suddenly one exploded a few hundred yards in front and bang on track. I left in a hurry, putting the aircraft on its back. I got the picture of the retreating Germans a few miles further on, so I returned to avoid the flak area. As I flew over Skopje I saw the Germans blow up the bridge just as I arrived South of the town. Knowing that I was in 'no mans land' all the way back to Salonkia, I went down to a couple of hundred feet flowing the main road. I then came across one of the most amazing sights of my life. Mile after mile of Cossack Horseman. Thousands of them coming from the area where I had previously been fired upon. They had probably never seen a Spitfire before so they took no chances. Rather than have a repeat performance, I waggled my wings vigorously for mile after mile. I don't know who was most surprised - them or me."

Operations carried on up the end of November, with only the weather hampering flying, and only one Spitfire had been lost in November, that being the one flown by Flight Lieutenant Rake. Wounded by flak, he had force landed, and had been treated by Bulgarian Cavalry. After a short hospital stay, he returned to the squadron on November 30th, escorted back by partisans.

Operational flying was somewhat restricted, and it was a quiet start to the month, Terry said this about that time: -

"It might be of interest to recall that during the weeks leading up to Christmas 1944 and the New Year, we did very little flying due to over a foot of snow on the runway and the surrounding area. Boredom was beginning to set in, even the weekly dicey drive in a lorry into Salonika began to lose its attraction. By day, due to the intense cold we were forced to seek logs to keep our log furnace going in our American School billet. One day we organised two of the Squadron

lorries to set off up into the mountains. After about an hours drive we drove through what we thought was an unguarded checkpoint. I was on the second lorry seated on the tailgate holding onto a rope, when after passing through some 30 yards beyond, a figure ran out and dropped to his knees, and put a round up the spout ready to fire.

He had obviously shouted halt - we were still moving. I think it was the loudest yell I have ever given when I shouted to the driver to stop. At the same time other guys were banging on inside the cab. I dropped off the back, gave a salute and signed the paperwork and off we went, coming back later laden with tree trunks ready to chop up later.

A few weeks later the logs had gone, a joint decision was made to chop down some of the telegraph poles on the road to Salonika as they did not have any wiring on. So we set off and had chopped down a number when we came to the top of a hill. A few hundred yards in front of us were members of the Indian Army putting up telegraph poles. We beat a hasty retreat."

32 Sqn Spitfires on a former Axis airfield.

They stayed at Sedes until their next move, this time they were off to Ramat David, in Palestine. Arriving on February 25th. As the squadron diary put it: -

"No flying was carried out due to the state of the aircraft picked up the Repair and Salvage Unit. Ramat David lent the squadron some Greek personnel and a few RAF bodies to try and get the aircraft shipshape pending the arrival of the squadron personnel."

The remainder of the squadron reached Ramat David on March 13th 1945. More serious flying commenced, mainly on recce sorties, so the pilots could fully familiarise themselves with the area, ready to take up the role as an 'internal security squadron'. April saw the flying increase, and numerous exercises were flown in cooperation with the Army. On May 8th, the Station Commanding Officer announced the surrender of Germany. Official permission had been received that there would be two days holiday on May 9th and 10th, and all personnel except those on essential duty were released at once. No 32 Squadron weren't destined to go home in the weeks that followed, however, for they stayed in the Middle East for some years to come. Terry O'Reilly left the Squadron in April 1946, (becoming one of the longest serving pilots on the unit), but not before Squadron Leader Silvester had written this comment in his log book: -

"W/O O'Reilly has been with the squadron as long as I have commanded it and has considerable fighting experience. At all times he has shown himself to be a good and reliable pilot."

Returning home in October 1946, Terry got married, and lived in Northfield for three years before moving back to Bromsgrove and setting up home on the Charford estate, where they later took over a shop and Mrs O'Reilly became a draper and sub postmistress, and ran the Post Office for about 18 years. Terry worked as an engineer for the Austin Motor Company, later becoming British Leyland.

However, in 1960 Terry O'Reilly became involved in politics at a local level, and there started a long an illustrious career involved in local government, where he was voted in as a County Councillor, for Bromsgrove, and when the counties of Hereford and Worcester joined in the early 1970's. During his time in the pre Hereford and Worcester days, he was Chairman of Further Education, and Bromsgrove College of Further Education.

Local government reorganisation loomed again in 1998, when Hereford and Worcester went their separate ways, and Terry became the last Chairman of Hereford and Worcester County Council prior to the split. He served his year in office, and retired from the council. He still displays an energy and keeness for his time serving as a Spitfire pilot, and his memories have been a great help in the completion of this chapter. Back in 1944 he took on a challenge and served his country, and upon return in the post war years, he served his town and county with just as much selfless vigour, and he is somebody who we all should be proud of.

Chapter Eleven

Sid Cleaver was born and grew up in Bretforton, in the heart of the vale of Evesham. Educated in Evesham, he joined the RAF in 1943 and was selected for pilot training. Shipped out to Canada, where he did his initial training, gaining his pilots wings before returning to England.

Sid Cleaver receives his 'wings' in Canada, 1944.

Sid Cleaver at the controls of a Harvard whilst training in Canada.

After a short spell back home, he was posted out to a fighter Operation Training Unit in Egypt, where he finally got to grips with the Spitfire. Sid remembered: -

"I'd already had a trip in a Hurricane, so I had that feeling that it wasn't like a first time, but when I got out of the aircraft it felt a lot different, and looking into the cockpit there wasn't a lot of room, but I was familiar with the cockpit layout as I'd already had time looking at one in the hangar, so I was familiar with all the bits and bobs, so it was a matter of getting in to it and getting it moving. This was a Fayed, near the Great Bitter Lakes, and we only flew in the mornings as it was too hot later in the day.

A Spitfire V has only got one radiator and when you're on the ground the oleo leg is right in front of the intake, so we were warned that we only has so much time to on the ground from start up to take off before the coolant temperature got out of range. We didn't get a lot of time to get accustomed, like as soon as we started up, our first thoughts were to get out to the end of the runway and get off. It got a bit dodgy I tell you! Once or twice when I took off I was watching the temperature needle, and as you took off it went up faster, then it would stop and come back down again. There were a few mishaps due to internal coolant leaks, but as to the actual flying it was much different to the Hurricane - the Hurricane you flew like getting hold of a pudding stick, but with a Spitfire it was just pressure, that's all. You hardly moved the stick.

When you got in it, you were almost a tight fit, and when you put the straps on, you know, you are as one. I felt it was a nice feeling but others felt it was a bit claustrophobic."

After completion of his Operational Training Unit Course, Sid was posted out to join 607 Squadron in December, based at Sapam, India, and under the command of Squadron Leader G Davies. The squadron were equipped with Spitfire VIIIs and were just about to embark on numerous escort sorties to Dakota transports dropping supplies to troops at the front line. It took a while to get used to the area, and Sid flew his first familiarisation flight on December 5th 1944, and had his first operational 'scramble' on December 12th in Spitfire LV654, when the squadron attempted to counter a flight of Oscars near Tamu. They were later reported over Kalewa, with the squadron flying to Maukkadaw before returning to base. It transpired that six Oscars had attacked a new pontoon bridge over the Chindwin, and had damaged it, but neither 607, nor 17 Squadron had spotted them.

Problems began to arise with the Spitfires using long range fuel tanks, especially when switching over from mains to long range. The sixth such incident resulted in Warrant Officer Townsend's engine cutting, with him stalling attempting a forced landing back at the airstrip. The Spitfire was written off, and Warrant Officer Townsend was admitted to hospital with minor injuries. Escort missions took the pilots to Taungdut, out over to the East of the river Chindwin, Chingyaung, Taukkyan, Thaungdut, Simlamaung and Naunkang.

By December 15th, the XIV Army had pushed the Japanese from its positions, and the squadron had been forbidden to use their long range tanks after their spate of problems. This tied them down to the Imphal Valley until the Army enter the Schwebo Valley, and capture some of the airstrips there.

The first fatality since Sid arrived on December 5th occurred on December 23rd when Sergeant Jackson had his engine cut out during an escort sortie. He had attempted to re start the engine, but had insufficient height to do so, and crashed into the jungle killing him. A second pilot, Warrant Officer Buck, was lost on

The Faithful Few

December 29th when he crashed after take off from the airstrip, and had impacted only 200 yards from the southern end of the strip.

Sid remembered the Dakota escort sorties: -

"During the escorts, there were occurrences with the odd Japanese aircraft, but just my luck I suppose, I didn't get involved, and I actually didn't see any enemy aircraft. Others did, but not me."

More Dakota escorts were undertaken between January 7th and 16th, with the squadron moving forward to Tabingaung in Burma, some 47 miles North West of Mandalay. Sweeps of the Mekteila airfields followed, but no enemy aircraft were encountered, however, the Spitfires were shot at by gun emplacements. Sid flew a Rhubarb on the roads between Mandalay and Myingyan on January 20th, with Flying Officer Round, Flight Sergeant McA.Boyd and Warrant Officer Peters. They shot up a tented camp, destroyed three lorries and some camouflaged bullock carts.

More Rhubarb sorties were flown over the next few days, shooting up enemy vehicle movements and attacking targets of opportunity. Two sections assisted Hurricanes bombing Japanese positions across the Irrawaddy River, and at subdued the enemy who had been firing upon Dakotas dropping supplies to the Army on the East bank of the Irrawaddy. On January 30th, five spitfires from 607 performed the first dive bombings by that type in Burma, making four direct hits on their target. Diving in from 9,000 feet, they released their single 250 lb bombs before returning to strafe the target for good measure.

On February 1st, a lone Lily bomber managed to bomb the airfield, releasing a canister of bomblets. It dropped in the dispersal area occupied by 17 Squadron, destroying one of their Spitfires, and damaging another three. The canister had not opened properly when it hit the one Spitfire. If it had, it was accepted that it would have caused a lot more damage. Three other Allied airfields were also bombed, with casualties inflicted at one.

The squadron were called upon to bomb and strafe gun flashes East of the Kyaukmyaung Bridgehead, with sorties being flown throughout February 8th, hunting for targets. It was reported the Japanese had the largest concentration of 75 mm and 105mm guns known in Burma, and it was essential to locate and destroy them. As Sid put it: -

The Faithful Few

"We certainly kept a look out to try and spot positions. If we saw a flash, then we tried to get down and sort them out, doing our best to shoot them up."

Four aircraft were scrambled to assist 17 Squadron who had engaged Oscars on February 17th, and it was the first time the pilots had seen enemy aircraft since June 17th 1944! They clashed with the fighters, but made no claim, however 17 Squadron destroyed two Oscars. Warrant Officer Newsam failed to return from this combat. The month finished with more ground attack sorties, as the Army began to push the Japanese troops back.

During the first five days of March, 607 flew 95 sorties, destroying numerous lorries, bullock carts, a bridge, and even shooting one Japanese soldier out of a tree. The constant attacks on troop and vehicle movements were having the desired effect, for fewer were being seen, having been forced to stay off the roads and in the jungle.

Pilots of 607 Sqn. Sid (3rd right) only just managed to get in the picture having landed from an operational sortie only minutes before!

On March 17th, Flight Lieutenant Logan Briggs, the 'B' Flight Commander, left the squadron for a spell of leave (eventually leaving altogether on April 14th) after nearly four years overseas. A desert veteran, he had been posted out to South East Asia Command, and joined 607 Squadron: -

The Faithful Few

"I had the privilege and honour of serving with 607 Squadron in India and Burma. How delightful and thrilling it was to drive around over the Irrawaddy and Chindwin in a superbly smooth Spitfire VIII. Surely this was the most impeccable, manoeuvrable and dynamic of all the marques. The styling was significantly better too, the pointed broader rudder, twin radiators and elongated air intake all enhanced its good looks. By the time I left, we had complete air superiority, with the rare appearance of the 'honourable' pilots of the Imperial Air Force in their Oscars, Zekes and Zeros."

The month ended on a sad note, with Warrant Officer Davison being killed during a VIP escort sortie on March 27th. His Spitfire was hit by a shell in the starboard wing root, causing it to flick over and nearly collide with his No 2, Sergeant Page. A total of 676 sorties had been flown by March 31st , covering 1231 flying hours, a new monthly record for the Squadron.

April was much quieter, with only 383 sorties, covering 696 hours, being flown. There were still hazards - Sergeant Vale collided with a truck as he came into land on April 2nd. The Spitfire ended up in its back, and on fire. Sergeant Vale was pulled clear by Flight Lieutenant Rewan and Leading Aircraftsman Sullivan, suffering cuts and burns to his hands and arms. The driver of the truck was killed. Flight Sergeant Connor had to bale out of his Spitfire after engine trouble on April 15th, managing to extract himself at just 500 feet. Landing on 50 yards away from the burning wreckage, he was spirited away by locals, and returned to Kyaukee by bullock cart, before re joining the squadron.

By now, Sid was Warrant Officer Sid Cleaver, in 'A' Flight under Flight Lieutenant Noble. The Squadron's CO was still Squadron Leader Davis.

The weather played a significant part in operations in Burma. Rain was of the monsoon variety, and it had the habit of flooding some of the forward airfields. Some Spitfires were actually tipped over when trying to land, as the standing water became too deep, causing them to nose in as soon as the wheels hit the water. By now the squadron were operating from Dwelha, their fourth airstrip since early December. Moves were again afoot in early May, with the aircraft operating from Tennant, then later at Thedaw, before moving to Mingladon, and old ex civilian airstrip on May 14th. There, in the middle of a fierce storm, they took over the buildings, with the Officers in a two story brick house, and the NCOs in a bungalow. This was luxury compared to previous living arrangements.

When established, the squadron started flying patrols, and dropping supplies from containers fixed to their bomb racks. The odd VIP escort was also flown. Sid recalled when he was detailed for such a duty:

"We got many VIP escorts - we had General Slim and Mountbatten. There was usually just the two of us, and the last one I did, I was No 1, leading, covering Mountbatten. He took off from the river at Rangoon (in a Sunderland) and I had to fly him just so far out to sea, as he was on his way out to Ceylon. It was just to make sure they got out of the area safely."

On May 25th, the Squadron held a farewell party to Squadron Leader Davis, who was leaving, handing command to Squadron Leader Humphreys, with him flying on operations on the last two days of the month, when the squadron managed to fly 36 sorties, despite the fact most of the dispersals were a quagmire. Flight Lieutenant Round amused himself in the meantime by making and sailing paper boats on the pools!

Sorties at the start of June included patrols and more supply dropping. Warrant Officer Farrell had a lucky escape on June 3rd when his Spitfire suffered a tyre burst on take off, careered into a ditch, and caught light. He managed to extract himself with slight burns and an injured shoulder. The next day, Flight Sergeant Simpson's Spitfire was hit by machine gun fire over the Sittang, but he managed to return safely.

The ever popular Flight Lieutenant Jimmy Round DFC was killed on June 5th after taking off on an early morning sortie. While completing a turn, and hit a tree, causing him to go straight in. A search party was despatched, and he was later found dead in the remains of the cockpit.

Concerns were raised about the Japanese build up on the east bank of the Sittang River. It was thought they were massing in an attempt to cross to support their troops withdrawing from the opposite bank. Orders were issued for patrols to destroy river craft and report any movement seen. Six craft were destroyed on June 17th, and further 41 destroyed or damaged on June 19th, another 30 on June 21st and 19 on June 23rd.

These offensive Sittang River patrols continued to bear results, with several camps being liberally shot up. The squadron lost two aircraft on June 25th when Flight Lieutenant Shi Sho had to return to base after his Spitfire suffered engine problems while on patrol. He turned for home, while Flying Officer Andrew continued with the flight. Neither returned to base. Flight Lieutenant

Pidgeon had a lucky escape the same day, when his Spitfire suffered a premature cannon explosion which split the leading edge of the port wing, but unlike Andrew and Shi Sho, he made it back.

The Sittang offensive continued into July, before the squadron went to support the Army in the Sittang Bend at Nyaungkashe, where a Battalion had been surrounded by Japanese troops. British troops were able to withdraw from Nyaungkashe two days later, and the squadron spent most of July 8th attacking the area.

Later sorties took the pilots to Amherst Harbour where they shot up moored Sampans, and attacked a village on the Salween River, North of Moulmein causing many Japanese casualties. More camps were attacked on July 12th, but Warrant Officer Goodenough was hit by return fire, crashed and was killed. Buildings held by the enemy at Pawnggyi Kyaung were bombed as were others in the Myitkyo area. A supply drop was carried out in adverse weather conditions to Captain Lindsey and his 'V' Force guerillas who had killed nearly 700 Japanese in a the last few days, and had run out of ammunition. Flight Lieutenant Colebrook and Flight Sergeant Dobbins got to the drop zone, flying under 10/10ths cloud at just 200 feet, and dropped in over 1,000 lbs of ammunition.
Their campaign finished off with sorties to Posabe and Winpa, where they attacked a concentration of over 4,000 troops, and targets Sitthwagyan, blowing snipers out of their trees. On July 31st, the Squadron Diary recorded: -

"Thus comes the end of the squadrons war history.. A good record and many are sorry that it has to be disbanded but RAF policy we realise can't stand on sentiment. Good luck to those who go to other jobs and a speedy finish to the Japanese is our wish. Maybe 607 will again be used as a county squadron and fly in peace with the object of using the air to better means and keeping that peace we all want."

Ironically, after all the sorties over Burma, it was a post war incident which came the closest to killing Sid. While serving in Naples in March 1946, he was given leave back to the UK, but had to find his own way back out to Italy. He managed to get a flight on board a Dakota taking a General out, along with a load of Dettol!

Near the Italian coast, one, then both engines 'ran away' causing the aircraft to lose height. The pilot just managed to make the coast and belly land at Anzio, right in the middle of what turned out to be an old minefield. The load of Dettol slid down the middle of the aircraft, jamming the crew cabin door, forcing the flight crew to escape from the roof hatch. Sid and the others (with General in tow) extracted themselves from the rear and got clear with minor bumps and bruises.

The Dakota having forced-landed in a minefield!

Sid returned home in 1946, and went back to civilian life, for good. Or so he had thought: -

"I was actually at work in the fields at the back of the village and there was a big exercise at that time and we were watching shoals of Meteors going over. I never dreamt I'd soon be flying one. One day I got home, and there was a letter for me, and in it they were asking me if I'd like to go back and do another period of service."

It was 1949, and with tensions between the West and Russia, the RAF were beginning to recall pilots and aircrew back to the service.. Sid agreed to return, and soon was at the Flying Refresher School at Finningley. Sid: -

"Everybody else went to a conversion unit to go onto jets, but they said 'you're not a rookie, you're going to go straight in there'! So two of us joined 92 Squadron at the same time. The other chap had been flying recon Spitfires during the war and he'd got a DFC. Of course we were put in front of the CO and asked if we had flown jets, and of course we said no - last thing we flew were Spitties! He said "well, it's all the same, you get in the cockpit and hopefully all the rest will follow". So the CO took over the other chap and got him away in the Meteor, and the Flight Commander took over me".

92 Squadron had a novel way of getting pilots accustomed to twin engine flying, for they had on charge a pair of Mosquitoes: -

"You see I'd never flown a twin engine before, and they thought it would be best if I did an hour or two on the Mossie and do a bit of single engined flying (asymmetric) and then carry on with the Meteor."

Flying Meteors was at times not a pleasant experience for Sid: -

"I wasn't happy with the Meteor IV. It hadn't got the range - it only had about 45 minutes flying, and in Burma I could get 2 ° hours out of my Spitfire VIII. If you came back , say in bad weather, low on fuel and you didn't get in first time, then it became an emergency!"

Sid stayed with the squadron until 1950, until one day he was called in to the CO's office and told that he was being posted out to Air Firing School at Acklington to fly target tugs: -

" The CO explained we were only at the squadron to get jet operational again, and I'd only got a short service of four years and he thought I'd be more use doing this for the remainder of my time. But as it turned out I quite enjoyed it."

The unit were equipped with Tempest Vs and later towed with some Meteors. Sid flew his first Tempest on July 12th 1950. They also had on strength a few Martinets, and Spitfire XVIs.

Sid Cleaver taxying a Tempest at Acklington prior to a towing flight.

The Faithful Few

" I liked the Tempest, but it was quite a handful, they could take over. The thing I remember most was at the end of the landing run you'd think that's it, everything hunky-dory, and the thing would swing and you had a hell of a job to control it. Just when you thought you were safe, things started to happen. You had to be on your toes right until you stopped. I also flew a Spitfire 16 from Acklington down to Lyneham, to the MU there. Of course I came over home with it. That was the only Spitfire I ever flew over home."

The list of squadrons who attended AFS Acklington reads like a Battle of Britain who's who, with 1, 19, 23, 41, 56, 65, 66, 151, 222, 257, 504, 600, 604 and 615 all attending. There they used to conduct the firing out over the North Sea, however it was a very busy time, and there was always room for error on behalf of the attacking pilot: -

"You always watched them coming in, because if they started coming in too line astern you could always turn away. Of course I've done some myself - firing at targets, and if you're happy with your sights, you tend to hang on a bit longer and all the time you're getting more and more line astern. A friend of mine, flying a Meteor, came back and when they were examining his plane they found bullet holes in one of his tailpipe. We towed either flags or gliders on flights. A flag was like a banner type target, the glider almost identical to a small V1, like a torpedo shape with squared wings and tail and it was rigged to be stable in the air. It was filled with microphones and connected to us along the cable into our radio, and the actual firing was recorded on a wire tape back at the station in the control tower, so that they could even record near misses."

Sid finished his second part of his flying career with the AFS at Acklington, and as before returned to civilian life near Evesham, continuing in market gardening and still living in the same village, just doors away from his old family home. Sid wasn't a decorated pilot, flying over Europe, but his efforts in the India and Burma, in hard arduous conditions, in unforgiving territory, and against a merciless enemy, must never be forgotten.

W/O Sid Cleaver upon conclusion of his second and final period of RAF service.

Chapter Twelve

As you can see from previous chapters, the service careers of the Worcestershire pilots varied, but it must be remembered that many trainee fighter pilots did not even make it to operational squadrons, having been killed in training accidents. The nearest fighter Operational Training Units were at Aston Down in Gloucestershire, and Rednal in Shropshire, and you only have to look through their operational diaries to see just how many were killed before reaching a squadron.

Sgt John Silvester on leave at his family's farm during training.

John Silvester shortly after receiving his 'wings'.

One such pilot was Sergeant John Silvester from Ombersley. Educated at Hartlebury Grammar, he was a natural athlete who went on to break many school records. He completed his education at Salter College, and did three months at Pershore Senior School. Prior to joining up, he was teaching at Bridge Street Boys School in Redditch, and had played hockey at county level, as well as playing for the Wolverhampton Wanderers Colts.

He joined the RAF on May 28th, 1940, and had been selected for pilot training, later being earmarked as a fighter pilot. He had joined 58 Operation Training Unit at Grangemouth, to gain experience on Spitfires before being posted to a squadron. He was very close to completing his course, when he was killed. He had taken off from base on February 14th, 1941, to complete a navigational exercise. Not long after, his Spitfire, L1059, was seen to dive into the ground, killing him. He was 22 years old. His body was returned to the family, and he was interred in Ombersley Church Cemetery.

John Silvester's grave at Ombersley Church.

Others had incredibly short operational careers - a good example is that of Pilot Officer Ralph Price (known as Ricky) from Evesham. He had survived his training and received his first posting to 504 Squadron in March 1941, but made few flights - his first being in Hurricane P3151 on March 19th. It wasn't long before he was posted from 504 to join 247 Squadron on April 25th, at Portreath, prior to them moving to Predannack on June 18th.

Here he was more fully engaged, flying coastal patrols, convoy cover, and providing standing cover over local harbours. However, his one and only engagement with the enemy came on July 31st, and was one in which he would lose his life.

The squadron diary recalled the incident: -

"During the night of 31st July/1st August Blue Section were ordered off at last light to patrol below cloud base south of the Lizard. Cloud base is 400 ft and conditions are generally poor. Blue 1 F/Lt Carver sights a Do 17Z and attacks. He uses all his ammunition and sets an engine on fire. Blue 2, P/O Price then followed up the attack and in doing so overshoots and rams the Hun. Ricky Price loses half a wing and crashes - there being little hope and no time to bale out. The Hun is confirmed as coming down in the sea. Our feelings are of exhilaration on a confirmed and sorrow at Ricky's unfortunate accident - for it is considered that we do not think that he rammed the Hun purposely. A hard working and popular pilot - we lose our officer in charge of night flying equipment which he looked after so well and which becomes unique in the sector as '247's box of night tricks' until our Drem lighting is installed."

The Faithful Few

The Do 17 was a Z-3 from 4/KG2, coded U5+GM. The crew of four also perished when their aircraft broke up and hit the sea.

247 Sqn at Predannack. P/O Ricky Price seated far right, wearing his 'Mae West'.

At the time of the incident, the pilots of 247 were a mix of new and experienced aviators. Flight Lieutenant John Carver who had been flying as 'Blue 1' had served with 87 Squadron in the Battle of Britain, while the squadron commander was Squadron Leader Peter O'Brian, who had also flown in the Battle of Britain, but with 152 Squadron.

Group Captain Peter O'Brian DFC* remembered the engagement:

"As I recall what happened, John Carver attacked first - followed by Ricky Price who pressed his attack so close and so thoroughly that he collided with the enemy aircraft, having presumably either misjudged his breakaway point or not realized his speed of closing with his eye on the target through his gun sight, and his guns firing. Perhaps these things are the same. A determined attack. In any case he was always an enthusiastic, affable and out-going individual who seemed to enjoy his short time with the squadron, and joined in all activities, on and off duty, in a very friendly and energetic way."

James Renvoize was also with 247 at that time: -

"At this time one flight was operating by day, the other by night, alternately, so that we were rarely all together in the squadron dispersal - in fact there are members of 'B' Flight I cannot recollect at all - I just remember him as one of the chaps: and of course, he had not been with the squadron long before he was killed. I believe he was quite enthusiastic to make his mark, and I expect this may have been part of the cause for his misjudgement when attacking the Do 17. My recollection is that F/Lt Carver made the first attack and then stood off for P/O Price to make his and he went on firing so long that he eventually collided with the tail of the Do 17."

Pilot Officer Ralph Ruskin (Ricky) Price was 22 years old, and is remembered on the Runnymede Memorial for those RAF fliers with no known grave.

Some pilots only completed a handful of operational missions before they too, lost their lives - like Pilot Officer Edward Lawson Walker from Worcester. An ex Worcester Royal Grammar School pupil, he joined his first operational squadron in November 1943. Posted in to 254 Squadron from No 1 Torpedo Training Unit, 254 were a unit equipped with Beaufighters, engaged on anti shipping strikes in the North Sea and around the Dutch islands.

Ricky Price in happier times, standing 3rd from left. His Flight Commander, John Carver DFC, is stoof far right.

Paired up with Sergeant Ernest Helps as his observer, they undertook their first mission on November 16th, when they were acting in a recce role, shadowing a small formation of enemy ships. During this flight, they were engaged by Bf 109s, with one managing to hit their Beaufighter. The starboard wing and engine were damaged, but they managed to make good their escape.

Their second sortie was just as eventful. 254 despatched 10 aircraft as part of a 'wing strike' to Texel, where they attacked shipping. Pilot Officer Walker returned to base after making his attack, as return fire had blown the nose out of the

A pair of Beaufighters strafing an enemy ship.

aircraft. Several other aircraft were also damaged during this engagement.

Walker flew four more operations over the Dutch islands, including a 'Coastal Roadstead' between Just and Ameland with rocket firing Beaufighters of 236 Squadron, with cover being supplied by 26 Typhoons of 3, 198 and 609 Squadrons. During this operation, the Wing Leader, Wing Commander Cliff DSO, collided with the Beaufighter flown by Flight Sergeant Yates of 254. Wing Commander Cliff managed to ditch his stricken aircraft, but Flight Sergeant Yates' Beaufighter lost its tail, and plunged into the sea.

During their next sortie on February 23rd 1944, they were chased by a German night fighter off Den Helder, and luckily, managed to get away. They only flew four sorties in February, and their final one on March 7th.

254 took part in a recce in force, along with aircraft from 143 and 236 Squadrons. Led by Wing Commander Burns DFC of 254, they attacked shipping, leaving some damaged and on fire. Two Beaufighters were in turn damaged, but 'M', flown by Pilot Officer Walker was shot down, with both crews being killed. Their operation career was just ten sorties long, and both are remembered on the Runnymede Memorial.

A low-level shipping attack: a risky business with little or no margin for error.

Acknowledgements

Over the period of time that this project has been ongoing, a vast number of people have willingly helped me with it's content, and have contributed to the final manuscript.

It would be a massive task to include all who have, at some stage assisted me, but I thank you one and all for your input, for it has truly been appreciated. However, there are some that I feel that I must not escape without a mention.

Firstly to my long standing friend Dilip Sarkar, who was always encouraging me to complete the manuscript, and was only a telephone call or email away to offer assistance or support. I owe him much for his faith in me, and for being instrumental in ensuring this project was finally completed. I must also thank Steve Cooper at Victory Books International for his friendship and support, without which this book could not have been published.

I would also like to express my appreciation to Group Captain Richard Haine for taking the time to read the manuscript and supply the foreword. As a one time CO of one of our most successful pilots, and one with a much distinguished wartime career, I could think of no-one better.

Numerous aviation historians have also helped me - and in no particular order they were: Jackie Withers of the CWGC, Dave Stubley, Gordon Permann, Christopher Shores, John Foreman, Brian Sadler, Steve Vizard, Bob Collis, John Vasco, Steve Brew (who runs the excellent 41 Squadron website) Don Aris, Alec Brew, Nick Beale, Ian Piper, John Vasco, Allan White, and Chris Goss; I thank you. Others which I feel need a special mention are Wing Commander John Elkington, Sid Cleaver, Terry O'Reilly, Mike Boucher, Anthony Whitehead, Larry McHale, Mark Postlethwaite, Eric Reeves, George Henderson, Sheila Thompson, Connie Storr, Andrew Kimbell, Rosamaund Wootten, Gerda Schlicting, Peter Swann, Claire Harrison, Amanda Stitson, Christelle Haurie, the Silvester Family, the Klee Family, and Les Smith. David & 'Dimple' Thatcher at Worcester's famous 'Sauce Factory' restaurant and bar provided a convivial venue for our frequent 'Think Tanks', greatly assisted by Wadworth's 6X ale, it must be said!

I must thank my partner Jackie Critchley, who has had to put up with this work, and has also been dragged down the National Archives at Kew to help me with note taking on more than one occasion! Her support was wonderful.

Bibliography

The sources for this book come from many and varied sources, including access to unpublished papers, photographs and papers kindly supplied by veterans and their families to the author; interview notes and the archive held by the National Archives at Kew. However I also make reference to:-

Battle of Britain: Then and Now MkV, Edited by Winston Ramsey, After the Battle 1989.

Men of the Battle of Britain: Ken Wynne, Gliddon Books, 1989.

Battle over Britain: Francis K Mason, Aston Publications, 1990.

The Blitz: Then and Now, Vols I-III, Edited by Winston Ramsey, After the Battle 1989 & 1990.

RAF Fighter Command Claims of WW2; Vol I & II, John Foreman, Red Kite 2003 & 2005.

RAF Fighter Command Losses of WW2, Vols I - III, Norman Franks, Midland Publishing 1998, 2000 & 2002.

Where a great day out **takes off**

JUNCTION 10 OFF THE M11

DUXFORD
Imperial War Museum

GO FREE